The Linguistic Heritage of Colonial Practice

Koloniale und Postkoloniale Linguistik
Colonial and Postcolonial Linguistics

Herausgegeben von Stefan Engelberg, Peter Mühlhäusler, Doris Stolberg, Thomas Stolz und Ingo H. Warnke

Band 13

The Linguistic Heritage of Colonial Practice

Herausgegeben von
Brigitte Weber

DE GRUYTER

ISBN 978-3-11-073651-9
e-ISBN (PDF) 978-3-11-062371-0
e-ISBN (EPUB) 978-3-11-062128-0

Library of Congress Control Number: 2018960713

Bibliographic information published by the Deutsche Nationalbibliothek
The Deutsche Nationalbibliothek lists this publication in the Deutsche Nationalbibliografie;
detailed bibliographic data are available on the Internet at http://dnb.dnb.de.

© 2020 Walter de Gruyter GmbH, Berlin/Boston
This volume is text- and page-identical with the hardback published in 2019.
Printing and binding: CPI books GmbH, Leck

www.degruyter.com

Foreword

It is an honor and a great pleasure to be given the opportunity to preface this volume, which offers a representative range of research evidencing *The Linguistic Heritage of Colonial Practice* via the prism of Colonial and Postcolonial Linguistics. The original workshop which formed the inspiration for the majority of the current contributions was gladly hosted by the Department of English, Alpen-Adria University Klagenfurt and served as an acknowledgment of the relevant research interests institutionally present in these fields. As well as possessing expertise in the literatures of the former settler colonies of Australia and Canada, the Department has also promoted internationally valued research into the linguistics of historically restructured Englishes (e.g. of Cameroon, Jamaica), hybrid Englishes (e.g. of India) and indigenously lexified Englishes (e.g. New Zealand) – all sociocultural and sociopolitical legacies of British colonialism overseas. With regard to the not uncontroversially labeled 'internal colonialism' within the British Isles themselves, referring to the increasing English political hegemony over 'the Celtic nations' dating from the 13th century onwards, the Department has been responsible too for considerable research on the linguistic consequences of the historical domination of England over Wales. Indeed, topics addressed in the present volume – toponomastics, language classifications, language contact/diglossia, the effects of local infrastructure development, (historical) lexicography and obsolescence/revitalization scenarios – can all be pinpointed as significant factors in a mapping of the linguistic heritage of British/English colonial practice in much the same way. By its good example, it is to be expected that the present volume will serve to focus and galvanize further international and co-disciplinary research on these and related areas of interest in the field of Colonial and Postcolonial Linguistics.

Allan James, Klagenfurt/Austria

Acknowledgments

I would like to thank Bremen University, in particular Prof. Dr. Thomas Stolz, for relocating one of their biannual conferences to the Alpen-Adria University Klagenfurt and accepting the editing of a volume in the series *Colonial and Postcolonial Linguistics* with the publishing house de Gruyter. My thanks also go to Prof. Dr. Allan James for helping me to launch and organize the conference in March 2015. I am also very grateful for all the help by Prof. Dr. Onysko and the whole organizing team, the secretaries and above all the kind help of the late Mrs. Helga Klopcic. Cakes for the coffee breaks were provided among others by my daughter Sigrun. Some folk music in the breaks contributed to an Austrian atmosphere. My heartfelt thanks.

Brigitte Weber, Klagenfurt/Austria

Contents

Foreword —— V

Acknowledgments —— VII

Brigitte Weber
Introduction —— 1

Thomas Stolz and Ingo H. Warnke
Saints, nobility, and other heroes. Colonial place-naming as part of the European linguistic heritage —— 13

Susanne Schuster
"The making of Greenland" – Early European place names in Kalaallit Nunaat —— 43

Paolo Miccoli
Colonial place-names in Italian East Africa (AOI) (with additional data from Tripoli). The linguistic heritage of colonial practice —— 75

Marina Wienberg
Linguistic missionary heritage. Capuchin missionary Father Laurentius and his unpublished German-Chuukese dictionary —— 93

Doris Stolberg
Positioning by naming: Constructing group affiliation in a colonial setting —— 115

Philipp Krämer
Third-hand colonial linguistics: Adolphe Dietrich's comparative study of Indian Ocean Creoles —— 139

Yliana Rodríguez
Spanish-Guarani diglossia in colonial Paraguay: A language undertaking —— 153

Wolfram Karg
Construction of (transcontinental) railways as a means of colonization. A corpus-based analysis on the German colonial discourse in postcolonial perspective —— 169

Valentyna Skybina and Natali Bytko
The Raj English in historical lexicography —— 191

Brigitte Weber
Anglo-Norman: Language contact and obsolescence —— 219

Index of Authors —— 245

Index of Languages —— 249

Index of Subjects —— 251

Index of Toponyms —— 253

Brigitte Weber
Introduction

Abstract: This introduction shows the history and development of the linguistic research field of *Colonial Linguistics* in an overview from the first conferences during the "Festival of Languages" in 2009 until the rich research activities today. Then some characteristic features of colonial languages are discussed in general and on the basis of Venetian in particular. The role of the Italian language at present is looked at as well and its possible future position in Europe is considered. The final part is concerned with English, the spread of which has been closely linked to a colonial process from the twelfth to the twentieth centuries. To several questions as to the future of English, answers are suggested.

Keywords: colonial language, Venetian, the Italian language, global language English

1 A short historical retrospect

The research field of *Koloniallinguistik* (colonial linguistics) was initiated by the Institute for General and Applied Linguistics (IAAS), University of Bremen, as one of the many disciplines dealt with during the *Festival der Sprachen* (International festival of languages) from Sept. 17th to Oct. 7th 2009. The festival was held in Bremen (www.festival.uni-bremen.de) under the patronage of UNESCO and the Mayor of the Free Hanseatic City of Bremen. It offered a multifaceted, resourceful and functional program with versatile conferences involved as well as several practical language days.

As regards the field of colonial linguistics, the ensuing activities of the many participants resulted in a number of conferences, workshops and publications in the following years. The conferences and workshops on *Language and Literature in Colonial and Postcolonial Contexts* were usually held at the University of Bremen, but also at the *Institut für Deutsche Sprache* (IDS) Mannheim and in 2015 at the Alpen-Adria University Klagenfurt. The publications based on these conferences have already attained a number of 12 volumes in the series *Koloniale und Postkoloniale Linguistik (KPL/CPL)*. In the introductory chapter of

---

Brigitte Weber, Alpen-Adria University Klagenfurt, Department of English, Universitätsstr. 65–67, 9020 Klagenfurt, Austria. E-Mail: weber_loets@yahoo.co.uk

volume 1 the concept of the research program "colonial linguistics" is discussed and special literature references are recommended. Furthermore, more details about colonial linguistics with regard to the *Festival der Sprachen* are indicated in the introduction of volume one. Apart from the series KPL/CPL there are numerous publications on language in colonial contexts, on missionary activities and above all on toponymy.

Colonial and Postcolonial Linguistics have been appreciated as additional disciplines in the field of Linguistics and Language Studies. An association called *International Association of Colonial and Postcolonial Linguistics* (IACPL) was founded in September 2014 during the Bremen Conference BCLL#2. This association is committed to the study of the relationships between language and colonialism from historical and contemporary perspectives (www.IACPL.net), trying to bring together linguists both from international universities and speaker communities who are interested in evaluating and discussing the historical base of their linguistic research.

2 Sociohistorical considerations regarding the evolution of colonial languages

Classical colonies in Africa were usually settlements of groups of citizens transplanted into another country but retaining their original citizenship as well as close political, trading and linguistic links with the mother country. This is the original meaning of the Greek term ἀποικία[1] meaning 'emigration', just as the Latin term *colonia* means 'cultivation, population, settlement'. This type of settlement was there almost two millennia before the age of Imperialism. The name subsequently took on its modern meaning. Ancient colonizations tended to be based on commercial relationships and this seems to have been true whether we are dealing with Greek, Carthaginian or Latin models. Carthage, for example, competed with Rome even in Sicily and in Spain for an economic rather than a political empire. Through the peoples of the Mediterranean the influence from Europe has always tended to be commercial rather than territorial (Weber 2008: 37ff.). The vehicular language, a later variety of Greek, known as *koiné* Greek, was spoken throughout the eastern Mediterranean from around the 4th century BC for nearly a thousand years (Crystal 1997: 303).

---

[1] ἀποικία ας ἡ (fr ἄποικος, away from home). Departure from home, emigration: – α colony (https://books.google.at/books: A Greek Reader).

Thinking of the Venetian Republic in the Middle Ages, we realize that it was the sea contributing to riches beyond measure, creating commercial wealth and a splendid maritime empire. That's why the Republic was called "Stato da mar" in their dialect. The crusades provided the Republic with its chance to ascend the world stage. For over five hundred years the Venetians became masters of the eastern Mediterranean and they nicknamed their city "La Dominante" (Crowley 2011: 3). Venice was organized to buy and sell. The Venetians were brilliant merchants, they calculated risks, return and profit with scientific precision. They communicated in their Venetian dialect, sometimes simplified but enriched by the lexicon of their conquering expeditions. The language, early Venetian, was spoken by a long-settled, ethnically Venetic population and emerged from the Late Latin spoken north of the Adriatic Sea. Ferguson (2007: 162) considers two hypotheses:
1. Venetian is the reflex of late Latin or proto-Romance from the north-eastern Veneto brought to the lagoon by the migration movements from the mainland. (6th and 7th centuries).
2. Or Venetian emerged organically from a koineization process. This involved converging migratory population streams, in the wake of the Germanic invasions, carrying linguistic features from both north-eastern and central-southern Veneto.

It is difficult to be certain. Historically, the areal spread and high status of Venetian were predicated on Venice's remarkable mercantile growth, maritime then territorial expansion, and consequent cultural prestige between c. 900 AD and c. 1500 AD. However, with regard to the Tuscan variety a possible negative influence on Venetian is discussed. Ferguson (2007: 35) is convinced that Venetian's subsequent functional contraction – first in the written sphere, then in the spoken domain – cannot be linked to economic and political decline. He points out that it is not unproblematic to label Venice's gradual imperial retrenchment and economic reconversion post 1500 as 'decline', and certainly not in relation to Florence. The impact of Italian (Florentine/Tuscan) on Venetian began well before 1500, when Venetian was still in part a language of state It predated by centuries the demise of the Serenissima and the absorption of the Veneto region into the new Italian state in 1866. In fact, the influence of Italian on Venetian was literary then, more broadly, textual and cultural. While it did have a limited effect on Venetian morphology, its main outcome was to progressively exclude *venexian* from the field of unmarked writing, establishing after c.1500 a rather clearcut writing-speech bilingualism.

By 1350–1400, following an intense period of urbanization and expansion, Venice was a major power, with merchants and outposts omnipresent from Egypt to the Black Sea. After 1100 she achieved dominance in the Adriatic and extensive influence in the eastern Mediterranean. Between 1200 and 1500 she acquired, partially or entirely, Istria, Dalmatia, Corfu, Zakinthos, Cephalonia, Methoni, Euboea, the Cyclades, Crete, Cyprus and Constantinople.

I have come to the conclusion that Venetian is a colonial language, spoken by the inhabitants of Venice, the colonial metropolis: With Venitian "de là da mar" (Folena 2015: 227), Venice provides a mercantile aristocracy contributing with a language enriched by influences from her acquisitions in Dalmatia and Greece and by features of the Mediterranean Lingua Franca. Special characteristic features are the processes of koneization and leveling as well as conservativeness. As a language of trade, it is the communication among speakers of different languages which is the main purpose of its use, not the grammatical correctness. This means simplification, access to a mediator language or koiné.

Italian today is spoken to a certain degree in the former Italian colonies (Africa Orientale Italiana) Somalia, Eritrea, Ethiopia, Libya, the Dodecanese islands and Albania. (See also the contribution of Paolo Miccoli this volume). Vedovelli (2011) in his *Storia linguistica dell'emigrazione italiana nel mondo* describes in detail the evolution of the Italian language in those geographical areas where millions of Italians had started a new life:

- in Europe (France, Belgium, United Kingdom, Switzerland and Germany);
- in Latin America (Argentina, Brazil, Venezuela, Uruguay – with smaller Italian settlements Bolivia and Paraguay, Chile, Colombia and Peru);
- in North America (USA, Canada);
- Australia and New Zealand;
- Africa (Italian between emigration and colonization, Contact varieties at the Horn of Africa, from the lingua franca to the koiné Sicilian-Tunisian, South African Italian, the role of Italian in the African "system";
- Japan.

It seems important to retrace all the places where Italians still communicate in the language of their ancestors. Apart from these places of emigration, Italian is spoken in Switzerland, in Monaco and Menton in the South-East of France, in Slovenia and Croatia, in Albania, on the Greek islands mainly by elderly people and in Malta. It is an international lingua franca for the clergy of the Catholic Church, at least for oral use. Furthermore, Italian is the universal language of **classical music, fashion (Alta Moda)** and **cuisine** – the last giving pleasure worldwide. Italian also provides language for advertising material, such as *Caro* for a boutique in Finland, *Andiamo* for a bar in Madrid and for an office of models in Finland, *Carissimo* for a clothes shop and a brand of instant coffee (company Nestlé) and many more (Ammon et al. 2001).

A possible future spread of Italian in an international context would certainly be facilitated by the attraction of Italian culture and lifestyle: but it would not serve as a lingua franca.[2] Italian just like the other 'former' European colonial languages will lose ground in favor of English, the language of informatics and the *new economy*. What will be the position of Italian in Europe in the near future – should be one of the next contributions in *Sociolinguistica*, by 2050 at the latest!

3 The English language: Colonial – postcolonial – global

Leith (2007: 117) indicates in *Changing English* that according to David Crystal's estimate during the period between the reign of Elizabeth I (1603) and the reign of Elizabeth II (1952) the number of mother-tongue English speakers in the world increased enormously: from 5–7 million to about 250 million, of whom four-fifth lived outside the British Isles. This growth was due to the colonial expansion of England. Leith suggests that the process of colonization had started when English first became established as the main language of the Celtic-speaking territories of Ireland, Scotland and Wales. The spread of English has thus been closely linked to a colonial process from the twelfth to the twentieth centuries.

The English language, its history and world-wide spread, has been a perennially popular subject throughout the 20th century. It has been a topic of interest to teachers, students, academics, business people, travelers, peace-makers, writers and to everyone who has a need, or a desire, to communicate internationally. If we wind the clock back 400 years – a mere tick of the timepiece that measures human habitation in Africa – there were no more than 7 million speakers of English in a world of, perhaps, 545 million people. Whereas the world's population has increased over twelvefold over the four centuries, the use of English has increased by a factor of 320, assuming, that is, that approximately one in three people on the planet now uses English for some or all purposes. We cannot be precise about the number of speakers of English because,

---

[2] "l'italiano non può diffondersi come lingua franca o lingua di servizio se non in ambiti ristretti [...] (Simone 1990: 71).

like the world's population, it grows too quickly. Some questions might suggest answers as to the fortune of English.

3.1 Will English take over the world?

It already has! In the 1990s, English became the first truly global language. Whether we think of internet usage or journalism, science, medicine, politics, trade or literature, tertiary-level study or international meetings, English is the language of choice. It has been so widely used throughout the world that it has developed an extensive and extremely subtle vocabulary. In the *Sunday Times* of February 5th, 2006, an article pointed out that the vocabulary of the English language was approaching one million words. Of course, the majority of us does not need or use anything like this number. David Crystal (2006) in *Words, words, words* suggests that the average English speaker today may have an active vocabulary of around 40,000 words and a passive knowledge of a further 20,000. That control of 60,000 words can be put into perspective by pointing out that the original *King James Bible* of 1611 contained approximately 8,000 words. Paul Payack (2008), who works for Global Language Monitor, a San-Diego-based consultancy firm, claims that the word-stock of English is increasing by approximately 20,000 new words a year. He suggests that French, by contrast, has a vocabulary of approximately 100,000 words. According to Payack, between 1997 and 2002 there was a drop of 24 % in the use of French in EU documents. The same period saw an increase of 32 % in the use of English in EU documents.

Until recently, English has been by far the most widely used internet language and the United States has had most internet users. About ten years ago, however, China became the largest net-using country in the world with over 253 million people on line (BBC News 28 July, 2008). Although this is 30 million higher than US usage, it should be remembered that net penetration in the US stands at 71 % compared to 19 % in China. If the Sinofication[3] trend continues, it is probable that Chinese will soon replace English as the most widely used language on the internet. For more on this, see www.earthtimes.org/articles/show/news_press_release,217790.shtml (accessed in July 2015).

---

[3] The conversion or adaptation of Western ideology or methods to accommodate Chinese values. (http://alphahistory.com/chineserevolution/chinese-revolution-glossary) (www.encyclo.co.uk).

3.2 What will happen to other languages?

The blunt answer to this question is simple: many will die. Of course, languages have died out from the beginning of time. They are unknown, unrecorded. We would have to acknowledge, however, that the rate of linguistic attrition has never been as high as it is now. It is estimated that we are losing as many as 10 languages a year and may have lost 50 % of the world's languages before the end of this century. Losing a language is not like losing one's money or one's job. Once a language is lost, it is virtually impossible to revive. In Ireland, in 2010, English is the most widely spoken mother tongue; the second is Polish; and the third is Chinese; Irish comes in a poor fourth and even that position it is already under threat from Portuguese.

3.3 How unassailable is the position of English as the leading 'world' language? Are there any potential 'rivals' waiting in the wings?

Given the evidence of the past few decades, it may look as if the position of English as the world's lingua franca, is unassailable. Linguistically speaking, that may well be true, but one thing we have learnt over the past 30 years is that mighty empires can crash with amazing speed, and unwanted walls of separation, that have stood for decades, can be broken down overnight. Although the status and strength of English internationally is not due solely or perhaps even mainly to the might of the United States of America, it may be prudent to ask the question:

3.4 What will happen to the prestige of English as a global language if the political and economic power of the United States should wane?

Once again, we cannot be certain, but we can wonder what will happen, if, at one and the same time, the USA declines as the world superpower while China becomes the richest and strongest authority on the planet. Perhaps we should remind ourselves of a number of facts:
- The USA is just as likely to suffer from global warming as, say, East Africa.
- Parts of the USA are geologically unstable. A large earthquake in California would devastate both its economy and its political power.

- English is not utterly secure even in areas of the USA. The numbers of mother-tongue speakers of Spanish is growing faster than the number of mother-tongue speakers of English in parts of California, Arizona, New Mexico and Texas. Moreover, in these areas bilingualism is far from universal. Many adult migrants from Mexico, the Spanish Caribbean and South America have no pressing need to learn English.
- Recent immigrants to the United States from Asia tend to live in their own communities, so we find areas where, for example, Korean is more frequently used than English. In the past, such communities became English-using within two generations, but immigrants seem to cling to their ethnic identities longer now than was once the case.

If the power of the USA should wane in this century, it is likely that the prestige of English would, indeed, diminish but it would still be the most useful lingua franca in the world. Nevertheless, it would be foolish to undervalue the potential of Chinese and, perhaps, Hindi. China, we must remember,
- has a population of well over one billion people;
- has a strong numerical base in Australia, Singapore, the UK, USA and increasingly in Africa, including Cameroon (!);
- could insist on business being conducted in Chinese, rather than in English. There is, so far, no evidence that this is happening but, if it did, the global dominance of English would be severely dented.

India, too, has certainly strengthened its economic role in the world over the last decade. Like China, it has a huge population with family connections worldwide. Unlike China, however, India has strengthened its position in part through the medium of English. Because it has a highly educated, English-speaking population, India has attracted 'Call-Centre Business' from all around the world. It is likely, for example, that if I buy an airline ticket on line in the UK, the business will be routed through India. So successful has India become at attracting English-speaking businesses to set up call centers in India that it has coined the term 'to bangalore', after the name of the city of Bangalore, which has been at the centre of much of this outsourcing. If call-centers are closed in England or the USA, and set up in India, they have been 'bangalored'.

3.5 Will all Englishes around the world become more alike – or will they all become different 'languages'?

In the past, when empires died or diminished, the language of power splintered, forming many new languages. If we take Latin, for example, it was the lingua franca of the known world 2000 years ago and Romans could boast of having food from three continents on their banqueting tables. As the power of the Empire waned, however, many Romance languages developed, including French, Italian, Portuguese, Romanian and Spanish, although Latin remained the language of Christianity and the link language of educated Europeans until the 17th century. Will English go the same way as Latin? From some points of view, it already has. Yet, when we want to, we can still accommodate to each other's English.

There have been lively discussions over the last ten years about the nature of possible standards for 21st century English. Some of the most interesting of these have appeared in journals such as English Today and many of these are the work of non-mother-tongue speakers. One of the themes is that 21st century Standard English may not be based on ANY variety of mother-tongue English, whether American, Australian, British, Canadian, Irish, South African or New Zealand. Mother-tongue speakers are not always the best models for international comprehensibility:

- They often speak too quickly and thus they are often less easy to understand than a non-mother-tongue speaker.
- They often use reduced forms that can cause confusion.
- They often use idioms that are incomprehensible to non-mother-tongue speakers. What is a Japanese speaker to make of a South African's advice that she should 'hold thumbs' (i.e. 'hope for success')?
- They often use intonation alone to ask questions and their negative questions, such as 'You didn't finish that on time, did you?' are hard to answer with a 'yes' or a 'no'.
- In addition, some sounds and sound combinations are difficult for non-native speakers. If more speakers say 'dis' and 'dat', why do we still urge everyone to say 'this' and 'that'?

In many ways, written English causes fewer problems, although many feel that its spelling system should be simplified.

3.6 Are pidgins and creoles likely to survive?

This is not an easy question to answer because pidgins and creoles, like all living languages, are perpetually evolving. They will survive and thrive as long as they serve a useful purpose as for example communication on social media or simply mailing. E-mailers regularly use pidgin, at least for part of their messages, also with abbreviations from texting: *Tank U Plenty/A glad say u wel. Me 2, a fine an di pikin dem di gro na dei.*

Finally, there are certainly many examples of global abbreviations as well, like the youth language using initials like LOL (Laughing out loud), XOXO (Kisses and Hugs), TTYL (Talk to you later), THNX (Thanks), 2DAY (today), B4 (Before), TIME (Tears in my eyes) [...] to mention but a few. All in English.[4] An emerging list of new-age abbreviations have begun to dominate the way social media users connect and communicate – and it is only set to get longer.

In connection with colonialism I would like to finish with an analogy: the languages of the conquered were threatened by the powerful colonial master's language just as we feel threatened today by the powerful global language.

This volume of the book series *Colonial and Postcolonial Linguistics* comprises topics of diverse interests within the field of language and colonialism. Most of the contributions were presented during a workshop at the Alpen-Adria University Klagenfurt in March 2015 and they offer both a diachronic and synchronic approach to aspects relating to different areas of colonial life. The short presentation will be organized according to the similarity of topics. Colonial place-naming is presented in a comparative perspective from several European and non-European geographical areas:

Stolz' and **Warnke's** linguistic analysis of anthroponyms sheds light on recurrent motives in the context of European colonialism. **Schuster** presents a toponymic case study of Greenland identifying a multitude of toponyms from various European source languages. **Miccoli** shows the naming practices of Italian colonizers during the fascist regime. **Wienberg's** study uncovers the contribution of linguistic missionary activity in the South Sea, unveiling hitherto unpublished manuscripts. **Stolberg's** paper analyses how the missionaries of the Rhenish Mission Society construct, define and position different population groups – by means of language – and what patterns emerge from these practices. **Krämer** presents Adolphe Dietrich's article of 1891, based on the materials from Schuchardt's collection, with a comparative study of the French-based

---

4 Social media speak: The 60 new abbreviations that are dominating the way young people communicate with one another.

Creole languages of the Mascarene Islands in the Indian Ocean (La Réunion and Mauritius). **Rodriguez** discusses the implications of Spanish missionary activity on the native language Guarani and the resulting changes through language contact. **Karg** presents an analysis of debates over constructing (transcontinental) railways in the context of German colonialism and thus contributes to the topic of infrastructure. **Skybina's and Bytko's** valuable lexicographic contribution examines the scope and methodology of the representation of the English language used in India during the Raj in historical lexicography. **Weber** traces language contact from the colonization of the Middle Ages up to the present day – with special consideration of the Channel Islands – relating to obsolescence or a possible revitalization.

The papers presented in this volume represent the linguistic fields of sociolinguistics, onomastics, historical linguistics, language contact, obsolescence, convergence and divergence, revitalization, (colonial) discourse, lexicography and creolistics. These studies add to a deeper understanding of the *Linguistic Heritage of Colonial Practice*.

References

Ammon, Ulrich, Klaus Mattheier & Peter H. Nelde (eds.). 2001. *Verkehrssprachen in Europa – außer Englisch* (Sociolinguistica 15). Tübingen: Niemeyer.
Crowley, Roger. 2011. *City of fortune. How Venice won and lost a naval empire*. London: Faber & Faber.
Crystal, David. 1997. *The Cambridge encyclopedia of language*. Cambridge: Cambridge University Press.
Crystal, David. 2006. *Words, words, words*. Oxford: Oxford University Press.
Ferguson, Ronnie. 2007. *A linguistic history of Venice*. Florence: Leo S. Olschki.
Folena, Gianfranco. 2015. *Culture e Lingue nel Veneto Medievale*. libreriauniversitaria.it.
Leith, Dick. 2007. English – colonial and postcolonial. In David Graddol, Dick Leith, Joan Swann, Martin Rhys & Julia Gillen (eds.). 2007. *Changing English*, 117–152. London: Routledge.
Payack, Paul J. J. 2008. *A million words and counting: How global English is rewriting the world*. New York: Citadel Press.
Simone, Raffaele. 1990. Il destino internazionale dell'italiano. In V. Lo Cascio (ed.), *L'italiano in Europa*, 62–71. Firenze: Le Monnier.
Social media speak: The 60 new abbreviations that are dominating the way young people communicate with one another. http://www.dailymail.co.uk/news/article-2689655/Social-media-speak-The-30-new-abbreviations-dominating-way-young-people-communicate-one-another.html (accessed July 10th 2018).
Vedovelli, Massimo. 2011. *Storia linguistica dell'emigrazione italiana nel mondo*. Roma: Carocci.

Thomas Stolz and Ingo H. Warnke
Saints, nobility, and other heroes

Colonial place-naming as part of the European linguistic heritage

Abstract: This paper reviews the major recurrent motives of place naming in the context of European colonialism. The focus is on colonial place names which involve a European anthroponym as one of the components of the toponym. It is examined to what extent patterns emerge which are common to all or most of the European colonizers. We adopt a comparative perspective to study assumed commonalities. There are two short case-studies which highlight especially the colonial toponomasticons of former German colonies in Africa (Cameroon) and Micronesia (Mariana Islands). On the basis of the findings made in relation to these two cases, a catalogue of motives for anthroponymically-based colonial place names is sketched with reference to all European colonialisms. The lesson to be learned from the recurrence of certain patterns and motives is outlined in the conclusions.

Keywords: place names, anthroponyms, Europeanization, Africa, Micronesia

1 Introduction

This contribution highlights a trait which all former European colonizer nations (henceforth: ECs) share in connection to the coining of new place names for geographical objects (henceforth: GO) in those overseas territories which they claim to possess. Our interest in focusing on the naming of colonial space through ECs is twofold: first, we assume that colonialism extends the factual exercise of power by ECs in so-called overseas territories. The control of space finds its expression in the subjection of foreign territories not least by way of colonial place-making. By this, we as linguists refer to linguistic practices of localizing space. While space can be understood as an unmarked and undi-

---

Thomas Stolz, University of Bremen, FB 10: Linguistics/Language Sciences, Universitäts-Boulevard 13, 28359 Bremen, Germany. E-Mail: stolz@uni-bremen.de
Ingo H. Warnke, University of Bremen, FB 10: German Studies, Universitäts-Boulevard 13, 28359 Bremen, Germany. E-Mail: iwarnke@uni-bremen.de

rected spatial figuration, places are **specific spaces** which are ascribed meaning and, importantly, produced through modes of perception as well as through symbolic and material practices; places can be remembered and assigned functions and interests. The coining of new place names is a crucial Euro-colonial praxis of place-making. Place names thus deserve far greater attention in the academic inquiry of colonialism than they have enjoyed up to this point. Apart from this general aspect of colonial place-making through naming, we are also interested in a second aspect that rather derives from the linguistic perspective proper: considering the massive naming of places in the colonial project, the naming of GOs constitutes a central object of study in comparative toponomastics. Regardless of the question of possible characteristics of colonial place-naming it is the task of linguistics to take stock of this large corpus of names and according to structure-oriented criteria. Especially those place names which occur across all ECs are of great importance. The place names we allude to are formed on the basis of proper names.

There is ample evidence of colonial place names (henceforth: CPN) which involve a component that is based on or is identical with a proper name that refers to a historically identifiable human being.[1] The options as to who was eligible as honoree can be shown empirically to be very limited across the different ECs throughout the entire era of colonialism and in all regions that were affected by colonialism. By this, we do not claim that this pattern is of relevance **exclusively** in CPN. However, it is obvious that it is of special significance in **CPN**. It is important to emphasize this significance for the description of types of place-naming as well as for specific functions of place-naming in Euro-colonial comparison. In this study we thus demonstrate that the place-naming practices of ECs yield a surprisingly homogeneous picture – and this homogeneity calls for being explained linguistically and in culture-historical terms. The homogeneity comes as a surprise above all because the historical circumstances of colonial practices are by no means consistent among different ECs. Accordingly, Castro Varela & Dhawan (2015: 23) point out that the process of colonization und the motivations to settle down overseas are heterogeneous. The authors state that the century-long process of colonization by no means took place in a uniform way; rather, very diverse colonial systems of rule were established in different ways.

---

[1] Another rather similar construction to be mentioned here are CPNs which contain components of ethnonyms. For the significance of the relation between toponyms and ethnonyms, see, for instance, Batoma (2006: 1).

We take the responsibility for the linguistic part of the evaluation of the empirical facts the vast majority of which still has to be taken stock of. In this study our focus is on the semantic patterns of motivation of CPNs whereas their formal properties are only touched upon summarily in a paragraph of this introductory section (cf. below). In this context, it should be noted that the question of the semantics of names is indeed discussed controversially. A lexical semantics in a more narrow sense can surely not be applied to name-transfer forms, but indexical meanings are of interest because names point to contexts and in this way have a crucial semantics.

We situate our study within the domain of the research program of *Koloniallinguistik* as outlined by Dewein et al. (2012) and *Postcolonial Language Studies* (Warnke et al. 2016). More precisely it forms part of a series of like-minded investigations of CPNs (Stolz & Warnke 2015, 2016, 2017, 2018a, 2018b, Stolz et al. 2016) all of which are meant to pave the way for *Comparative Colonial Toponomastics (CoCoTop)*, a joint project which aims at collecting, systematizing, and evaluating comprehensively and in a comparative-linguistic perspective the toponomastic manifestations of the Europeanization of the maps of extra-European regions during the era of colonialism. The data are taken mainly from cartographic representations of European colonies, registers and indexes of atlases, (semi-)official lists of place names, and gazetteers as well as an assortment of various other sources all of which date back to the period of European colonial rule. We look exclusively at macrotoponyms (i.e. names of GOs) that are known beyond the city-limits, in a manner of speaking (Nübling et al. 2012: 206–207) as coined by ECs independent of their acceptance and employment by the autochthonous population of the colonies. Since the project is primarily about what the ECs thought to be suitable designations of GOs in their extra-European dependencies, we deliberately skip the similarly interesting issues of precolonial and postcolonial toponomastics for the time being.

Furthermore, we are interested in CPNs which involve an anthroponymic component that is connected to the EC's culture. The place names we account for are representative of exactly three construction types, namely
- compound/syntagm (the prototypical CPN with two possible linearizations):
 $[\{N\}_{ANTH}\text{-}\{N\}_{CLASS}]_{TOP} \sim [\{N\}_{CLASS}\text{-}\{N\}_{ANTH}]_{TOP}$
 Wilhelmsfeste = $[\{Wilhelm\text{-}S_{GEN}\}_{ANTH}\text{-}\{feste\}_{CLASS}]_{TOP}$ – a military station in Deutsch-Südwestafrika (henceforth: DSWA) in the vicinity of Swakopmund, named after either the German *Kaiser* **Wilhelm**[2] I in 1889 (Möller 1986: 442–

---

[2] Boldface highlights those parts of a proper name of an individual human being which form the anthroponymic component of a CPN.

443) or after his son *Kaiser **Wilhelm** II* in 1898 (Kausch 1903: 118) – the historiographers of the German colonial period in DSWA disagree on this issue, *Port Francqui* = [{*Port*}$_{CLASS}$-{*Francqui*}$_{ANTH}$]$_{TOP}$ – an important town in the Province du Kasaï (Congo Belge), named after *Émile Lucien Joseph **Francqui***, leader of several military campaigns in the early 1890 on behalf of the then État Indépendant du Congo (Michiels & Laude 1953: 344);
– conversion (~ zero-derivation):
[{N}$_{ANTH}$]$_{TOP}$
Crispi = [{*Crispi*}$_{ANTH}$]$_{TOP}$ – an agricultural village in the Italian colony Libia, founded in 1938 and named after the politician *Francesco **Crispi*** (1818–1901) who was instrumental in the creation of the first Italian colonies on African soil in the late 19th century (Labanca 2002: 70–73);
– derivation (by way of suffixation of a Latin-based derivational morpheme):
[{N}$_{ANTH}$-{___}$_{DERIV}$]$_{TOP}$
Georgia = [{*George*}$_{ANTH}$-{*ia*}$_{DERIV}$]$_{TOP}$ – one of the British colonies on the Atlantic coast of North America, named in 1732 after *King **George** II* (1683–1760) (Room 2006: 143).

These three construction types can be unified in the formula

$$[\{N\}_{ANTH} \ (\left\{ \begin{array}{c} -\{N\}_{CLASS} \\ -\{\_\_\}_{DERIV} \end{array} \right\})]_{TOP}$$

This means that there are two general types of CPNs (= (a) simple [{N}$_{ANTH}$]$_{TOP}$ vs. (b) complex [{N}$_{ANTH}$ + X]$_{TOP}$). One of these types consists of only one constituent which is identical with an anthroponym whereas there are other CPNs which require the co-presence of either a classifier or a Latinate derivational suffix. Both of the latter strategies are clear instances of toponomastic Europeanization. The use of Latin-like patterns for the formation of CPNs connects them directly to the cultural traditions of Europe which have their roots in Roman antiquity. The classifier is indicative of the ontological class membership of the GO thus named. Since the classifier overwhelmingly stems from the language of the EC, most of the CPNs under review belong to the category of full exonyms, i.e. to the class of formations which consist entirely of elements which are taken from the EC's language.

CoCoTop covers the colonial toponomasticons of fourteen ECs, viz. Austria (= AU), Belgium (= BE), Brandenburg-Preußen (= BP), Courland (= CO), Denmark (= DK), France (= FR), Germany (= GE), Italy (= IT), the Netherlands (= NL), Portugal (= PG), Russia (= RU), Spain (= SP), Sweden (= SW), and the United

Kingdom (= UK) which are compared to those of extra-European colonizers such as Japan and the United States. Space restrictions do not allow us to account for all of these colonialisms in this study. We therefore limit the presentation to a handful of show-cases which we consider to be largely representative of the ECs in general. For practical reasons, we refer to the GO exclusively by the CPNs given to them by the relative ECs. No attempt at homogenization via general Anglicization of proper names, titles, and classifiers is made. In the case of orthographic variation in the sources to which we have access, we give preference to the more frequently attested of the competing versions. We approach our subject-matter qualitatively. Quantitative methods will be applied in follow-up studies. These will have to show which average and diverging distribution results from construction patterns, as e.g. of types of formal morphological correlation (e.g. between place-name types and name types) and of sundry correlations (e.g. that between EC and structure types). In terms of toponomastic theory, taxonymy, and terminology we follow the guidelines laid down by Anderson (2007), Van Langendonck (2007), and Nübling et al. (2012). It is understood that, at this early stage of CoCoTop, we can only present a small selection of the data and our conclusions must remain preliminary.

The paper is organized as follows. In Section 2 we take advantage of a recent publication on CPNs in the German colony Kamerun (= KA) which serves as our point of departure. To check whether or not the picture which results from the toponomastic evaluation of the data from Kamerun may serve as a basis for further generalizations, we look at the situation in the erstwhile Spanish Mariana Islands. Based on the observations made in Sections 2–3, the subdivisions of Section 4 explore the main motivation patterns of CPNs separately. Section 5 is dedicated to the evaluation of our findings and contains the conclusions.

2 A source of inspiration

Colonial matters are hardly touched upon in those linguistic contributions which provide a general theory of modern toponomastics. Nübling et al. (2012: 217 and 237), for instance, mention CPNs only in passing when they discuss the co-existence of several systems of place names or the renaming of GOs in the postcolonial period. The properties of CPNs thus remain to be investigated thoroughly.

The extant linguistically-minded studies of CPNs are by no means numerous. They usually focus on the toponomasticons of individual colonies. A recent example is Weber's toponomastic exploration of the erstwhile German colony

KA. Weber (2012: 105–107) discusses the newly coined place names which were introduced by the German colonizers. The author emphasizes specifically that

> [f]amous German personalities, usually from the colonial government, served for the appellation of newly discovered places [...]. Famous and important persons also serve as a source for new names. (Weber 2012: 105)

Weber (2012: 105) illustrates this with two examples. The rapids on the river Nyong were named *Tappenbeck-Schnellen* after the Prussian military-man and explorer *Leutnant Hans **Tappenbeck*** who died in the colony on his way back from an expedition to the hinterland of KA in 1889 (DKL III, 459). *Sodeninsel* is the name of an island just off the Pelikan-Halbinsel on the Atlantic coast of Cameroon. The name of the island honors *Julius Freiherr von **Soden*** who served as first German governor of KA and Togo (= TO) (1885–1890) and later also as governor of Deutsch-Ostafrika (= DOA) until 1893 (DKL III, 369). At this point it can already be recognized clearly – and we would indeed like to stress this – that the so-called famous personalities are nothing but emblems of colonial power. Precisely CPN with an anthroponymic component can, by way of semantic analysis, be understood as emblematic formations which indexically refer to power relations and power representations. This points again to our understanding of semantic analyses of CPNs.[3] CPNs declare positions of powerful superiority also by way of anthroponymic integration in CPNs.

Additionally, Weber's (2012: 108–118) index of toponyms provides further evidence of similar instances of anthroponymically-based CPNs which we present shortly below.

- *Cap Nachtigal* – a promontory on the coast close to Victoria, and *Nachtigal-Fluss* – a river in the east of KA; both of these GOs were named after the explorer *Gustav **Nachtigal*** (1834–1885) who served as Reichsbeauftragter with the task of acquiring TO and KA for the Second German Empire; Nachtigal died of tuberculosis during his mission (LzÜG 567–568);
- *Johann-Albrechtshöhe* – a governmental station and town in central KA, named after *Herzog **Johann Albrecht** von Mecklenburg-Schwerin* (1857–1920), temporary prince regent of the Großherzogtum Mecklenburg-Schwerin and the Herzogtum Braunschweig, president of the Deutsche Kolonialgesellschaft and member of the Kolonialrat (DKL II 130–131);
- *Kaiser-Wilhelmsburg* – a station in the Wuteland, founded in 1890, named in honor of ***Kaiser Wilhelm*** *II* (Kausch 1903: 48);

---

3 Cf. Agha's (2003) concept of emblems and indexicality.

- *Manns-Quelle* – the spring of a river on the slope of the Kamerunberg, named after the German botanist *Georg **Mann*** who was the first European to reach the peak of the Kamerunberg where he located the above spring (Kausch 1903: 130);
- *Viktoria ~ Victoria* – an important settlement on the coast at the foot of the Kamerunberg; Kausch (1903: 115) and Weber (2012: 118) are undecided whether the CPN refers to ***Victoria** von England* (1840–1901), wife of the German Kaiser Friedrich III, or to *Queen **Victoria*** (1819–1901), Queen of Great Britain and Ireland, Empress of India. Since the station was a British foundation dating back to 1877 which was ceded to the German Empire only in 1886, it is plausible to assume that the CPN was originally meant to honor the ruler of the British Empire (DKL III 619–620).

In connection to the eight anthroponymically-based CPNs of Weber's we can observe several features which are of interest for our line of argumentation in the subsequent sections of this study. The honorees belong to three classes of personalities. First of all, there is the ruling nobility whose main representatives are the monarchic rulers of the empire(s). The proper names of Kaiser Wilhelm I and/or II as well as that of Queen Victoria are represented on the map of KA. Secondly, important (noble) supporters of the colonial policy of the European metropolis are honored by CPNs as is the case with the Duke of Mecklenburg, Johann Albrecht. The third group of CPNs comprises all those cases in which the honoree is a person who was active in the colony to the benefit of the EC. This criterion applies to the governor von Soden, the explorer Mann, the Reichsbeauftragte Nachtigal, and Leutnant Tappenbeck. Especially the latter two fit the description of heroes of the EC because both Nachtigal and Tappenbeck died on duty, i.e., from the point of view of the EC, they sacrificed their lives to guarantee the success of imperialistic politics.

Not only are the above examples illustrative of place-naming practices of all ECs but they also testify to the multiple employment of a given anthroponym in the toponomasticon of even in one and the same colony of an EC. Besides the above mentioned *Cap Nachtigal* and *Nachtigal-Fluss*, there are also the *Nachtigal-Insel* and the *Nachtigal-Schnellen* on the map of KA (GDKA Map 3) whereas in DSWA we find the *Nachtigalberg* in the vicinity of Windhuk (Möller 1986: 356). The *Nachtigal-Bucht* is located in Kiautschou (= KI) (GDKA Map 30), meaning: the former Reichsbeauftragte has left onymic traces on the colonial map of both Africa and Asia. The anthroponym is used to form CPNs which belong to different toponymic sub-classes, namely that of settlements as well as those of choronyms, hydronyms, oronyms, and others. The Duke of Mecklenburg's name appears on the map of DSWA, too. Möller (1986: 316) registers two

GO which bear a CPN that involves the component Johann-Albrecht, viz. the militarily important traffic junction *Johann-Albrechtshöhe* (thus named officially in 1903) and the spring *Johann-Albrechtsquellen*. The German botanist Mann was also honored twice toponymically since his last name is attested also as the initial constituent of *Man<n>-Insel* – an island located to the north of Neu-Pommern in the Bismarck-Archipel in Deutsch-Neuguinea (= DNG) (Kausch 1903: 68). The recurrence of anthroponyms which refer to identical personalities contribute to a certain degree of uniformity of the colonial toponomasticon (not only of) imperial Germany.

It comes as no surprise that the German Emperors' names recur throughout the German colonial toponomasticon. Not every attestation of the anthroponym *Wilhelm* in a German CPN is connected to Kaiser Wilhelm II. The above case of *Wilhelmsfeste* is suggestive of the possibility that the component Wilhelm might refer to Kaiser Wilhelm I instead. In addition, the anthroponym *Wilhelm* also forms part of the following twenty German CPNs in (1)–(2):

(1) CPNs which involve a monarchic title
 a. *Kaiser-Wilhelmsberg* (DSWA)
 b. *Kaiser-Wilhelms-Berge* (DOA)
 c. *Kaiser-Wilhelmsfluss* (KA)
 d. *Kaiser-Wilhelm-Höhlen* (DOA)
 e. *Kaiser-Wilhelmspitze* (DOA) (Kausch 1903: 48)
 f. *Kaiser-Wilhelmbaai* (DSWA)
 g. *Kaiser Wilhelmberg* (DSWA) (Möller 1986: 319)
 h. **Kaiser-Wilhelmsland** (DNG)
 i. *Kap König Wilhelm* (DNG) (Kausch 1903: 50)
 j *Prinz-Wilhelm-Fluss* (KI) (GDKA Map 30)

(2) CPNs without additional title
 a. *Wilhelmberg* (KI) (GDKA 30)
 b. *Wilhelmsthal* (DOA) (Kausch 1903: 118)
 c. (2x) *Groß-Wilhelmbank* (DSWA)
 d. *Wilhelmst<h>al* (DSWA)
 e. *Wilhelmshöhe* (DSWA)
 f. *Wilhelmsfeld* (DSWA)
 g. (2x) *Wilhelmsruh* (DSWA)
 h. *Wilhelm-Albrechtstal* (DSWA)
 i. *Wilhelmberg* (DNG)
 j. *Friedrich-Wilhelmhafen* (DNG) (Kausch 1903: 35–36)

Those CPNs which are marked out with double underlining have an honoree other than Kaiser Wilhelm II. Single underlining is used to identify CPNs for which the identification of the honoree is controversial. In the case of (1a–e) (Kausch 1903: 48) and (2a–b) (Kausch 1903: 117–118), it seems clear that we are facing CPNs which honor Kaiser Wilhelm II. In contrast, (1f–h) are CPN-formations in honor of Kaiser Wilhelm I (Möller 1986: 318–319 and Kausch 1903: 48) whereas (1i) refers to the British *King **William** III of Orange*. The name *King William's Cape* was coined originally in 1700 by Dampier (DKL II, 232). Its later German shape allowed the association with *König **Wilhelm** II von Württemberg* (1848–1921) (Sokop 1993: 13). The *Prinz-Wilhelm-Fluss* (= 1j) is a river in KI that was named after **Prinz Wilhelm** *von Preußen* (1882–1951), the oldest son of Kaiser Wilhelm II and designated heir to the imperial throne (Sokop 1993: 26). The CPN *Groß-Wilhelmsbank* (= 2c) occurs twice on the map of DSWA (GDKA Maps 9–10). The referent of the anthroponymic component of these CPNs has not been identified yet. In the case of (2d), Möller (1986: 444) mentions three scenarios. Kaiser Wilhelm II is a possibility. However, the anthroponym may also reflect the Christian name of the first owner of the place, **Wilhelm** *Goerlitz*. Thirdly, *Wilhelmstal* is also assumed to be a case of transferal of the name of a Swabian town *Wilhelmstal* to DSWA. Similarly, there are two options for the origin of the CPN (2e). Either the GO was named after its first owner, **Wilhelm** *Hampel*, or it was a direct copy of the name of the Prussian castle *Wilhelmshöhe* on the edge of Kassel (Möller 1986: 443). The CPNs (2f–h) refer to **Wilhelm** *Halberstadt*, **Wilhelm** *Grabow*, and **Wilhelm-Albrecht** *Engelhard*, respectively, who were first settlers at or owners of the GOs thus named (Möller 1986: 442–443). The honoree of (2i) is **Wilhelm** *von Bismarck*, the younger son of Otto von Bismarck (Kausch 1903: 117), whereas *Friedrich-Wilhelmshafen* was named in 1885 in honor of *Kronprinz* **Friedrich Wilhelm** *von Preußen* (1831–1888), the later Kaiser Friedrich III (1888) (Kausch 1903: 35–36).

Owing to the popularity of the male first name *Wilhelm* not only in Germany but also as *Willem* in the Netherlands and *William* in the British Isles, there is an abundance of CPNs which involve this anthroponym as a constituent. Relatively often the honoree is a monarch of this name. However, this does by no means imply that each CPN that is based on *Wilhelm, Willem*, or *William* celebrates nobility. Several of the German CPNs from DSWA show that a frequently occurring motivation for the employment of this male Christian name in the coining of CPNs is the autoreferential claim of ownership and/or primacy of pioneer-settlers.

Unsurprisingly, this motivation is strong numerically only in those colonies which belong to the category of settler colonies. In the case of German colonialism, DSWA is the sole representative of this category. It is therefore also the only

German colony in which the first names of the female consorts or daughters of the male pioneers are commemorated in the guise of CPNs as, e.g., *Charlottental*, *Elisenore* (a telescope-formation of *Elise* + *Eleonore*), *Elsenhof* (based on the initials *E.L.* of the settler's wife's name and the final morpheme of the patronymicon *Paulsen* of the settler's last name), *Emiliental*, *Idatal*, etc., all of which refer to a female member of the settler's family and designate GOs in DSWA (Möller 1986: 257). For referential-semantic analyses, it would be necessary to take a closer look at how these female anthroponyms are distributed in space and which meaning these places have. Following Meyers's (2003: 175) study of colonial Maryland und her reference to Anne Norton, there is indeed a correlation between ascribed meaning of a place and its gendered naming; this also awaits systematic examination with regards to CPN. Within the German colonial toponomasticon, this type of privately motivated CPNs is as scarcely represented as that of CPNs which are based on overt hagionyms, i.e. names of saints which are identified as such by the saintly title *Sankt* 'Saint'. The gender bias should also be noted in connection to these phenomena. The genuinely German coining of CPNs which involve the name of a Christian saint plus title amount to just eighteen cases. All of these CPNs are indicative of the presence of a Catholic mission. The list in (3) is based on the entries in Kausch (1903: 99–100).

(3)   German CPNs with an overt hagionymic component
    a.   *Sankt Ambrosius* (DOA)
    b.   *Sankt Anton* (DOA)
    c.   *Sankt Antonius* (DOA)
    d.   *Sankt Bonifaz* (DOA)
    e.   *Sankt Franziscus* (DOA)
    f.   *Sankt Franz-Xaver* (DOA)
    g.   *Sankt Joseph* (DOA)
    h.   *Sankt Michael* (DOA)
    i.   *Sankt Paul* (DOA)
    j.   *Sankt Peter Claver* (DOA)
    k.   *Sankt Peter und Paul* (DOA)
    l.   *Sankt Peter Tulii* (DOA)
    m.   *Sankt Bruno* (DNG)
    n.   *Sankt Josef* (DNG)
    o.   *Sankt Josefsthal* (DNG)
    p.   *Sankt Otto* (DNG)
    q.   *Sankt Peter* (DNG)
    r.   *Sankt Marienfluss* (DSWA)

Two thirds of all attested cases are located in DOA. All other hagionymically-based CPNs in the German colonial toponomasticon are inherited from a former EC or explorer of a nationality other than German. A case in point are the Mariana Islands (= DNG/MA) which are discussed in Section 3.

3 Where sanctity dominates

After the defeat of Spain in the Spanish-American War of 1898 and the cession of the Philippines and Guam to the USA, the German Empire purchased the remaining Spanish island possessions in Micronesia in 1899. In this way, the Mariana Islands changed hands after some 230 years of de facto Spanish dominion (and almost 380 years of contact with this EC). The long-lasting Spanish overlordship over these islands left its mark on the insular toponomasticon. The archipelago whose modern endonym is the Chamorro binary construction *Tano' Tasi* 'land of the sea' boasts as many as seven colonial aliases of Spanish origin, viz. *Islas de los Ladrones* 'Thieves Islands', *Islas de las Velas Latinas* 'Islands of the Latin sails', *Islas de los Jardines* 'Garden Islands', *Islas de los Placeres ~ las Placeres [Prazeres]* 'Islands of the [masculine] Sandbanks/[feminine] Desires', *Archipiélago de S. Lazaro* 'Archipelago of Saint Lazarus', and *Islas Marianas* 'Maria-Anna Islands'[4] with the latter honoring the Spanish queen regent **María Ana d'Austria** for giving her support to the Christianization of the Chamorros in 1668–1690 (Rogers 1995: 46).

The individual islands of the archipelago bore Spanish names too. When Germany acquired the Marianas attempts were made to wipe out the Spanish toponomastic heritage. Hiery (2001: 22) argues that

> [d]ie ersten wirklichen Umbenennungen führte Bezirksamtmann Fritz auf den Marianen durch, als er am 23. September 1901 durch »Erlaß« die alten Chamorronamen der verschiedenen Inseln wiederherstellte.

This is remarkable insofar as no German CPNs were used to replace those of the previous EC. As Table 1 suggests the above administrative act abolished a plethora of Spanish CPNs based on hagionyms in one go. These hagionymic CPNs are identified by underlining. Note that several of the islands had more than one

---

[4] Except the modern endonym, all of these names are registered as alternatives on Map 28 of the GDKA albeit in Germanized orthography.

name. No Chamorro replacement for Spanish *Farallón de Pajaros* or *Santa Rosa (Reef)* has been reported.[5]

Table 1: Spanish CPNs and their Austronesian replacements in the Marianas.

Chamorro	Spanish
Urak(as)	Farallon de Pajaros 'Birds Rock'
Ma(d)ug	S. Lorenzo ~ Las Monjas 'The Nuns'
Asongsong[6]	Asunción 'Ascencion'
Agrigan ~ Agrihan	Francesco Xavier
Pagan	S. Ignacio
Alamagan	Concepción 'Conception'
Guguan	S. Felipe ~ Piedras 'Stones' ~ Farallon de Torres
Sarigan	S. Carlos
Anatahan ~ Anatagan	S. Joaquin
–	Farallon de Medinilla
Saipan	S. José
Tinian	Buenavista 'Good sight'
Aguihan ~ Aguigan	S. Ángel

---

5 For reasons of practicality, we exclude a number of further toponyms associated with the Marianas from Table 1. Esmeralda Reef, Supply Reef, and Zealandia Bank are not represented cartographically on all of the maps we have consulted. Moreover, Map 28 of the GDKA also mentions a number of terms (in brackets) which are treated as potential alternative designations of a given island but, on closer inspection, do not seem to fit the definition of CPN. A case in point is *Volcano grande* 'huge volcano' which is presented as one of the aliases of *Asongsong ~ Asunción*. It seems plausible to assume that the syntagm was taken from a Spanish map on which certain physical aspects of the individual islands were noted down – in this case the presence of a notably huge active volcano. Similarly the German cartographer of the Marianas provides the information "tätiger Vulkan, 355 m hoch" (= 'active volcano, 355 m high') on the above Map 28.
6 It is likely that the Chamorro name of the island *Asongsong* is a nativized rendering of the Spanish CPN *Asunción*. On the other hand, it cannot be ruled out completely that the Chamorro *songsong* 'plug up, close up (hole), stopper, plug; village' (Topping et al. 1975: 190) functions as the host of the reciprocal prefix *a-* 'one another' (Topping 1973: 175) to yield a genuinely Chamorro place name which resembles its Spanish competitor only outwardly. Note that *Songsong* is also the name of the principal village on the island of Rota.

(Table 1 continued)

Chamorro	Spanish
Rota ~ Luta[7]	S. Ana ~ Zarpana 'Weighing of anchors'
Guam ~ Guahan[8]	S. Juan
–	S. Rosa (Reef)

S. Lazaro, S. Lorenzo, S. Ignacio, S. Felipe, S. Carlos, S. Joaquín, S. José, S. Ángel, S. Ana, S. Juan and *S. Rosa* refer to Catholic saints. *Francesco Xavier* honors the memory of the first Jesuit missionary to work overseas, **Francisco de Yassu y Xavier** (1505–1552). *Asunción* and *Concepción* refer to important events in the life of Mary, mother of Jesus. *Las Monjas* might be indicative of the presence of nuns on the island. *Farallón de Torres* and *Farallón de Medinilla* bear the names of two government officials of the Marianas, namely *Sargento Mayor* **Luís de Torres** (1788–1792) (Rogers 1995: 85) and the military commander and later governor *Don José de* **Medinilla** *y Pineda* (1812–1822, 1826–1831) (Rogers 1995: 90, 95–97). *Farallón de Pájaros, Piedras, Buenavista,* and *Zarpana* are place names of a descriptive nature. With fourteen out of twenty CPNs in Table 1 there is thus a clear preference for employing anthroponyms within place-name constructions – and these anthroponyms, more often than not, are drawn from the religious calendar of the Catholic Church.

If we add to these island names the (modern) names of the villages *San Antonio, San José, San Roque, San Vicente* on Saipan as well as *San Luís de Apra* and *Santa Rita* on Guam[9] to this list of toponymic reflexes of the Spanish reign over the Marianas, we get twenty hagionymic coinings of CPNs – a turnout which ousts by two that of the entire German colonial toponomasticon as shown in (3) above. The surface of the Marianas covers 1,140 km^2, almost half of which go to the credit of Guam alone (DKL II, 504) whereas the German colonial empire occupied a territory of almost 3,000,000 km^2 (Speitkamp 2005: 40). The size of the German colonial empire is more than 2,600 times as large as the archipelago formed by the Marianas. Nevertheless, the absolute numbers of hagionymic CPNs are almost identical for both of the compared territories. This

---

[7] A Spanish origin is also probable in the case of *Rota ~ Luta* which might go back to Spanish *ruta* 'route'.
[8] Whether or not Chamorro *Guam ~ Guahan* represents the phonological adaptation of Spanish *San Juan* is a question we cannot dare to answer in this study.
[9] For further information about the history of CPNs on Guam, we refer the reader to Onedera et al. (1983).

means that there is a striking disproportion in the distribution of hagionymically motivated CPNs across the German colonial empire. The conclusion to be drawn on this basis is that the place-naming preferences of the ECs Spain and Germany widely differed among each other. On the Spanish side, the hagionymic patterns constituted the preferred option whereas they were clearly of marginal importance for the German colonial toponomasticon.

The example of the Spanish impact on the toponymy of the Marianas is indicative of a tendency that can be observed also elsewhere in the domain of colonial place-naming. The ECs often opt for baptizing GOs in a more or less sizeable segment of their sphere of influence according to a virtual system so that clusters of CPNs arise which reflect one and the same motive and motivation. In the above case of the Marianas, the density of hagionymically-based CPNs lends a high degree of homogeneity to the local toponomasticon and, at the same time, connects this relatively marginal territory of the Spanish crown to the bulk of the Spanish colonial empire where hagionyms play an equally important role for the creation of CPNs. The CPN clusters serve the double purpose of claiming the GOs for Spain and making explicit the religiously-tinged state ideology of the EC. In Section 4, we will encounter further examples of clusters of identically motivated CPNs.

In spite of the different preferences of the ECs reviewed above, the Spanish and German practices of coining CPNs still resemble each other at least in certain aspects. The commemoration of important local representatives (e.g. governors) of the EC by way of supposedly immortalizing their names as parts of CPNs is common to the Spanish and the German colonial toponomasticon. Commonalities of this kind are also shared by the bulk of the other ECs.

4 Commonalities

On the basis of the data discussed in the foregoing Sections 2–3, we have identified the major categories of human honorees whose names are prime candidates for being employed in the creation of European CPNs. In this section, we provide evidence of the wide distribution of these patterns from across all European colonialisms.[10] To this end we set up three macro-classes of honorees, namely

---

10 Since several of the ECs only held ephemeral colonial empires which also were relatively small, there are gaps in the distribution of some of the categories we address below. ECs like Austria, Brandenburg-Preußen, Courland, and Sweden never managed to coin more than say,

SAINTS, NOBILITY, and HEROES. This list of categories is not meant to exhaust the phenomenology of anthroponymically-based CPNs. Moreover, the distinctions we make in this study are still very coarse-grained and need to be refined in the future. The above three categories have been selected exclusively because they enjoy a certain prominence in the colonial toponomasticons which facilitates their identification. For each of the three categories we provide an explanation that is intended to shed light on the motives and motivations which determine the choice of a given CPN pattern. To save space, we restrict the empirical documentation to one example per category and EC. This practical solution should not give rise to the false impression that we are dealing with rara and rarissima. Likewise it cannot be assumed that all types were distributed equally. To the contrary, as mentioned above, most of the categories are attested relatively frequently within the different colonial toponomasticons. In addition to the data review for each category we also touch upon instances of clusters of CPNs with identical motivation. The sources from which we draw the examples are identified in the footnotes where we also disclose any further piece of information that might turn out to be relevant in connection with a given CPN. In the main body of the text we address exclusively those issues which transcend the individual cases.

4.1 Saints

We open the presentation by way of illustrating that hagionyms can be found in the vast majority of the colonial toponomasticons of the European brand. Brandenburg-Preußen (= BP) is exceptional insofar as this EC does not participate in the general pattern. The CPNs in (4) prove that thirteen out of fourteen ECs boast hagionymically-based CPNs in their colonial toponomasticons. Since the case-study of the CPNs attested in the Marianas already shows that saintly CPNs may come in great numbers in a relatively small territory, there is no need to prove additionally that there are place-name clusters of this type.

(4)   Overt hagionyms as components of European CPNs
       AU: *St. Joseph*[11]

---

half a dozen of CPNs each so that some of the categories we are interested in were never realized within their colonial toponomasticons.

11 This CPN identifies one of two short-lived forts the Austrians built on the shores of the Delagoa Bay in 1777 only to lose them to the Portuguese again already in 1781 (Randa 1966: 75).

BE: Saint Joseph[12]
CO: St. Andreas[13]
DK: St. Thomas[14]
FR: St. Pierre[15]
GE: Sankt Anton[16]
IT: S. Stefano[17]
NL: Sint Maarten[18]
PG: São Martinho[19]
RU: St. Paul[20]
SP: San Antonio[21]
SW: St. Barthélémy[22]
UK: St. Helena[23]

---

[12] This village was the residence of the apostolic vicar of Luluabourg in the District du Kasaï (Province du Kasaï) of Congo Belge (Michiels & Laude 1953: 297).

[13] St. Andreas was a fortified station situated on an island in the mouth of the Gambia River on the West African coast held by Herzogtum Kurland in the 1650 (Mattiesen 1940: 130). The CPN is probably a Portuguese coining which dates back to the mid-16th century (https://de.wikipedia.org/wiki/Kunta_Kinteh_Island, last accessed 12 April, 2016).

[14] This is the name of the first island of the later Dansk Vestindien (= Danish Virgin Islands) Denmark acquired and colonized in the Caribbean in 1672 (Bro-Jørgensen 1968: 57).

[15] The island of St. Pierre forms part of the French archipelago of St. Pierre-et-Miquelon just off the coast of Newfoundland. This island group is the remainder of Nouvelle France the mainland territories of which were ceded by France to the UK in 1763 (Havard & Vidal 2003: 451).

[16] According to Kausch (1903: 99), Sankt Anton is a village in the Nguru Mountains near Bagamoyo in DOA.

[17] This CPN refers to an island in the Lago Háic in Eritrea (Africa Orientale Italiana). The CPN is not a new coining by the EC but an Italianization of the original Amharic hagionym *Estifanòs* of the Coptic Church (GAOI 321).

[18] The CPN goes back to Christopher Columbus who visited the island on 11 November 1493 "which is the feastday of St. Martin" (Room 2006: 327), *San Martín* in Spanish. The Dutchmen took possession of the island for the first time in 1631 and accommodated its name to the Dutch language as *Sint Maarten* (Hulzen 1946: 91–92).

[19] This CPN (aka *São Martinho do Bilene*) refers to a village in Mozambique prior to the country's independence from Portugal (Gaz 109, 447).

[20] The CPN refers to a fortified Russian settlement which was established on the coast of Kodiak Island in the 1780 (Littke 2003: 108–114).

[21] San Antonio is very popular in the Spanish colonial toponomasticon. Of the many GOs which bear this name we pick out *San Antonio* (aka *San Antonio de Palé*) and *San Antonio de Ureca* both of which are settlements in Guinea Española (Gaz 108, 75).

[22] The French colony St. Barthélemy was sold to Sweden in 1784 only to be handed back to France a century later (Sjögren 1966: 21). The French CPN was kept throughout the Swedish reign over this Caribbean island.

Superficially, it seems as if all ECs alike introduced hagionymically-based CPNs. However, this conclusion is not entirely correct. In (4) boldface marks out those ECs whose official religious orientation was protestant during the age of colonialism. Single underlining identifies the cases of the religiously divided Germany where Catholicism and Protestantism have coexisted for centuries, and the UK whose Anglican Church is not averse to the concept of Saints. With the exception of Orthodox Russia, the remaining ECs can be considered to be bona fide representatives of Catholicism. Given the religious antagonism in Europe in the crucial period of time (= 16th through 19th century) protestant ECs cannot be expected to coin CPNs which involve an overt hagionym since this practice was associated strongly with (especially Iberian) Catholicism.[24]

On closer inspection, however, it turns out that none of the supposedly problematic cases in (4) is a genuine coining of the protestant EC but an inheritance from an earlier Spanish or Portuguese act of place-naming. Bro-Jørgensen (1968: 31) remarks somewhat flippantly in connection to the behavior of the Spaniards in the Caribbean that

> [t]ilmed var spanierne fra første færd indstillet på at trænge længere frem for at finde den eftertragtede vej til Asiens rigdomme. I deres forhold til de mindre øer nåede de derfor ikke videre end til at give dem navne – de talrige Santos og Santas, der viser, at man så at sige rejste med helgenalmanakken i hånden [...].[25]

Val Julián (2011: 74–78) highlights this practice which was especially dominant during the early years of the Spanish expansion in overseas but never ceased to be employed also in later phases of Spanish colonialism. She shows that it was par-

---

23 According to Room (2006: 326) the CPN was introduced as *Santa Helena* by João da Nova who reached the island on 22 May 1502, the feast day of the Catholic St. Helen. The island remained a Portuguese possession until 1651 when the British took control of it.

24 The various Christian denominations represented by the ECs of the early modern age held different views as to the concept of sainthood. Where Catholicism and Orthodoxy clearly favored and continue to favor the adoration of saints, the Protestant churches disagree as to this issue. In the case of Anglicanism, the stance taken depends on how close a congregation associates with the High Church which tolerates sainthood. Lutherans accept those saints whose sainthood was established prior to the schism whereas the Reformed Church strictly disapproves of sainthood (cf. Beyer et al. 2003). What can be concluded on this basis is that it is highly unlikely that Protestant ECs coined hagionymically-based CPNs themselves but some of them had no problems with accepting already established CPNs of this kind.

25 Our translation: [Besides, the Spaniards were intend from the first to advance further to find the searched for passage to Asia's riches. As to the smaller islands they therefore did not achieve more than baptizing them – the many Santos and Santas, which show that, in a manner of speaking one travelled with the calendar of Saints in one's hands...].

ticularly important for an act of place-naming to coincide with the feast day of a saint that was prestigious because of the supposedly powerful protection s/he could offer to the inhabitants of the newly baptized settlement. The aspect of guaranteeing saintly support by naming a GO after a given saint is also essential for the survival of hagionymically-based CPNs in situations of a change of EC.

Several of the minor Caribbean islands which the Spaniards chose to neglect were occupied by rivals in the colonial competition which appeared on the scene in the 17th century. The Spanish government usually protested in vain against the appropriation by foreign powers of what the Spaniards considered their rightful possession (Rella 2010: 135–152). Since the islands thus acquired already bore names introduced by the Spaniards, the new possessors more often than not kept these CNPs with the occasional adaptation to their own language. It is not too farfetched to assume that it was exactly the hagionymic character of many of the originally Spanish CPNs which prevented their replacement with more mundane CPNs. The religious animosity between Catholic and Protestant ECs notwithstanding, it appears that the overt sanctity of the CPNs protected them against toponymic profanation. This protection safeguarded the survival also in many other cases of a change from erstwhile Catholic EC to new Protestant EC as the historical commentary in the footnotes demonstrates.

Hagionyms prompt us to note something general about CPNs. A CPN is characterized by being shaped by colonizers (place-naming) und being used for colonial territories (place-making). The patterns which are used in this context are evidently not necessarily reduced to colonial naming practices. In order to be able to describe a specificity of the colonial, it will be mandatory to conduct comparative studies of respective national or metropolitan toponymicons. Regardless of the question, however, whether patterns are specific for colonial naming practices, we should at first determine, by way of precise description, which patterns are being used in the first place. We do not assume that a toponomastic analysis, as a basic principle, has to provide evidence of specifics in domains, but that it should rather and above all begin with a precise description of which naming practices can be registered in which naming contexts. In this respect, our concern is explicitly descriptive. Only a precise description facilitates comparisons as well as qualitative and quantitative correlation analyses on which bases colonial specifics can then also be highlighted. This said, we do already assume that the colonial appropriation of space is characterized precisely by the transferal of metropolitan patterns. In this sense, the specificity of the colonial may lie in its unmarkedness, that is, in its analogy to non-colonially situated patterns.

4.2 Nobility

The category to be illustrated in this section allows for further subdivisions. The term NOBILITY is meant to cover not only the rulers of monarchies and their families but also politically and/or socio-economically influential members of the nobility of a given EC as well as not necessarily blue-blooded republican heads of state and superordinated members of the metropolitan government. For each of these groups, it is possible to define a distinct sub-category. Space restrictions disallow us to elaborate on these sub-categories. For the purpose of this study, we give examples of toponymically exploited names of monarchic rulers or members of the royal family of ECs in (5).

(5) Names of monarchs as components of European CPNs
AU: *Teressa*[26]
BE: *Léopoldville*[27]
BP: *Groß-Friedrichsburg*[28]
CO: *Jacobusstadt*[29]
DK: *Frederiksøerne*[30]
FR: *Louisbourg*[31]

---

26 One of the Nicobar Islands still bears the name of *Maria **Theresia** von Habsburg* (1717–1780), de jure Queen of Hungary and Bohemia and de facto German empress who encouraged the attempts of her subjects to build a colonial empire in the Indian Ocean – all of which were unsuccessful (Randa 1966: 84).
27 This CPN honors **Léopold** *II* (1835–1909), Roi des Belges, whose private possession, the *État Indépendant du Congo* (founded in 1885) became a state-run colony of Belgium in 1908. The CPN was created by Henry Morton Stanley who explored the Congo region on behalf of the Belgian king (Michiels & Laude 1953: 337).
28 The GO originally received the name *Groß Friedrichs-Berg* on 1st January 1683 when the Brandenburgian Major Otto Friedrich von der Groeben came ashore on the West African Gold Coast. The anthroponymic component *Friedrich* refers to *Kurfürst **Friedrich** III von Brandenburg* (1657–1713) who initiated the colonial adventure of Brandenburg-Preußen (Heyden 2001: 25).
29 **Jakob** *Kettler* (1610–1681), *Herzog von Kurland*, tried to turn his relatively small duchy on the eastern shore of the Baltic Sea into an EC. For a short period of time, Courland possessed inter alia the Caribbean island of Tobago where the settlement *Jacobusstadt* was named in the duke's honor. In the relative literature, the Latvian version of this CPN is sometimes used (Rella 2010: 120–121). However, *Jekaba pilsēta* is an unlikely candidate for the status of an officially recognized CPN since the language of administration in the duchy and the native language of the duke was German.
30 In 1756, this CPN was proposed as a replacement for the original name of the Danish-owned Nicobar Islands (Struwe 1967: 228). The honoree of this CPN was *Kong **Frederik** V* (1723–1766).
31 This CPN refers to the "ville-forteresse" built in 1720 by the French on the Île Royale in the mouth of the St. Lawrence River to protect their Canadian possessions. The CPN honors the *Roi*

GE: *Kaiser-Wilhelmsland*[32]
IT: *Margherita*[33]
NL: *Mauritius*[34]
PG: *Princesa Amélia*[35]
RU: *Alexandrowsk*[36]
SP: *Islas Carolinas*[37]
SW: *Gustavia*[38]
UK: *Victoria Island*[39]

It is striking that direct toponymic references to royalty are scarce within the Portuguese colonial toponomasticon. Metzeltin's (1977) study of the place-naming practices of the Portuguese in the early years of their expansion in Africa does not yield a single CPN which involves the name of a member of the royal family of the country. The same turnout results from Mota's (1950) detailed account of the toponymic manifestations of the Portuguese presence in West Africa. What one can find in lieu of anthroponymically-based CPNs are coinings which refer exclusively to the princely title of the honoree such as *Ilha do Prín-*

Soleil **Louis** *XIV de Bourbon* (1638–1715) who was still alive when the decision was taken in 1714 to erect the fortification (Havard & Vidal 2003: 80).

32 Cf. the information given in connection to the data presented in (1h) above.

33 *Margherita* is the name given by the Italian authorities to a village in Somalia to commemorate **Margherita** *di Savoia-Genova* (1851–1926), Regina d'Italia and royal consort of Umberto I (Paolo Miccoli, p.c.).

34 The Dutch took control of the island in 1598 and baptized it in honor of the *Stadhouder* (regent) **Maurits** *van Oranie-Nassau* (1567–1625) (Room 2006: 242).

35 This CPN identifies a Portuguese fort on the Cubango River in southern Angola which was erected in 1886 (Pélissier 1997: 106). It involves the name of *Maria* **Amélie** *de Orléans* (1865–1951), royal consort of the King of Portugal, Carlos I (Sokop 1993: 58).

36 Alexandrowsk was a fortified Russian settlement on the tip of the Kenai Peninsula on the southern coast of Alaska. The CPN refers to *Tsar* **Alexander** *I Romanow* (1777–1825) who was still Tsarevich when the GO was given his name (Littke 2003: 111).

37 This group of Micronesian islands was "named *Islas Carolinas* [original italics] by the Spanish in 1686 in honor of their king, *Charles II* (1661–1700)" (Room 2006: 79) whose Spanish name is **Carlos** *II de España*.

38 *Gustavia* is the capital of the Caribbean island St. Barthélemy, named after the Swedish king **Gustav** *III Vasa* (1746–1792) who bought the island from France for Sweden (Sjögren 1966: 20–21).

39 "Canada's third largest island [...] was discovered by Thomas Simpson in 1838 and named for Queen *Victoria* [original italics] (1819–1901), who had come to the throne the previous year" (Room 2006: 395).

*cipe*⁴⁰, *Ilhéu do Rei*⁴¹, and *Rio d'El-Rei*⁴² which involve the components *príncipe* 'prince' and *rei* 'king'.

As to the creation of clusters of similarly motivated anthroponymically-based CPNs, we draw the reader's attention to the CPNs in (6).

(6) CPNs in the South Pacific which honor British noblemen
*Auckland*⁴³, *Brisbane*⁴⁴, *Cape York*⁴⁵, *Hobart*⁴⁶, *Melbourne*⁴⁷, *Murray River*⁴⁸, *Norfolk Island*⁴⁹, *Palmerston*⁵⁰, *Port Moresby*⁵¹, *Sydney*⁵²

---

40 This CPN identifies one of the former Portuguese island possessions in the Gulf of Guinea. It was named "in honor of *Prince* [original italics] Alphonso, the future Alphonso V (1432–1481), king of Portugal" (Room 2006: 304). The act of place-naming must have taken place during the 1470s (LzÜG 714).
41 This CPN identifies a small island in Guinea Portuguesa and dates back to the year 1796 but may be much older (Mota 1950: 148–149). Thus, it cannot be stated with any certainty to which of the Portuguese rulers of the 18th century the CPN refers.
42 Mota (1950: 130) assumes that this CPN which refers to a GO in Guinea Portuguesa has arisen in the second half of the 19th century. It is unclear therefore to which of the three kings who ruled Portugal at that time the CPN refers.
43 According to Room (2006: 39) the city of Auckland "was founded in 1840 as the capital of British colonial New Zealand and was named for George Eden, Earl of *Auckland* [original italics] (1784–1849), first lord of the Admiralty."
44 Room (2006: 68) states that "[t]he capital of Queensland is named for Sir Thomas Makdougall *Brisbane* [original italics] (1773–1860), the Scottish general who was governor of New South Wales [...] from 1821 to 1825."
45 This peninsula in Queensland is Australia's northernmost point. The CPN was coined by Captain Cook in 1770 to honor *Edward Augustus, Duke of* **York** *and Albany* (1739–1767), a brother of King George III (Room 2006: 413).
46 The British colonial secretary, *Robert* **Hobart***, 4th Earl of Buckinghamshire* (1760–1816) is the honoree of the name of the capital of Tasmania (Room 2006: 166).
47 Melbourne is the capital of the Australian state Victoria and "was so named in 1837 in honor of William Lamb, 2nd Viscount *Melbourne* [original italics] (1779–1848), the British prime minister of the day" (Room 2006: 244).
48 As to the origins of this CPN, Room (2006: 258) explains that "Australia's principal river was discovered in 1824 by the English emigrant explorer W. H. Hovell and Australian bushman Andrew Hume, and the former originally named it for his companion as the *Hume* [original italics]. In 1830 it was renamed by the British explorer Captain Charles Sturt in honor of Sir George *Murray* [original italics] (1772–1846), colonial secretary at that time."
49 Captain Cook discovered the island in 1774. The CPN refers to *Edward Howard, 9th Duke of* **Norfolk** (1686–1777) (Room 2006: 272).
50 This CPN replaced the earlier toponym Port Darwin in 1869 and refers to the British Prime Minister *Henry John Temple, 3rd Viscount* **Palmerston** (1784–1865). The old place name was re-established in 1911 (Room 2006: 105 and 286).
51 The modern capital of independent Papua New Guinea received its name in colonial times in 1873 when the explorer Captain John Moresby "named it for his father, Admiral Sir Fairfax

The CPNs in (6) are interesting insofar as most of them involve that part of a British nobleman's full name which identifies the GO for which the honoree bears the noble title, i.e., *Norfolk* in the CPN *Norfolk Island* is indirectly also connected to the toponym *Norfolk*, a county in eastern England.

These ten CPNs from Australia, New Zealand and nearby areas do by no means exhaust the inventory of GO which were named after representative of the British oligarchy starting from the late 18th and continuing throughout the 19th century. It is true that this pattern of place-naming is also common elsewhere in the British Empire. However, the CPNs of this kind abound especially in the area under review. It suggests itself that the choice of honoree was motivated by patriotism which supported the existing political system of the United Kingdom by way of commemorating some of those who held office at the time of the coining of the CPN. At the same time, this practice can also be seen as an attempt at endearing oneself to the politically powerful honorees. In regard to this issue, it is telling what Room (2006: 404) tells us about the motivation for the creation of the CPN *Wellington* for the capital of New Zealand (which can be added to the list in (10)):

> The city [...] was founded in 1840 and named for Arthur Wellesley, 1st Duke of *Wellington* [original italics] (1769–1852) [...]. The name commemorated not so much the duke's victory at Waterloo (1815) as the generous aid he gave to the New Zealand Company, whose colonizing members had arrived the previous year with the task of finding a suitable site for their proposed settlement.

This means that baptizing a GO after a prominent personality may have the function of showing one's gratitude to a socially superior generous supporter who was or would be helpful politically and/or economically for one's projects. In this way, the map of the colonies can be used as an ostentatious means of communication with the politically powerful in the metropolis.

4.3 Heroes

Our provisional category of so-called HEROES is very heterogeneous and thus calls for being thoroughly revised in studies to come. For the time being, how-

---

Moresby [original italics] (1786–1877). Locally the city is known simply as *Moresby* [original italics]" (Room 2006: 301).

52 Sydney is "[t]he capital of New South Wales, Australia's largest city and its first British settlement, [it] was founded in 1788 and named for the British home secretary, Thomas Townsend, 1st Viscount *Sydney* [original italics] (1733–1800)" (Room 2006: 364).

ever, it has the purely practical advantage of permitting us to collect a multitude of data without having to determining how exactly the single items have to be classified. At this early stage of our research this is admissible methodologically. In the future further sub-divisions of the category of HEROES have to be defined and distinguished from each other.

The notion of HEROES we employ in this study is intensionally vague and thus has a very large extension. We admit in this category any honoree who has actively contributed to a given EC's imperialistic enterprise and/or is representative of the putative cultural and political superiority of the EC in comparison to the colonized people. This allows for an assemblage of honorees who are administrators, adventurers, conquerors, explorers, merchants, missionaries, pioneers, poets, scientists, settlers, etc. Some of these potential sub-categories are represented in (7). This type of CPN is not found in the colonial toponomasticons of BP, CO, and SW.

(7) Names of heroes as components of European CPNs
   AU: *Fort Benjowski*[53]
   BE: *Vankerckhovenville*[54]
   DK: *Egedeminde*[55]
   FR: *Rabelais*[56]
   GE: *Schopenhauer-Berge*[57]

---

[53] With US-American support the Austro-Polish adventurer and multiple turncoat *Graf Moritz August* **Benjowski** (1746–1786) erected a fort in Madagascar in the mid-1780ies which he held nominally for Austria until he was killed on occasion of a French attack in 1786 (Littke 2003: 235–238). The CPN is an instance of autoreferential place-naming since Benjowksi used his own last name to baptize the fort.

[54] The Belgian officer *Guillaume* **Vankerckhoven** was killed accidentally in 1892 (elsewhere the year given is 1893) during a military expedition to conquer new regions for the État Indépendant du Congo, the predecessor of the Congo Belge. Masoin (1913: 263, fn. 1) remarks that "[p]our perpétuer son nom, le gouvernement donna au chef-lieu de la zone des Makaras dans le Haut Uelé le nom de Vankerckhovenville (1897)."

[55] In 1760, Egedesminde (lit. 'Egede's memory') was founded on the west coast of Greenland to fill the empty space between the northerly and southerly Danish establishments. The founder was Niels Egede who named the new settlement after his father *Hans* **Egede** (also known as Greenland's Apostle) who had initiated and mostly also conducted the Herrnhut missionary activities in Greenland in 1721 (Lidegaard 2001: 88–102).

[56] This CPN was given to a settlement in the western part of Algiers (ACI-F 26). It bears the name of *François* **Rabelais** (1494–1533), one of the most outstanding representatives of French literature in the Renaissance.

[57] This CPN refers to a mountain range in Kaiser-Wilhelmsland. It is named after the German philosopher *Arthur* **Schopenhauer** (1788–1860) (Kausch 1903: 101).

IT: *Dante*[58]
NL: *Fort Ernestus*[59]
PG: *Silva Porto*[60]
RU: *Ostrova Pribylova*[61]
SP: *Villa Cisneros*[62]
UK: *Hamilton*[63]

It strikes the eye that in five of the eleven cases mentioned in (7) the CPN honors a person who died at least indirectly as a consequence of his activities in the colony. The commemoration of those who sacrificed their lives for the cause of the EC is a very common motivation for the coining of CPNs. In the case of the French colonization of the Chad region, it has become the dominant pattern of the colonial toponymy introduced by the EC.

In (8) we provide a selection of French CPNs in the Chad, the second component of which consists of the last name of a French officer or non-commissioned officer killed in action in this colony of France (Montagnon 1988: 289 footnote 10; Guillorel 2008: 7).[64]

---

[58] The famous national poet of Italy, **Dante** *Alighieri* (1265–1321) is the honoree of this CPN of a town in the north of the Italian colony Somalia (GAOI 620).

[59] This is the name of two fortifications the Dutch erected on the island Antonio Vaz to protect the capital of their possessions in Brazil, Mauritsstad or Mauritia. Fort Ernestus was built in 1640 and was given the name of *Johan* **Ernst** *van Nassau* (1618–1639), the younger brother of the governor of the Dutch colony, Johan Maurits van Nassau. The honoree died in Brazil during the Dutch conquest of Salvador de Bahía (Bouman 1947: 66).

[60] This CPN replaced that of *Belmonte* in the Bie region of Angola. It commemorates the elderly Portuguese merchant-explorer *Silva Porto* who was involved in the frustrated attempts of Portugal to claim possession of the inner-African territory that could have joined Angola and Mozambique. He committed suicide in 1890 because of the failure of this project and "est immédiatement promu en métropole au rôle de héros national, martyr romantique" (Pélissier 2004: 131).

[61] The islands which bare this CPN are located to the west of Alaska of which they form part. They are named after the Russian explorer *Gavril* (aka *Gerasim*) **Pribylov** who discovered the islands in 1788 (Littke 2003: 90).

[62] The CPN Villa *Cisneros* was created by the Spanish authorities on occasion of the annexation of the West Sahara (Rio de Oro and Saguía el Hamra) in 1884/7 in commemoration of *Gonzalo Jímenez de* **Cisneros** (1436–1517), the archbishop of Toledo, confessor of Isabela de Castilia and propagandist of the strict anti-Moor policy of Spain at his time (https://de.wikipedia.org/wiki/Gonzalo_Jim%C3%A9nez_de_Cisneros, [last accessed 12 April, 2016]).

[63] Hamilton is a city in New Zealand which goes back to a British military settlement founded in 1864 "on the site of a deserted Maori village. It was named for Captain John *Hamilton* [original italics], a British naval officer killed fighting Maoris" (Room 2006: 158).

[64] Several of the honorees of the CPNs in (8) and further cases of the same type have not been identified yet. We therefore refrain from giving any biographical information about the French military-men at all.

(8) CPNs in the Chad which commemorate French casualties
Fort Archambault, Fort Bretonnet, Fort Crampel, Fort de Cointet, Fort-Foureau, Fort Lamy, Fort Millot, Fort Possel

This practice began in 1900 with the introduction of the CPN *Fort Lamy* and continued until the end of the First World War. The GO thus named usually were forts or fortified settlements located in the vicinity of the battlefield on which the honoree received his lethal wound.

Since the toponymic commemoration of the EC's casualties in the Chad yielded a sizeable turnout of CPNs which refer to GOs in one and the same geographic region, the map of this French colony resembles a war cemetery, in a manner of speaking. In contrast, the British practice of place-naming discussed in connection with the data in (7) above give rise metaphorically to the image of the government benches or the House of Lords. The Spanish CPNs in the Marianas as discussed in Section 3, on the other hand, invoke the setting of a religious function of the Catholic Church. It is tempting to assume that these different images reflect in some way the ideology and/or self-perception of the different ECs. We cannot pursue this topic here because it deserves to be studied properly and in depth within the framework of discourse linguistics. Therefore, the thorough investigation of this issue has to be relegated to a separate dedicated study.

5 Conclusions

The previous sections have shown that it makes sense linguistically to investigate thoroughly the toponymic manifestations of colonialism. The cases reviewed above are indicative of a relatively restricted set of motivations for the choice of honorees of CPNs assigned by ECs to a GO in the colonies. Since many of the similarities are shared either by all or the majority of the fourteen ECs accounted for in this study, it can be concluded that there is strong evidence of pan-EC patterns of colonial place-naming. The common motivations of CPNs cannot be explained sufficiently in terms of the undeniable structural similarities of the languages of the ECs alone; we assume that the general convergence of the place-naming practices is explicable much rather as the effect of the permanent competition for hegemony which impelled the ECs to copy the patterns their rivals employed.

However, this tendency does not preclude the possibility of different ECs giving preference to different motivation categories. In the absence of robust statistical data, we can only hypothesize on the basis of our prior qualitative research that the colonial toponomasticons of say, France, Spain, and the UK differ from each other in terms of how many of the CPNs belong to categories such as saints, nobility, and heroes. The differences seem to be of a gradual nature and not of the categorical kind. To determine conclusively to what extent the colonial toponomasticons of the ECs agree with each other and/or display individual traits, it is necessary to take stock empirically of the entire wealth of CPNs – a task that will have to be tackled in the near future. What is clear already at this stage of our project is that the ECs treated the maps of their colonies as largely empty, i.e. as an area in which they were entitled to mark their claims by way of naming places.

Acknowledgments: This study forms part of our joint project *Comparative Colonial Toponomastics (CoCoTop)* which has developed within the framework of the *Creative Unit (CU) Koloniallinguistik/Language in Colonial Contexts* at the University of Bremen/Germany (2012–2016). We are grateful to the members of our project teams for their kind support and their intellectual input. We especially mention by name Barbara Dewein, Sonja Kettler, Nataliya Levkovych, Daniel Schmidt-Brücken, Susanne Schuster, Cornelia Stroh, and Marina Wienberg. The organizers of the workshop on colonial linguistics in Klagenfurt/Austria in March 2015 deserve an extra word of thanks for giving us the opportunity to present our ideas to an interested audience. We are also indebted to Stefan Engelberg and Philippe Krämer for their thought-provoking comments on the talk we gave on occasion of the above workshop. Rosa Salas Palomo kindly gave us access to an important publication on place names on Guam. We assure Brigitte Weber and Alexander Onysko of our gratefulness for commenting on the draft version and accepting our revised paper for publication in the proceedings of the workshop. Whatever our many helpers have contributed to making us think twice about our original ideas, we as authors assume the entire responsibility for what is said how and why in this study.

Abbreviations

ANTH	anthroponym
AU	Austria
BE	Belgium
BP	Brandenburg-Preußen
CLASS	classifier

CO	Courland
CPN	colonial place name
DK	Denmark
DERIV	derivational morpheme
DNG	Deutsch-Neuguinea
DOA	Deutsch-Ostafrika
DSWA	Deutsch-Südwestafrika
EC	European colonizer
FR	France
GE	Germany
GEN	genitive
GO	geographical object
IT	Italy
NL	The Netherlands
KA	Cameroon
KI	Kiautschou
MA	Mariana Islands
PG	Portugal
RU	Russia
SA	Samoa
SP	Spain
SW	Sweden
TO	Togo
TOP	toponym
UK	United Kingdom

References

(a) Atlases and encyclopedias

ACI-F = *Atlas colonial illustré. Géographie, voyages & conquêtes – productions, administration.* Paris: Librairie Larousse, 1904.

DKL = *Deutsches Kolonial-Lexikon.* I Band: A–G, II Band: H–O, III Band: P–Z, herausgegeben von Dr. Heinrich Schnee. Leipzig: Quelle & Meyer, 1920.

GAOI = *Guida dell'Africa Orientale Italiana*, a cura della Consociazione Turistica Italiana. Milano: C.T.I., 1938.

Gaz 108 = *Gazetteer No.108 Spanish Guinea.* Official Standard Names approved by the United States Board on Geographic Names. Prepared in the Office of Geography, Department of the Interior, Washington D.C., June 1962.

Gaz 109 = *Gazetteer No. 109: Mozambique.* Official Standard Names approved by the United States Board on Geographic Names. Prepared in the Office of Geography, Department of the Interior, Washington D.C., June 1969.

GDKA = *Großer Deutscher Kolonialatlas*, herausgegeben von der Kolonialabteilung des Auswärtigen Amtes (bearbeitet von Paul Sprigade und Max Moisel). Berlin: Dietrich Reimer (Ernst Vossen), 1901–1915. Reprint with addenda: Köln: Komet, 2002.

LzÜG = *Lexikon zur Überseegeschichte*, herausgegeben von Hermann Hiery im Auftrag der Gesellschaft für Überseegeschichte. Stuttgart, Steiner, 2015.

(b) Monographs and scholarly articles

Agha, Asif. 2003. The social life of cultural value. *Language & Communication* 23(3–4). 231–273.

Anderson, John M. 2007. *The grammar of names*. Oxford: Oxford University Press.

Batoma, Atoma. 2006. African ethnonyms and toponyms. An annotated bibliography. *Electronic Journal of Africana Bibliography* 10. 1–40.

Beyer, Jürgen et al. (eds.). 2003. *Confessional Sanctity (c. 1550 – c. 1800)*. Mainz: Philipp von Zabern.

Bouman, P. J. 1947. *Johan Maurits van Nassau. De Braziliaan*. Utrecht: N.V.A. Oosthoek.

Bro-Jørgensen, J. J. 1968. *Vore gamle tropekolonier. Bind 1: Dansk Vestindien indtil 1755. Kolonisation og kompagnistyre*. København: Fremad.

Castro Varela, María do Mar & Nikita Dhawan. 2015. *Postkoloniale Theorie. Eine kritische Einführung*. Bielefeld: Transcript.

Dewein, Barbara et al. 2012. Forschungsgruppe Koloniallinguistik: Profil – Programmatik – Projekte. *Zeitschrift für Germanistische Linguistik* 40(2). 242–249.

Guillorel, Hervé. 2008. Introduction. In Hervé Guillorel (ed.), *Toponymie et politique. Les marqueurs linguistiques du territoire*, 1–9. Bruxelles: Bruylant.

Havard, Gilles & Cécile Vidal. 2003. *Histoire de l'Amérique française*. Paris: Flammarion.

Heyden, Ulrich van der. 2001. *Rote Adler an Afrikas Küste. Die brandenburgisch-preußische Kolonie Großfriedrichsburg in Westafrika*. Berlin: Selignow.

Hiery, Hermann Joseph. 2001. Zur Einführung: die Deutschen und die Südsee. In Hermann Joseph Hiery (ed.), *Die deutsche Südsee 1884–1914. Ein Handbuch*, 1–26. Paderborn: Schöningh.

Hulzen, Johan van. 1946. *Onze westindische geschiedenis*. 's-Gravenhage: van Hoeve.

Kausch, Oskar. 1903. *Deutsches Kolonial-Lexikon*. Dresden: Kühtmann.

Labanca, Nicola. 2002. *Oltremare. Storia dell'espansione coloniale italiana*. Bologna: Il Mulino.

Lidegaard, Mads. 2001. *Grönlands historia*. Stockholm: Boviggen.

Littke, Peter. 2003. *Die Geschichte Russisch-Alaskas. Vom Zarenadler zum Sternenbanner*. Düsseldorf: Magnus.

Masoin, Fritz. 1913. *Historie de l'État Indépendant du Congo*. 2 tomes. Namur: Picard-Balon.

Mattiesen, Otto Heinz. 1940. *Die Kolonial- und Überseepolitik der kurländischen Herzöge im 17. und 18. Jahrhundert*. Stuttgart & Berlin: Kohlhammer.

Metzeltin, Miguel. 1977. La toponimia de los primeros descubrimientos. Contribución a una teoría de la toponimización. In Manuel Alvar (ed.), *Actas del V Congreso Internacional de Estudios Lingüísticos del Mediterráneo*, 622–634. Madrid: CSIC.

Meyers, Debra. 2003. *Common whores, virtuous women, and loving wives. Free Will Christian Women in Colonial Maryland*. Bloomington, IN: Indiana University Press.

Michiels, Albert & Norbert Laude. 1953. *Notre colonie. Géographie et notice historique*. Bruxelles: L'Édition universelle.

Möller, Lucie A. 1986. *'n Toponimies-linguistiese ondersoek na duitse plekname in Suidwes-Afrika*. Voorgelê ter vervulling van 'n deel van die vereistes vir die graad Doctor Philosophiae in die Departement Afrikaans en Nederlands. Durban: Universiteit van Natal.

Montagnon, Pierre. 1988. *La France coloniale. La gloire de l'empire. Du temps des croisades à la seconde guerre mondiale*. Paris: Éditions Pygmalion.

Mota, A. Teixeira da. 1950. *Topónimos de origem portuguesa na costa ocidental de África desde o Cabo Bojador ao Cabo de Santa Caterina*. Bissau: Centro de Estudos da Guiné Portuguesa.

Nübling, Damaris, Fabian Fahlbusch & Rita Heuser. 2012. *Namen. Eine Einführung in die Onomastik*. Tübingen: Gunther Narr.

Onedera, Peter et al. 1983. *Nå'an lugåt siha gi ya Guåhan*. Hagåtña: Kumision i fino' Chamorro.

Pélissier, René. 1997. *História das campanhas de Angola. Resistência e revoltas 1845–1941*. Vol. II. Lisboa: Estampa.

Pélissier, René. 2004. *Les campagnes coloniales du Portugal (1844–1941)*. Paris: Pygmalion.

Randa, Alexander. 1966. *Österreich in Übersee*. Wien: Herold.

Rella, Christoph. 2010. *Im Anfang war das Fort. Europäische Fortifizierungspolitik als Instrument der Welteroberung. Guinea und Westindien 1415–1678*. Münster: Aschendorff.

Rogers, Robert F. 1995. *Destiny's landfall. A history of Guam*. Honolulu: University of Hawai'i.

Room, Adrian. 2006. *Placenames of the world. Origins and meanings of the names for 6,600 countries, cities, territories, natural features and historic sites*. Jefferson & London: McFarland & Co.

Sjögren, Bengt. 1966. *I Västindien: Ön som Sverige sålde*. Uddevalla: Zindermans.

Sokop, Brigitte. 1993. *Stammtafeln europäischer Herrscherhäuser*. Wien & Köln & Weimar: Böhlau.

Speitkamp, Winfried. 2005. *Deutsche Kolonialgeschichte*. Stuttgart: Reclam.

Stolz, Thomas & Ingo H. Warnke. 2015. Aspekte der kolonialen und postkolonialen Toponymie unter besonderer Berücksichtigung des deutschen Kolonialismus. In Daniel Schmidt-Brücken et al. (eds.), *Koloniallinguistik – Sprache in kolonialen Kontexten*, 195–266. Berlin & Boston: De Gruyter Mouton.

Stolz, Thomas & Ingo H. Warnke. 2016. When places change their names and when they do not. Selected aspects of colonial and postcolonial toponymy in former French and Spanish colonies in West Africa – the case of Saint Louis (Senegal) and the Western Sahara. *International Journal of the Sociology of Language* 239. 29–56.

Stolz, Thomas & Ingo H. Warnke. 2017. Anoikonyme und Oikonyme im Kontext der vergleichenden Kolonialtoponomastik. In Axel Dunker, Thomas Stolz & Ingo H. Warnke (eds.), *Benennungspraktiken in Prozessen kolonialer Raumaneignung*, 205–229. Berlin & Boston: De Gruyter Mouton.

Stolz, Thomas & Ingo H. Warnke. 2018a. Auf dem Weg zu einer vergleichenden Kolonialtoponomastik: der Fall Deutsch-Südwestafrika. In Birte Kellermeier-Rehbein, Matthias Schulz & Doris Stolberg (eds.), *Sprache und (Post)-Kolonialismus. Linguistische und interdisziplinäre Aspekte*, 71–103. Berlin & Boston: De Gruyter Mouton.

Stolz, Thomas & Ingo H. Warnke. 2018b. Comparative colonial toponomastics: Evidence from German and Dutch colonial place names. In Rita Heuser et al. (eds.), *Sonstige Namenarten – Stiefkinder der Onomastik*, 45–68. Berlin & Boston: De Gruyter Mouton.

Stolz, Thomas, Ingo H. Warnke & Nataliya Levkovych. 2016. Colonial place names in a comparative perspective. *Beiträge zur Namenforschung* 51(3/4). 279–355.

Struwe, Kamma. 1967. *Vore gamle tropekolonier. Bind 6: Dansk Ostindien 1732–1776. Tranquebar under kompagnistyre.* København: Fremad.
Topping, Donald. 1973. *Chamorro reference grammar.* Honolulu: University of Hawaii Press.
Topping, Donald, Pedro M. Ogo & Bernadita C. Dungca. 1975. *Chamorro-English dictionary.* Honolulu: University of Hawaii Press.
Val Julián, Carmen. 2011. La realidad y el deseo. Toponymie du découvreur en Amérique espagnole (1492–1520). In Julien Roger et al. (eds.), *La realidad y el deseo. Toponymie du découvreur en Amérique, suivi de textes en hommage à l'auteur,* 30–148. Lyon: ENS.
Van Langendonck, Willy. 2007. *Theory and typology of proper names.* Berlin & New York: Mouton de Gruyter.
Warnke, Ingo, Thomas Stolz & Daniel Schmidt-Brücken. 2016. Perspektiven der Postcolonial Language Studies. In Thomas Stolz, Ingo H. Warnke & Daniel Schmidt-Brücken (eds.), *Sprache und Kolonialismus. Eine interdisziplinäre Einführung zu Sprache und Kommunikation in kolonialen Kontexten,* 1–26. Berlin & Boston: De Gruyter Mouton.
Weber, Brigitte. 2012. Exploration of Deutsch-Kamerun: A toponymic approach. In Stefan Engelberg & Doris Stolberg (eds.), *Sprachwissenschaft und kolonialzeitlicher Sprachkontakt. Sprachliche Begegnungen und Auseinandersetzungen,* 101–122. Berlin: Akademie Verlag.

(c) Online sources

https://de.wikipedia.org/wiki/Gonzalo_Jim%C3%A9nez_de_Cisneros [last accessed 12 April, 2016].
https://de.wikipedia.org/wiki/Kunta_Kinteh_Island [last accessed 12 April, 2016].

Susanne Schuster
"The making of Greenland" – Early European place names in Kalaallit Nunaat

"[...] and it may be mentioned that the really valuable English, Danish and Dutch maps of Greenland, which were published in the 17th century, were founded upon their [the Englishmen, Hall, Hudson and Baffin, the Danes, Lindenow, Jens Munk and David Danell, and the Dutchman, Joris Carolus and others] experiences and observations. In spite of their great inaccuracies [...] these maps not only supplied a solid basis, hitherto lacking, for **the making of Greenland** and the establishment [...] of the principal courses along its coasts [...]" [emphasis added] (Garde 1929: 225).

Abstract: Place names play a crucial role in understanding how people relate to landscapes through language. By giving names to geographical features, colonizers claim authority not only over these places but also over indigenous cultures and people. For this reason, the evaluation of colonial toponyms is an important aspect of colonial and postcolonial linguistics. With its long-lasting colonial history, Greenland (Kalaallit Nunaat) is a suitable candidate for such a toponymic case study. The arctic island shows a multitude of toponyms from various European source languages. This paper intends to give an account of their structural and functional properties in order to reveal similarities which could support a prototypical practice of colonial name giving, as well as differences to show how specific naming patterns might be motivated by the intentions of the colonizers and by particular contact situations.

Keywords: Greenland, linguistic place-making, colonial place names, mapping

1 Introduction

The phrase quoted in the title of this paper is taken from an essay on the navigation of Greenland and gives clear evidence for colonial attitudes and place-making in the sense of Busse & Warnke (2014). The author of the quotation, Danish naval officer Thomas Vilhelm Garde, puts into words – centuries before the "cultural turn" in the humanities of the late 1980s – the construction of landscape via place-naming as has been formulated in Busse & Warnke (2014: 2):

Susanne Schuster, University of Bremen, FB 10: Linguistics/Language Sciences, Universitäts-Boulevard 13, 28359 Bremen, Germany. E-Mail: suschu@uni-bremen.de

https://doi.org/10.1515/9783110623710-003

> Raum existiert nicht unabhängig von sprachlichen Kategoriensystemen, Raum ist kein fixiertes materielles Denotat – [...] –, sondern wird durch diese überhaupt erst in spezifischer Weise wahrnehmbar und hervorgebracht. Sprache verweist also nicht nur auf Raum, sondern bringt diesen zugleich hervor. Und es ist nicht nur der Raum, der hervorgebracht wird durch Sprache, sondern es sind vor allem auch Orte im Raum, die erst durch sprachliche Praktiken und sprachliche Interaktion von Akteuren identifizierbar und erinnerbar bzw. als solche kreiert werden.[1]

Mapping and exploring Greenland was an important project mainly of 17th century's English navigators in search for a north-western passage to Asia. In doing so, they created "exploratory mapping environments in which knowledge is constructed" (Crampton 2001: 236). However, not only were the British heading towards Greenland but also many other European nations and for many different reasons. They all left traces, more or less visible nowadays, in the Greenlandic toponomasticon. This diachronically oriented paper intends to shed light on the linguistic colonialism executed by Norse settlers, Dutch whalers, English navigators, Danish and German missionaries and traders. They all claimed authority interpreting unstructured space, as well as inhabited places, by individuating geographical entities and naming them in their language (cf. Vuolteenaho & Berg 2009: 10 and Stolz & Warnke 2016).

It is important to emphasize that this paper is by no means intended to perpetuate colonialism nor colonial practices. The fatal impacts of foreign rule on Greenland's population are well-known and cannot be overrated (cf. for an indigenous view: Petersen 1995). Still, it is beyond the scope of this study to examine the difficult process of decolonization or the re-indigenization of place names. Instead, it aims at reflecting historical practices of naming places in order to contribute to the understanding of language uses an important factor in constituting and reinforcing unequal power relations in colonial contexts. Because of their visibility not only in ancient text sources and on historical maps but also in contemporary discourse (just consider the country's international name *Greenland* which has been coined by early medieval settlers from Iceland) they are witnesses of "the power and possibilities of 'making places'" (Vuolteenaho & Berg 2009: 9). Naming places as a demonstration of power highlights the relevance of language for colonial and postcolonial affairs as has

---

[1] My translation: [Space does not exist independently from linguistic categorical systems, space is no fixed physical denotatum [...], instead these systems make it perceivable in a specific way and thus generate it. Language does not only refer to space but produces it at the same time. Furthermore, it is not only that space is generated by language, but first of all there are places in space which are being made identifiable, memorable and are thus created as such by linguistic practices and linguistic interaction of agents].

been pointed out in various articles (Warnke 2009; Stolz & Warnke 2015) who speak of "language based and language generated colonialism" (Stolz & Warnke 2016: 32). Vuolteenaho & Berg (2009: 10) are right to cite Carter (1987: xxiii–xxiv): "the hegemonic acts of naming transform polymorphous and uncontrollable 'space' into a finite system of neatly isolatable, stabilized and interconnected 'places'". This is especially true for places like Greenland, or in Carters case Australia, which were supposedly terra nullius.

With its strictly data based approach, this paper is written within the framework outlined in Warnke (2009), Stolz et al. (2011) and Dewein et al. (2012). It is embedded in a research program termed "Language in Colonial and Postcolonial Contexts" and with its inductive methodology it contributes to the data collection and analysis asked for in Stolz & Warnke (2016).

Earlier studies (Stolz & Warnke 2016, 2018a and 2018b) have given rise to the assumption that there might be "common principles of the linguistic appropriation of foreign territory by way of place-making [...]" (Stolz & Warnke 2016: 32). These principles seem to vary according to the kinds of colonization: "There is evidence, however, that the toponomasticons of settler colonies, on the one hand, and fort and plantation colonies, on the other hand, may differ from each other systematically" (Stolz et al. 2016: 283, fn. 7). These two observations allow us to formulate two hypotheses which will be tested with a comparative analysis of 129 historically documented toponyms from five European nations:

Hypothesis I: Place names in colonial contexts share characteristic features, even if they originate from different source languages.

Hypothesis II: Besides these similarities, there are differences which are rather related to the type of colonization than to the type of territory.

Nowadays, Greenland or Kalaallit Nunaat 'Land of the Kalaallit' is a self-governing part of the Kingdom of Denmark, it had the status of a colony from 1721 until 1953 (Nuttall 2005a: 784, Kleivan 1977: 197). Besides this de jure colonial rule, it had been affected by multiple foreign influences in the course of time, caused by its exposed geographical position. Due to climatic conditions all colonial activities were concentrated on the south and west coast. This situation – many different groups and nations being confronted with the same geological conditions – provides the preconditions for the testing of the two hypotheses: variability of source languages in combination with stable territorial conditions.

A considerable body of literature has investigated toponyms in Greenland. Since the authority of naming places has been given to the indigenous people of Greenland in 1984, the *Nunat Aqqinik Aalajangiisartut* [Place Name Committee] is responsible and has published a list of 96 authorized place names.² They are all Kalaallisut toponyms except for six Danish station names such as *Daneborg*. The article of the committee's chairman Carl Christian Olsen (2008) gives valuable information about the aims and the development of the committee whereas Lisathe Møller Kruse (2012), as an active member of this committee, contrasts in her paper indigenous and European naming practices.

Besides these works on toponyms from an indigenous perspective, there are numerous other notable works on the European legacy in Greenland mirrored in place names: Among them is Laursen's collection of place names of North Greenland (1972). Laursen was especially interested in the origin of the place names that he encountered as a member of several geological expeditions in the late 1930s (Laursen 1972: 7). Inge Kleivan (1996) collects place names of the very early state of colonization. Her critical view on cultural imperialism is made explicit in Kleivan (1977). The more recent work of Higgins (2010) focuses on toponyms from the northern part of East Greenland (north of 69°N). This literally uninhabitable area was first reached by Europeans in 1822.

The value of these works notwithstanding, they all tend to focus on the etymology of the toponyms. Much less is known about their linguistic structure, however. The aim of this paper is therefore to explore and to compare systematically the place names given by various European nations to the same or similar landscape in the course of time. According to Stolz et al. (2016: 35) I will deal with these toponyms as "colonial place names", being aware of the ideological perspective of the term "colonial" (Warnke et al. 2016: 3) but still lacking a more appropriate term. My understanding of "colonial" does thus not only comprise its narrow and rather innocent sense as "a settlement in a new country: a body of people who settle in a new locality" (Oxford English Dictionary online) but a more general meaning as stated in Loomba (2005: 11): "the takeover of territory, appropriation of material resources, exploitation of labour and interference with political and cultural structures of another territory or nation [...]".

Throughout this paper the indigenous population of Greenland is referred to with the rather general term Inuit or more specifically Greenlanders, as the commonly used ethnonym *Kalaallit* might be considered an expression of unequal power relations as well: it is not the name of all inhabitants of the island but only of the western and dominant ones of three Greenlandic populations (cf. Nuttall 2005a: 780 and 2005b: 791). Thus the name *Kalaallit*

---

2 *Nunaqarfiit illoqarfiillu aqqi akuerisat* [Overview of the Greenlandic city-and settlement names and their abbreviations approved by the Greenland Place Names Committee].

Nunaat 'Land of the Kalaallit' is an "example of cultural imperialism among the Greenlanders themselves" (Kleivan 1977: 199). For this reason, I prefer to use the English term "Greenland".

The paper is organized as follows: After a short introduction of the historical background and today's situation of Greenland's toponomasticon, I will lay out the methodological approach following Anderson (2007), Nübling et al. (2012) and Stolz & Warnke (2018a). The European based place names and their analysis are then presented according to their source languages and arranged in roughly chronological order. The remaining part of the paper is concerned with a concluding discussion.

A contemporary map of the respective area is included at the end of the text to facilitate orientation.

2 Historical background

2.1 Waves of immigration

Archaeological findings show that first Inuit cultures immigrated to Greenland from Alaska via Canada. They inhabited the coastal regions of the island and lived as hunters for centuries (Higgins 2010: 18; Nuttall 2005a: 783). The ancestors of today's Greenlanders (Inuit of the Thule culture) populated the country 800 years ago (Nuttall 2005b: 791). They mainly lived close to the coast in a nomadic lifestyle and, in doing so, were able to cope with the challenging climatic conditions. No place names are recorded from this period of time.

Around the same time the first European immigrants, Icelanders with Norwegian origin, arrived in Greenland. They settled at the southern west coast and built the Norse settlements, staying in vivid contact with their home countries Iceland and Norway and trading with the Inuit (Nuttall 2005a: 783 and 2005b: 792). Due to reasons still unknown their prospering settlements vanished around 1500 A.C. (Nuttall 2005a: 783). Possible explanations are dramatic changes of the climatic conditions and conflicts with the Inuit about the diminishing resources (Nuttall 2005a: 783).

The Norse settlements were the reason and the legitimating for the united Danish-Norwegian Kingdom to claim power over the island from the early 17th century onwards (Kleivan 1996: 138). King Christian IV sent out expeditions in the search for "his" former colonies. However, not only the Danes were interested in Greenland, but also many other European nations for different reasons: Besides whaling, the British were primarily in search for a shorter passage to

Asia for mercantile reasons and explored the west coast of Greenland and Baffin Bay as far north as Upernavik. At the same time Dutch whalers followed their prey from Spitsbergen to Greenland and built up trading stations mainly in the Disko Bay area (near Qeqertarsuaq). They engaged in dynamic trading activities with the indigenous population (Nuttall 2005a: 783) and were the leading traders in fish oil (Higgins 2010: 19). With this activity they were in hard competition with the Danish-Norwegian regime (Cavell 2008: 436 and Nuttall 2005a: 783) which still claimed power over the island and emphasized this claim by building colonies and organizing trading monopolies. In 1721 the actual missionary work began with the arrival of the priest Hans Egede who built up the missionary station named *Godthaab* ('good hope') (Cavell 2008: 435), in the location of today's Nuuk. Twelve years later German Moravian Brethren arrived in Greenland to strengthen the protestant missionary work.

Under the direction of the *Kongelige Grønlandske Handel* [Royal Greenland Trade Company] Danish activities expanded northwards in establishing more and more settlements (Nuttall 2005a: 783 and Ostermann 1929: 184ff.). After World War I, Denmark declared its sovereignty over the whole island though many parts of Greenland (especially the eastern regions) were not inhabited. In 1933, after some disputes with the now independent Norway, the Permanent Court of International Justice decided in favor for Denmark and granted it the sovereignty over all Greenland (cf. Cavell 2008: 434f.).

2.2 From *The Place Name Committee* to *Nunat Aqqinik Aalajangiisartut*

The various foreign influences described above resulted in a complex and multi-layered name system. This fact was a thorn in the side of the Danish sovereignty and in 1934 the *Stednavneudvalget* [Place Name Committee for Greenland] was formed as a subcommittee of the *Commission for Scientific Investigations in Greenland* (Higgins 2010: 13). Its aim was to ratify places names in Greenland (Higgins 2010: 13 and Olsen 2008: 185). Laursen (1972: 182) summarizes:

> Simply, the place name committee has the authority to decide on all matters regarding the place naming of Greenland with the result that no place name within the Greenland territory is liable to be approved by the Danish State unless the name in each individual case has been authorized by the place name committee.

Obtaining control over Greenland's toponomasticon by dictating which names in which language can or cannot be used in official contexts is an important power strategy as described in Helander (2009: 256). Interestingly though, in this case it was not the indigenous Greenlandic names which were regulated or oppressed. Whenever possible a double authorization of Greenlandic and Danish names was the committee's aim (Olsen 2008: 186). The objects of the regulations were European place names given by other – possibly competing – nations. The committee took care of the "Danification" of all foreign place names, which mainly meant that the classifying part of the place name from any European language should be translated into Danish (Laursen 1972: 184 and Higgins 2010: 14). This process transformed, for instance, the German toponym *Koldewey Inseln* into the Danish *Koldewey Øer* 'Koldewey islands' (Higgins 2010: 233).

With the increasingly growing independence of Greenland from Denmark (in 1978 the Greenland Home Rule and in 2008 the Self-Government Act was granted)[3], the authority for place names was transferred into the Greenlanders' hands: In 1984 the *Nunat Aqqinik Aalajangiisartut* [Place name committee] was established (Olsen 2008: 185). Today's task of the committee is to collect, register and authorize macrotoponyms.[4] One of the most important criterions for the authorization is that non-Greenlandic place names can only be authorized if the proposal is well-founded. This does not mean that all European based place names have been eliminated or transferred into Greenlandic – many have been kept as "historisk betydningsfuldt material"[5] (Olsen 2008: 188).

For this reason there are still many European place names to be found on some maps, depending on what kind of political reality is intended to be conveyed. Maps by *NunaGIS* (The National Geographic Information System for Greenland) exclusively display Greenlandic place names, while on geological maps of the *Danish Ministry of Energy, Utilities and Climate* there are many cases of double naming or even only Danish names.[6]

Many of these names have their origin in the 18th century, when the Danish colonization was fully underway. But there are even earlier witnesses of European contact with Greenland, place names which can serve as a good data base for a comparative analysis.

---

3 *Politics in Greenland*: Naalakkersuisut: Government of Greenland.
4 *The Place Name Committee*: Oqaasileriffik. The Greenland Language Secretariat.
5 [historically important material], my translation.
6 *Grønlandskort, Geologiske kort 1:2 500 000.* Udsnit 7: Nuuk, Godthåb, Julianehåb, Sønder strømfjord.

3 Data sources and method of analysis

I chose the toponyms from Inge Kleivan's paper (1996) as a starting point as she has compiled place names from a long period of time (10th–18th century). In the cases of the Norse and English toponyms it was possible to extend the list with data from additional sources. The dataset (129 types), despite its still rather small size, allows not only a quantitative but also a qualitative approach.

The toponyms of my sample generally denote major geological entities such as fjords or islands and thus belong to the class of macrotoponyms (Nübling et al. 2012: 206). Some smaller items, such as churches, are included in the case of Norse names. All places and entities discussed in this paper are located on the southwest and west coast of Greenland (as far north as 72°N). This area is surrounded by open water, whereas the access to the east coast is widely hindered by pack ice (Nuttall 2005a: 779).

For methodological reasons, I will concentrate on pure exonyms where every part of the place name is recognizably taken from the colonizers' language. It is beyond the scope of this study to examine hybrid forms with one part from the indigenous language and one from the colonizers' language or endonyms with only indigenous elements.

I will analyze the place names in two ways: The first step is a formal analysis of the internal morphological properties of the names. This includes the syllabic and morphemic structure, the internal inflection, as well as the order and the lexical category of the components. In this regard I refer to Stolz et al. (2016) who categorize the components as classifier (CLASS) being the head of the construction, and its modifying determiner (DET). Throughout this paper, the term "compound" is used to refer to any combination of at least two of these lexical components resulting in a complex toponym, regardless of whether this construction is written as one or in several words, this decision being largely a question of orthographic convention. The term "simplex" ore simple toponym will be used to refer to names that are based on a single lexical item possibly provided with grammatical morphemes.

After having examined these formal properties, I will turn to the functional aspects of the place names. As each component fulfils a clearly distinguishable function they are analyzed separately: the CLASS denotes the geological feature to which the entity belongs (Stolz & Warnke 2015: 138). It indicates which features or entities the name givers consider to be worth being individuated from the whole of the landscape or, in other words, how people dissected the polymorphous geographical space into places of their interest (cf. Vuolteenaho & Berg 2009: 10 and Stolz & Warnke 2016). *Frobisher Strait* is a good illustration of this interpretive and highly subjective aspect of name giving: the CLASS *strait* was given to an inlet on Baffin Island in honor of Martin Frobisher who sailed this area in 1576 on the false assumption of having reached Greenland. The fact that this CLASS described reality in an inappropriate way was only realized in 1861 when Charles Francis Hall discovered *Frobisher Strait* not to be a strait but a bay.[7]

While the classifier denotes the specific interpretation of reality and thus deals with the question: "what is named?", the determiner on the other hand (in this example: *Frobisher*) specifies and individuates the referent of this classifier. It indicates the meaning and relevance the name givers ascribe to the place and is therefore concerned with the question of "how to name?".[8] Therefore, the toponym *Frobisher Strait* is meant to commemorate Martin Frobisher as an early European seaman to sail these territories.

Commemoration is only one function a toponym can fulfill with its determiner. There have been several ways of classifying the different functions. Laursen (1972), for instance, suggests a very fine-grained typology (based on Stewart)[9] distinguishing the following ten categories which are then further subdivided: descriptive, commemorative, tribute, symbolic, incident, shift, ethnic, mythological, whimsical and Greenlandic names (Laursen 1972: 178ff.). I adjusted this categorization according to my data ending up with the following four categories: i) Descriptive names which describe the permanent characteristics of the location (*Vlakke groene Eilanden* 'plain green islands'); ii) incident names referring to an accidental or temporal property of the place (*Hvalsey* 'whale's island'); iii) commemorative and iv) transfer names which are given to pay tribute to a person (*Frobisher Strait*) or a place (*London coast*). I decided to add an additional category v) emotive names in order to cope with place names which express a sentiment the name giver experienced when encountering the place, like for example *Cape Desolation*.

In my opinion, there is one essential difference which groups these five categories into two higher-level functional categories: one group refers to the locality itself (comprising descriptive and incident names) while the other refers to something or someone from outside the place (commemorative, transfer and emotive names). Even if we do not know the exact coordinates of the *Vlakke groene Eilanden*, we can faithfully expect them to be plain and green, whereas we will not encounter something Londonish at *London Coast*. Inspired by

---

7 Finlayson, Douglas. 2006. *Frobisher Bay*. The Canadian Encyclopedia.
8 Questions inspired by George R. Stuart. 1943. What is named? – Towns, island, mountains, rivers, capes. *California University Publications in English* 14, 223–232, cited in Nicolaisen (1995: 389).
9 Stewart, George R. 1954. A classification of place names. *Names. A Journal of Onomastics* 2(1). 1–13. Cited in Laursen (1972: 168).

Nübling et al. (2012: 229) who use the terms in a slightly different context, I will call the first group internally motivated and the second externally motivated.

Together with the structural properties of the first part of the analysis, this gives us two parameters to systematically scrutinize the data set on a formal and on a functional level enabling us to test hypothesis I. In order to test the second hypothesis, the type of colonization has to be included as an additional variable. The assignment of these types to the different nations is necessarily subject to certain simplifications, but might still reveal some interesting correlations.

4 European place names

4.1 Norse place names

The outlawed Norseman Erik the Red is said to be the first European to have built permanent settlements in Greenland. In 985 he sailed from Iceland to Greenland and established colonies on the south and southwest coast of the island (Nuttall 2005a: 783). With its long-term character this enterprise can be described as a settler colony. The names the immigrants used for places like fjords, for their farms, settlements and churches are only passed down to us by written sources such as the *Grænlendinga saga, Eiríks saga rauða, Íslendigabók* and the *Landnámabók* (Andersen 1982: 167). As they did not use any maps (Kleivan 1996: 128), it is very difficult to identify and locate the exact position of these places. *Eystribyggð* 'eastern settlement' illustrates this point clearly: It was not until the end of the 19th century that it was realized that this settlement was not on the east coast as had been assumed for many centuries but on the south west coast, near Narsaq (Kleivan 1996: 132). *Vestribyggð* 'western settlement' was located in the vicinity of today's Nuuk. This lack of information might have been the reason why hardly any of the Norse place names, except for the countries name *Groenland* 'Greenland', have survived (Kleivan 1996: 129).

The following list of place names includes all toponyms that Kleivan (1996: 130) cites in her article, plus 15 names (underlined) which are certain to have existed in the Eastern Settlement (according to Andersen [1982: 173]) as they were mentioned in more than two sources. The list does not include uncertain names of hunting grounds. I adopted the spelling convention of my sources.

Agnafjörðr, Anavík, Andafjörðr, Bjarney, Brattahlíð, Eið, Einarsfjörðr, Eiríksfjörðr, Eyjarfjörðr, Eystribyggð, Garðar, Grønland, Gunnbjarnarsker, Herjólfsfjörðr, Herjólfsnes, Hornafjörðr, Hóp, Hrafnsfjörðr, Hvalsey, Hvalseyjarfjörðr, Ísafjörðr, Kambstaðafjörðr, Ketilsfjörðr, Langey, Leirafjörðr, Loðinsfjörðr, Lýsu-

fjörðr, Miðfjörðr, Pétrsvík, Rangafjörðr, Sandnes, Siglufjörðr, Slettufjörðr, Sólarfjöll, Straumsfjörðr, Svartfjörðr, Vágar, Vatnahverfi, Vatnsdalr, Vestribyggð.

All place names are polysyllabic, except for *Eið* 'isthmus', 'neck of land' and *Hóp* 'small landlocked bay' or 'inlet'. Both are bare nouns without any modification and their function as proper names (and not as common nouns) seems most likely as *Hóp* has lost its lexical meaning denoting a church instead (Kleivan 1996: 131). There are two more place names which are polysyllabic but still consist of only one lexical element plus a plural marking morpheme: [{Garð}$_{NOUN}$-{ar}$_{PL}$]$_{TOP}$ 'enclosed spaces' was the seat of the bishop and [{Vág}$_{NOUN}$-{ar}$_{PL}$]$_{TOP}$ 'creeks' denotes a church with surrounding farm buildings (Lynnerup 1998: 30). Still, the majority of the Norse place names (36 types) are compounds, consisting of at least two lexical items: the CLASS and the DET. Toponyms being a sub-group of the category NOUN, the CLASS as the head of the construction is necessarily a noun, too. In this sample it always comes on the right side of the construction further modified by a single preceding DET like in: [{Vestri}$_{DET}$-{byggð}$_{CLASS}$]$_{TOP}$ 'western settlement'. The DET on the other hand can belong to different lexical categories: in this data set it is most often a common noun as in [{Bjarn}$_{GEN.PL}$-{ey}$_{CLASS}$]$_{TOP}$ 'island of the bears' (15 types) or an anthroponym: [{Eirík-s}$_{GEN}$}$_{ANTH}$ {fjörðr}$_{CLASS}$]$_{TOP}$ 'Erik's fjord' (11 types). In both cases the DET is genitive-marked to show its syntactic dependency. In case the DET is an adjective (8 types) it agrees with the head noun as can be seen in [{Bratta}$_{ADJ.FEM}$-{hlið}$_{CLASS.FEM}$]$_{TOP}$ 'steep hillside'.

These binary right-headed compounds (BRH) make up nearly 95 % of all morphologically complex toponyms. There are only two deviant cases where the toponym consists of three constituents (ternary right-headed: TRH) as the DET is binary: [{Hval-s}$_{GEN}$}$_{NOUN}$-{eyjar}$_{GEN}$-{fjörðr}$_{CLASS}$]$_{TOP}$ 'fjord of the whale's island' (Kleivan 1996: 130) and *Kambstaðafjörðr* which is presumably named after a dwelling called *Kambstaðir* with *kamb* denoting a mountain (Kleivan 1996: 131 and Jónsson 1899: 292). Figure 1 below shows the distribution of the structural features in a pie chart with the total of types indicated. The bar next to the pie chart splits up the compounds into their various forms.

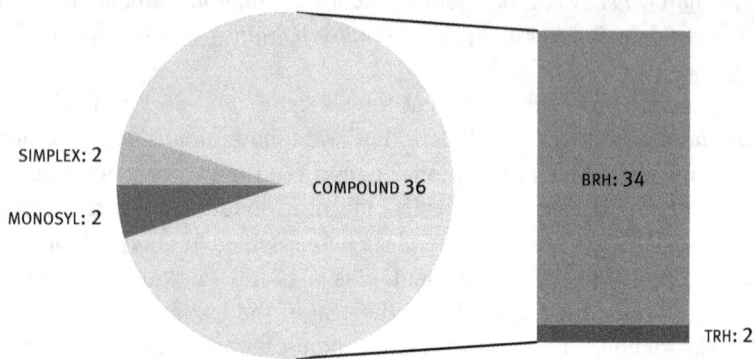

Figure 1: Structure of Norse place names.

If we now turn to the functional aspects of the two elements of the toponyms we notice a clear tendency for the CLASS: *fjörðr* 'fjord' is by far the most frequently used item (21 cases), followed by *ey* 'island' (3 cases). *Byggð* 'settlement', *nes* 'point' and *vík* 'bay' occur twice each, while all others are hapaxes (*hlíð* 'side', *Garðar* 'enclosed spaces', *land* 'land', *sker* 'skerry', *fjöll* 'mountains', *vágar* 'creeks', *hverfi* 'cluster of farms', *dalr* 'valley'). It is striking that out of 40 toponyms 29 are associated to the sea (*fjörðr, ey, nes, vík, sker*, etc.). This predominant choice, the biased "classification of space" (Stolz et al. 2016) is not too surprising, keeping in mind that the Norse sailed the west coast heading north and mainly settled in fjord areas.

Evaluating the function of the determiner on the basis of the above introduced classification, we find that 25 of the complex toponyms have a determiner which describes the place in a certain way, either by the accidental occurrence of some animal (incident) like *Lýsufjörð* 'fjord of the whiting' (5 types) or some stable geological properties (descriptive) like *Vatnsdalr* 'water valley' (20 types). They refer to the place itself and are therefore internally motivated. 11 Types are referring to a person related to that place, they are therefore externally motivated. What is special in terms of the anthroponyms is that more than half of them (7 types) occur in connection with the geo classifier *fjörðr* which strengthens the thesis of Marcus (1980: 63) who assumes that the anthroponymic names indicate possession as the "The lesser chieftains each took possession of a fjord and in most cases named it after himself. Thus Herjólf took Herjólsfjörd; Ketil took Ketilsfjörd; [...]". Figure 2 shows the percentage distribution.

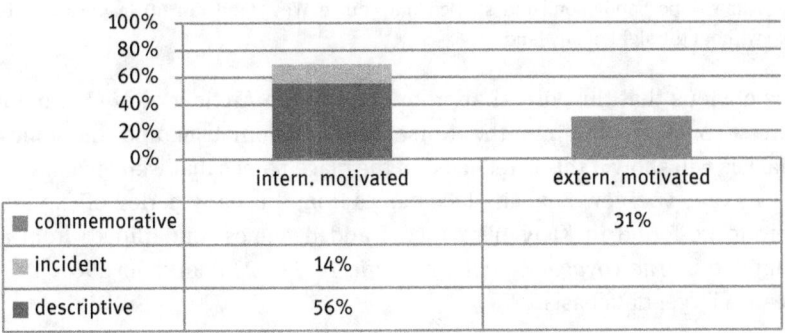

Figure 2: Semantic motivation of Norse place names.

It is obvious that internally motivated toponyms outnumber externally motivated names by far. The main function of the determiners in the Norse place names of my sample is thus to describe places of interest, mostly fjords as points of orientation, as well as fishing grounds, safe harbors and dwelling places. If Marcus is right, then anthroponyms are used to mark possession rather than in a commemorative function.

4.2 English place names

After the decline of the Norse settlements during the Little Ice Age, Greenland faded into oblivion for centuries (Higgins 2010: 9). It was only in the 16th century that British explorers came across the island in the search for the Northwest Passage to Asia. John Davis was one of the first in a long line of explorers who sailed the strait between Greenland and Canada (today known as Davis Strait in his memory) trying to make his way through the ice to pass by the American landmass. He, and many others after him, explored and charted the western coastline of Greenland scattering place names to be eternalized on their maps without taking already existing indigenous toponyms into consideration:

> Now having coasted the land, which we called London coast, from the 21 of this present till the 30, the sea open all to the Westwards and Northward, the land on starboard side East from us, the wind shifted to the North, whereupon we left that shore, naming the

same Hope Sanderson, and shaped our course West, and ran 40 leagues and better, without the sight of any land.[10]

It is obvious that this virtual appropriation of the Arctic territory via mapping differs considerably from the Norse settler colonialism and the following analysis will show if this is reflected in the place names that were given.

As only very few English place names from this early period of exploration were to be found in Kleivan's paper, I added names (underlined) from a list compiled in *The voyages of William Baffin 1612–1622* (Markham 1969: 181f.) to create a larger data basis.

Ball's River, Burnil Cape, Cape Desolation, Cary Islands, Cockin Sound, Comfort Land, Cumberland Isles, Cunningham Fiord, Cunningham Mount, Davis Strait, Desolation, Dudley Digges Cape, Farewell Cape, Frobisher Strait, Gabriel Mount, Hakluyt Island, Hatclife Mount, Hope Harbour, Hope Sanderson, Horne Sound, Jones Sound, King's Fiord, Lancaster River, Lancaster Sound, London Coast, Queen Anne's Cape, Queen Sophia's Cape, Ramel's Fiord, Smith's Sound, Throughgood Island, Whale Sound, Wilkinson Islands, Wolstenholme Sound, Women's Islands

This list only comprises exonyms meeting the above specified selection criterion. Interestingly though, and just as an aside, there are no endonyms nor hybrids mentioned at all in Baffin's or Davis' journals, even though there must have been contact with the indigenous population as Davis describes them in quite some detail (Nuttall 2005a: 783). All English toponyms are polysyllabic and complex multi-word constructions, except for *Desolation*. This south eastern coastline, on similar latitude as *Qaqortoq*, had been named so by Davis in 1585 when he saw the coast for the first time but was prevented from getting closer due to the pack ice.[11] The name refers to the noise of the ice going into the sea (Markham 1970: 4) and it is re-occurred with one of the three left-headed toponyms in this sample: *Cape Desolation* west of *Narsaq* and the outmost point of this coastline. *Hope Sanderson* and *Harbour of Hope* are the two other left-headers, assuming that the element *Hope* in *Hope Sanderson* is the Middle English word for 'valley' used only in place names and related to the Norse *Hóp* we encountered above. It is thus a typical CLASS just as *Harbour* is in the prepositional phrase *Harbour of Hope* where *Hope* is clearly used as a

---

10 *Third voyage northwestward, made by John Davis* (From the journal account of John Janes) June 1587 in Markham (1970: 44).
11 McCaskill Popini, Eloise: *John Davis*. Encyclopedia Arctica Vol. 15, Biographies.

determiner in its modern meaning as can be seen in the text passage which reports the act of name-giving:

> This day we look'd for a harbour with our shallops, for the ships to ride in safety, and found one, which our general call'd **harbour of Hope**; for here we came to land with our ships; the which we could not come near, the time we sail'd along the land, from the sight of Cape Farewel until we came to this place.[12] [emphasis added]

All other 30 toponyms are right-headed compounds, or rather multi-word units, and most of them (27 types) are binary, meaning that DET and CLASS are single lexical items each. More often than not the former is represented by an anthroponym (24 types). We can distinguish two structural sub-types here: the minority is genitive-marked (6 types: *Ball's River, King's Fiord, Queen Anne's Cape, Queen Sophia's Cape, Ramel's Fiord, Smith's Sound*), while the majority is uninflected (18 types). Seven out of the 33 complex place names have a common noun as a determiner, either marked with the possessive 's (1 type): [{*Woman-s*$_{GEN}$}$_{NOUN}$ {*Islands*}$_{CLASS.PL}$]$_{TOP}$ or with a prepositional phrase (1 type) [{*Harbour*}$_{CLASS}$ {*of*$_{PREP}$ *hope*$_{NOUN}$}$_{PP}$]$_{TOP}$ or, most frequently, unmarked (5 types) like for example: [{*Whale*}$_{NOUN}${*Sound*}$_{CLASS}$]$_{TOP}$. One place name has another toponym as its determiner: [{*London*}$_{TOP}$ {*Coast*}$_{CLASS}$]$_{TOP}$, another one an adjective: [{*Throughgood*}$_{ADJ}$ {*Island*}$_{CLASS}$]$_{TOP}$. Three toponyms are made up of three components (TRH), all with the CLASS 'cape' as their heads: [{*Dudley Digges*}$_{ANTH}$ {*Cape*}$_{CLASS}$]$_{TOP}$, [{*Queen Anne-s*$_{GEN}$}$_{ANTH}$ {*Cape*}$_{CLASS}$]$_{TOP}$ and [{*Queen Sophia-s*$_{GEN}$}$_{ANTH}$ {*Cape*}$_{CLASS}$]$_{TOP}$. Figure 3 displays the distribution of the internal structure of the English place names (in total numbers).

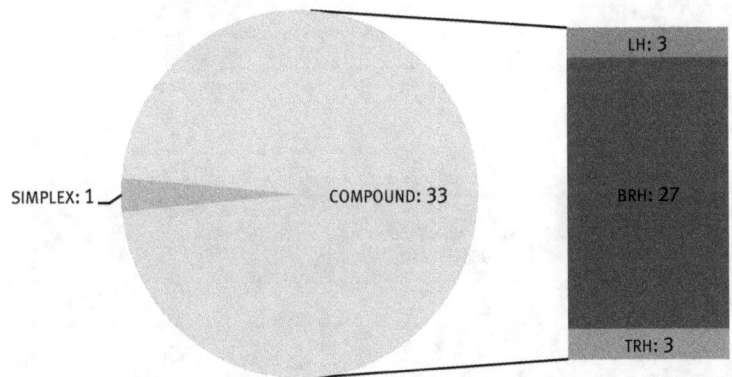

Figure 3: Structure of English place names.

---

12 First recorded voyage of William Baffin. In Markham (1969: 12).

With respect to the functional characteristics of the CLASS we find a similar situation as with the Norse data: the vast majority is associated with the sea and the coastline respectively: *sound* (7 types), *cape* (6 types), *island(s)* (6 types), *fjord* (3 types), *river* (2 types), *strait* (2 types), *coast* (1 type), and *harbor* (1 type). This clearly reflects the declared goal of the English naval officers to chart the shoreline. As to the determiners, we find that the high frequency rate of anthroponyms in this position leads to quite a different situation than in the previous case of Norse toponyms. British national pride shows in the authority to interpret the landscape according to the navigators' perception and in imposing a nomenclature which promotes a British worldview via maps. However, it is not only those commemorative toponyms that transport the colonizers ideas, beliefs and views but also other externally motivated place names like the transfer names (*London Coast*) or emotive names (*Desolation, Comfort Land, Farewell Cape*) which put the name giver and his sentiments into focus rather than the place itself.

As Figure 4 shows there are only very few internally motivated toponyms which are related to the locality itself: one can be considered descriptive (*Throughgood Island*) and three being incident by referring to events that have taken place there: *Horne Sound, Whale Sound,* and *Women's Islands*.

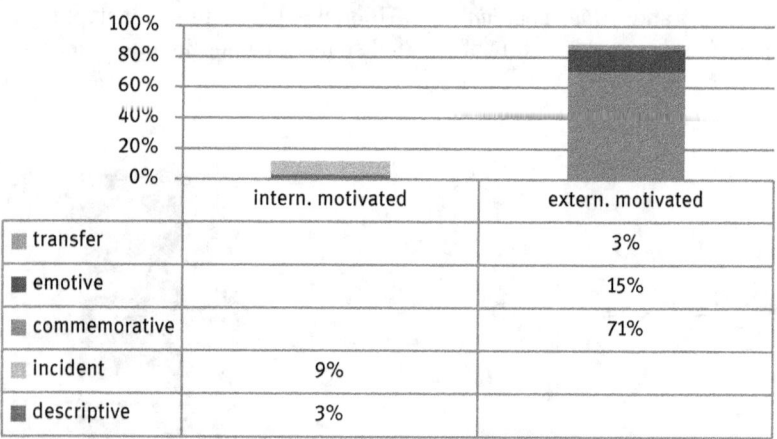

Figure 4: Semantic motivation of English place names.

This data suggests that the main aim of the English explorers was to perpetuate names of national importance on the coast line by charting and indicating the names on the maps, as noted by Grant (2010: 71): "While 'naming' was considered just reward for financial support, their appearance on published maps was also a means of identifying the extent of a nation's discovery claims." By mapping and thus controlling formerly (for Europeans) unknown spaces the explorers constructed knowledge (in the sense of Vuolteenaho & Berg 2009: 8) and thus "made" Greenland ascertainable.

4.3 Dutch place names

In the 17th century Dutch whalers entered the scene in their expanding their hunting grounds from Spitsbergen to Davies Strait (cf. Bobé 1929: 81ff. and Kleivan 1996: 139ff.). They had detailed knowledge of the western coastline and were engaged in trading activities with the Inuit (Nuttall 2005a: 783). This can be interpreted as a third type of colonization: the Dutch's objective was to run trading posts rather than to settle permanently. Their geographical knowledge was of practical relevance rather than for the sake of national prestige. The following 31 toponyms are all taken from Kleivan's paper.

> *Bonkebay, Bonke-Eiland, Boots-Klamp, de Schans, Delftsche Haven, Disko, Fortuynbay, Hunde Ejland, Kloekhuk, Liefde Bay, Nordbay, Onbekande Eiland, Rifkol, Rommelpot, Roobay, Rotgans Eiland, Skinderwalen, Spiring-Bay, Statenhouk, Suikerbrood, Vlakke groene Eilanden, Walvis Eilanden, Waygat, Wilde Eiland, Wildebay, Witteblink, Ysfioert, Zuidoost-Bay, Zuydbay, Zwartenhuk, Zwartevogelbay.*

All but two place names are polysyllabic and morphologically complex; the exceptions being *Disko* and *de Schans*. *Disko* has not only an unclear etymology but even an unclear denotatum, referring to both the whole bay at 69°N 52°E, and the island *Qeqertarsuaq* located in the bay (cf. Kleivan 1996: 140). The mountain's name *de Schans* 'entrenchment' (Kleivan 1996: 140) consists of only one lexical morpheme provided with the definite article: [{de}$_{DEF}${Schans}$_{CLASS}$]$_{TOP}$.

In terms of the complex toponyms all of the CLASS are again nouns but what is different from the before mentioned is that at least five of them are no classifiers in a strict sense designating a geological entity, but rather common nouns: *Suikerbrood* 'sugar loaf' (Kleivan 1996: 139) and *Wittenblink* 'white, shine/glitter' (Kleivan 1996: 140) illustrate this functional shift from a common noun to a part of a proper name. More than half of the DET are nouns, resulting in noun-noun-compounds as for example in [{Ys}$_{NOUN}$-{fioert}$_{CLASS}$]$_{TOP}$ 'ice fjord' (17 items), followed by adjectives (9 items) as in: [{Wild-e}$_{ADJ}$-{bay}$_{CLASS}$]$_{TOP}$ 'wild bay' and one foreign toponym *Delft* which had been transferred to Greenland.

Skinderwalen cannot be analyzed beyond doubt, though Kleivan (1996: 139) gives as etymology 'that which looks like a whale'.

An interesting aspect in this data set is the distinction between multi-word and one-word compounds. As already mentioned before, this differentiation is challenging due to inconsistent orthographic conventions. Nonetheless, there seems to be a tendency worth being mentioned here: Multi-word constructions are possibly triggered by an inflected determiner, as is the case in [{{*Delft*}$_{TOP}$-{*sche*}$_{DER}$}$_{ADJ}$ {*Haven*}$_{CLASS}$]$_{TOP}$ 'harbor of Delft' with its adjectival DET derived from the place name *Delft*. Uninflected determiners, by contrast, tend to be merged with their CLASS as can be seen in [{*Suiker*}$_{NOUN}$-{*brood*}$_{NOUN}$]$_{TOP}$ 'sugar loaf'. The following ratios support this hypothesis: 7 of the 9 multi-word units (78 %) and 3 of the 4 hyphenated forms (75 %) have an inflected determiner, whereas inflectional affixes are only present in 4 types of 18 one-word-units (23 %). However, with such a small sample size and the spelling inconsistencies of the medieval sources, these findings cannot be taken as a general rule. Yet, the fact that all toponyms in my data set are right-headed, is beyond all doubt and confirms the finding of Stolz & Warnke (2018a: 58): "In Dutch-based exonyms, the classifier does not normally occur in the initial position in the construction." Most of them (26 items) are binary elements with a single DET like in: *Fortuynbay*. There are three three-part toponyms with a binary DET: *Vlakke groene Eilanden*, *Zuydoost-Bay* and *Zwartevogelbay*. Figure 5 illustrates the distribution just described:

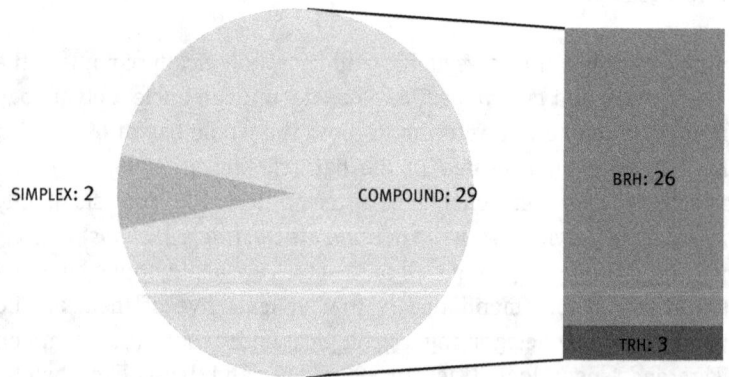

Figure 5: Structure of Dutch place names.

As to the function of the classifiers a similar situation as with the English place names can be observed: the overwhelming majority is related to the sea and the coastal area respectively: *bay* 'bay'(11 types) and *eiland* 'island'(7 types) are most frequent, followed by names with no CLASS in a strict sense (7 types) as exemplified above. Furthermore, *H(o)uk* 'cape' has 3 types while *fioert* 'fjord', *gat* 'hole', *haven* 'harbor' and *schans* 'entrenchment' are all hapaxes. The determiners are mainly used in a descriptive or incident function, designating the place itself as can be seen in *Zwartevogelbay* 'bay of the black bird'. There are very few toponyms referring to something other than the place and most of these convey the sentiment the name givers had when encountering the place: *Fortuynbay* 'bay of happiness', *Liefde Bay* 'bay of love' and *Roobay* 'bay of rest' are telling examples. There are two transfer names: *Delftsche Haven* and *Disko*, a name which has probably been taken from Spitsbergen (Kleivan 1996: 140). Interestingly, there are no anthroponyms in the determiner slot; the only commemorative name *Statenhouk* refers to the Dutch parliament *Staten-Generaal*. The distribution is shown in Figure 6:

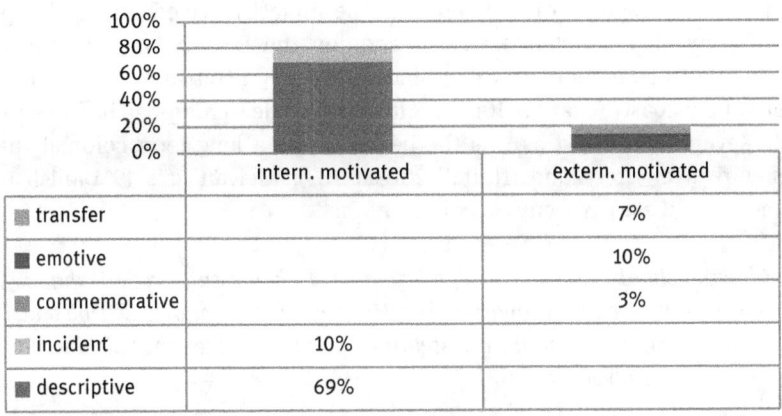

Figure 6: Semantic motivation of Dutch place names.

The contrast to the English toponyms could not be any clearer: whereas the English explorers used almost only commemorative names, the Dutch whalers and trader seemed to be much in favor of naming places in a descriptive way. With their seasonal hunting and trading activities (Bobé 1929: 84) practical information and orientation, conveyed by place-related names, were of much more importance than honoring people. In their being predominantly descriptive, they resemble Inuit toponyms which are always descriptive (Møller Kruse 2012: 2f.).

4.4 Danish place names

The Dutch's very efficient whaling and trading activities had been a constant source of irritation to the Danish empire as Greenland had been considered to be part of the Danish-Norwegian realm since the Norse communities had agreed to pay taxes to the kingdom around 1260 AD (Petersen 1995: 119). The Danish-Dutch conflict dragged on for decades culminating in the mutual burning down of trading stations (Bobé 1929: 93).

In order to cope with the competition from the Dutch and to retain sovereignty, a Danish-Norwegian colonization project was initiated in 1721 by the minister Hans Egede. He and his *Bergen Grønlandske Compagnie* [Bergen Greenland Company] had a vital interest in immigration and permanent settlement to Greenland to reclaim the territory (Bobé 1929: 89). In this respect the undertaking had many similarities to the Norse settler colony but Egede pursued, besides agricultural and mercantile plans, another important objective: to convert the Inuit, who were thought to be the descendants of the still missing Norsemen, to Christianity. This added not only a religious but also a strong socio-cultural aspect to the enterprise. The project received financial support from Norwegian merchants and in addition the Danish king established a Greenland trade monopoly which hindered "foreign ships to trade within four miles of the coast" (Grant 2010: 83). Although Egede's enterprise had to struggle with severe setbacks, this was the beginning of a long term colonial rule of Denmark over Greenland (Nuttall 2005a: 783). Kleivan lists 19 Danish place names from these early days of colonization:

Christianshaab, Claushavn, Egedesminde, Fiskenæsset, Frederikshaab, Godhavn, Godt-Haab, Gunnbjarnarsker, Haabets Havn, Haabets Ø, Holsteinsborg, Jakobshavn, Julianehaab, Præstefjord, Ritenbenck, Sletten, Solsiden, Sukkertoppen, Sydprøven.

All Danish toponyms are polysyllabic and complex except for [{$Slette_{NOUN}$-n_{DEF}}]$_{TOP}$ 'the plain'. Being provided with the definite article it is structurally similar to the Dutch *de Schans*. As far as the CLASS of the remaining toponyms are concerned, we can observe a much bigger semantic variety than in the other data sets: only *havn* 'harbor' is used four times, all others are hapaxes (*borg* 'castle', *fjord* 'fjord', *næs* 'point', *ø* 'island', *side* 'side', *top* 'top'). Five CLASS are provided with the suffixed definite article: [{$Fisk$-e}$_{NOUN.PL}$-{$næs_{NOUN}$-et_{DEF}}$_{CLASS}$]$_{TOP}$ 'the fish point' [{$Slette_{NOUN}$-n_{DEF}}]$_{TOP}$ 'the plain', [{Sol_{NOUN}-{$side_{NOUN}$-n_{DEF}}$_{CLASS}$]$_{TOP}$ 'the sun side', [{$Sukker$}$_{NOUN}$-{$topp_{NOUN}$-en_{DEF}}$_{CLASS}$]$_{TOP}$ 'the sugar loaf', [{Syd}$_{NOUN}$-{$prøve_{NOUN}$-n_{DEF}}$_{CLASS}$]$_{TOP}$, 'south proof' probably to ensure the mono-referential function of the name, as four of them are common nouns taken from the Danish lexicon (*slette* 'plain', *side* 'side', *top* 'top' and *prøve* 'proof'). The DET position is most often occupied by a proper name which is always genitive-marked (10 types). We can distinguish between anthroponyms as is the case in *Jacobshavn* (8 types) and a ship's name (*Haabets Havn* and *Haabets Ø*). The second most frequent DET are common nouns as in *Solsiden* (4 types) followed by adjectives (2 types) agreeing in gender with their heads: [{*Godt*}ADJ.N-{*haab*}CLASS.N]TOP vs. [{*God*}ADJ.C-{*havn*}CLASS.C]TOP. *Ritenbenck* cannot be analyzed properly as it is supposed to be a "manufactured name" made up by mixing the order of the letters of Count C.A. von Berckentin (Kleivan 1996: 146).

The majority of the Danish toponyms are one-word units (16 types). In contrast to the Dutch place names, this merging is also possible with an inflected determiner as can be seen in [{*Egede-s*GEN}ANTH-{*minde*}CLASS]TOP '(in) remembrance of Egede'. There seems to be a general tendency towards merging instead of using multi-word constructions, as the pietistically inspired *Godt-Haab* 'good hope' has been changed to a one-word-unit (*Godthaab*) in the course of time (Kleivan 1996: 141). Only determiners marked for definiteness by a suffixed article seem to resist this trend as [{*Haab-et*DEF-SGEN}NAME {*Havn*}CLASS]TOP 'harbor of Hope' and [{*Haab-et*DEF-SGEN}NAME {*Ø*}CLASS]TOP 'island of Hope' clearly show. The definite article is used in both cases to refer to Egede's ship *Haab* 'Hope' that brought him to Greenland. Figure (7) illustrates the distribution just described:

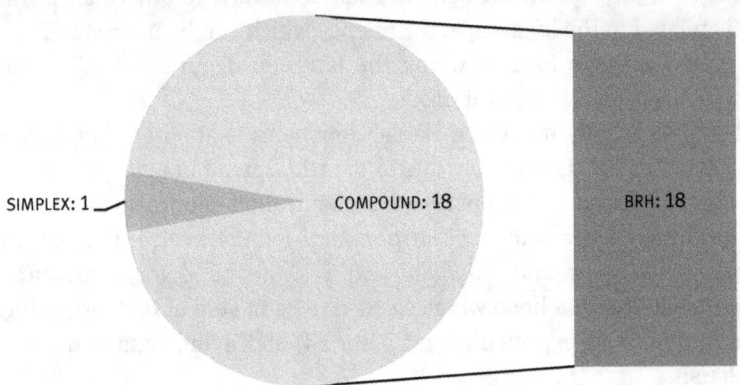

Figure 7: Structure of Danish place names.

Considering the functional side of the classifiers, we notice that a significant amount of CLASS has experienced the very common shift from a meaningful lexeme to a meaningless part of a name (Nicolaisen 1995: 391). *Haab* and *minde* are good examples in this respect: They lost their appellative function and became toponymic markers instead. This onymization of lexical items is a regular process (Nübling et al. 2012: 16) and the respective place names are presumably no ad-hoc constructions but "names-of-the-peg" created by the "analogical application of name models" (Nicolaisen 1995: 391). This assumption is supported by the relatively high type frequency of this model in the metropolis (2473 toponyms with the affix -*minde* and 297 place names including -*haab* in Denmark).[13]

There are only five internally motivated names describing the landscape and its properties, which is rather low in frequency compared to the other settler colony which the Norse had established. This might be due to the fact that the first Danish missionaries were probably not so much engaged in the direct utilization of natural resources, an endeavor which would require appropriate spatial knowledge, but rather in trading and religious activities which in turn entails some kind of socio-cultural transfer. This can be illustrated by the name of the trading post *Sukkertoppen* 'sugar loaf' which is internally motivated on the surface as it describes the shape of the surrounding environment. Using a European concept for description, however, by referring to the Dutch *Suikerbrood* (Kleivan 1996: 139) gives it a rather imperialistic connotation.

Half of the place names are related to the sea, similar to the English data, but rather with regard to settling activities like in *havn*. The other half of the toponyms is related to the landscape, a tendency which can be interpreted as a changing of the settler's focus towards the landside. Figure 8 displays the distribution of the semantic motivations.

The rate of externally motivated Danish toponyms is almost as high as in my English sample. This is probably due to the widespread practice of naming places after persons who had supported the colonization enterprise financially as exemplified in *Frederikshaab* and *Christianshaab* (cf. Bobé 1929: 113). The two emotive names *Godhavn* and *Godthaab* express the hope for a favorable progress of the endeavor; a hope which seemed to be in vain at first, as trading was not as profitable as expected (Grant 2010: 84) and living conditions were extremely harsh.

---

13 *Danmarks Stednavne*: Nordisk Forskningsinstitut. Total number of place names in this database: 210.000.

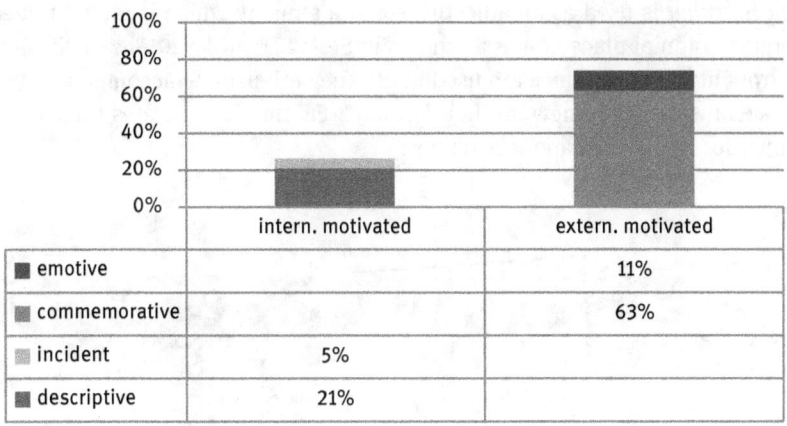

Figure 8: Semantic motivation of Danish place names.

4.5 German place names

In 1733, after the Danish colonization project had almost been given up, three Moravian Brethren from Herrnhut (Bohemia) were sent to Greenland by the Danish court in order to support Egede's missionary project (Bobé 1929: 101 and Grant 2010: 85). The objective of this colonial missionary undertaking is thus comparable to the Danish. The Germans built up six mission stations on the south and west coast of Greenland. Two of the stations kept their indigenous place names *Uummannaq* and *Illorpaat* (Kleivan 1996: 142) while the other four were given German names:

Friedrichstal, Lichtenau, Lichtenfels, Neu Herrnhut.

Again all of the exonyms are polysyllabic and complex. They are all binary right-headed and at least three of them come in the shape of one-word units, whereas the spelling of *Neu Herrnhut* is inconsistent: some sources refer to it as *Neuherrnhut* with the adjectival stem *neu* 'new' being fused with the toponymic classifier (Genft 1820: 3). Three of the CLASS are common nouns (*Au* 'meadow', *Fels* 'rock', *Tal* 'valley'); one is a toponym (*Herrnhut*). The determiners are either adjectives (*licht* 'bright', *neu* 'new') or a genitive-marked anthroponym: [{*Friedrich-s*}GEN]ANTH-{*tal*}CLASS]TOP 'Friedrich's valley'. [{*Licht-en*}ADJ-{*fels*}CLASS]TOP and [{*Lichte-n*}ADJ-{*au*}CLASS]TOP are both provided with an epenthetic element *-(e)n-* between the DET and the CLASS, a formal dissociation which is often an indicator of older onymization processes as stated in Nübling et al. (2012: 16f.). {*Neu-*} in

Neu Herrnhut is used as an adjective stem, a strategy which is often applied in German colonial place names as shown in Stolz & Warnke 2018a: 64 "if German metropolitan place names are used at all, they are usually accompanied by the adjectival stem *Neu-* 'new' to their left [...]". Figure (9) illustrates the structural properties of the German place names:

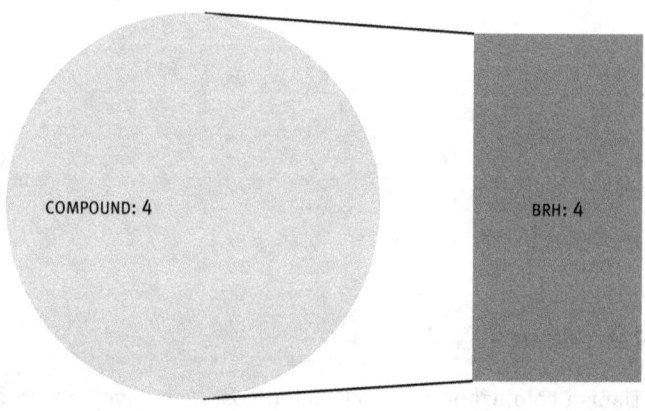

Figure 9: Structure of German place names.

Considering the functional aspects of the classifiers, we find that there is no preferred CLASS, all of them are idiomatic. Those which denote a geological item (*Tal, Au, Fels*) are clearly oriented towards landside, there is no reference at all to the sea, although the places are all located directly at the coastline (*Lichtenfels* in the vicinity of Nuuk, *Lichtenau* and *Friedrichsthal* near Nanortalik). As to the determiners we find that one is commemorative (*Friedrich*), paying tribute to the contemporary Danish king, one is clearly transferred from the metropolis (*Herrnhut*), while the other two seem to be descriptive at first sight (*licht*). The archaic form mentioned above, however, suggests that the names were not ad-hoc constructions used to give an appropriate description of the surrounding landscape, but have been transferred using a widespread pattern [{*Lichte-n*}$_{ADJ}$-{x}$_{CLASS}$]$_{TOP}$ from the homeland of the missionaries (Sturmfels & Bischof 1961: 149). This supposition being only hypothetical, I still opt for classifying them as descriptive, especially since the adjective *licht* can easily be related to the Greenlandic coastline free of trees. This gives us the following distribution:

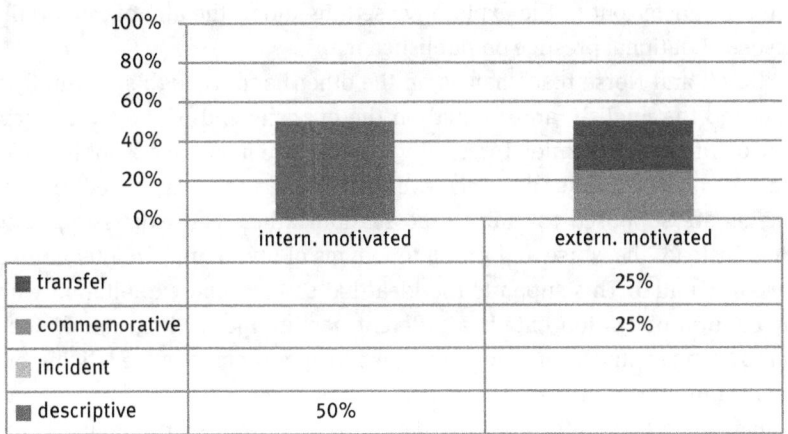

Figure 10: Semantic motivation of German place names.

5 Conclusions

Although very limited, this last sample of German toponyms still highlights an interesting aspect of naming practices in specific colonial contexts: creating place names in a missionary setting differs considerably from naming places in an exploratory context. Mission with its clear commission to spread the Christian faith seems to involve various kinds of other socio-cultural transfers of norms, beliefs, traditions and values, and this is, among others, mirrored in place names. *Lichtenfels* and *Lichtenau* exemplify this transfer: Despite of being descriptive, and thus internally motivated on the surface, they are prototypical instances of German place names and their being implemented in Greenland reflects the missionaries' attempt of transferring concepts of their homeland to the unknown territory. A similar tendency can be observed with the Danish place names which are the result of a comparable situation with missionary and trading activities. The cultural transfer is obvious even in descriptive place names like *Sukkertoppen*. Due to the continued financial support, a high number of externally motivated names were given to pay tribute to the financiers.

If we place the naming motivations on a scale from extremely internally to predominantly externally motivated, then the English place names would surely range at the external end: more than 80 % of the names are not related to the geological features themselves but mostly to English persons of importance. Unlike the German and Danish names, this choice was not so much due to cultural transfer but to the explorative setting and to the aim of immortalizing persons of national prestige on published maps.

Dutch and Norse place names on the other hand, though structurally very similar to the English, are situated on the opposite end of the scale, showing quite a different motivation for naming. Their place names were not intended to impress competing nations, since even the Norse toponyms based on anthroponyms are supposed to indicate possession rather than expressing national pride. Instead, the Norse and Dutch toponyms of my sample are predominantly place-referential. This supports the idea that settling and exploitation without any cultural obligation entails a different naming motivation, mainly focused on providing spatial orientation which is indispensable to make a living on the basis of hunting and fishing.

Returning now to the two hypotheses posed at the beginning of this paper, the structural prototype suggested in Stolz & Warnke (2018a) can be confirmed: the overwhelming majority (87 %) of the European based place names in my sample are binary compounds, with the classifier as the right-hand part and the determiner to the left. It cannot be excluded, however, that the observed similarities might be due to structural similarities of the examined languages, as all of them are Germanic. Further studies using unrelated source languages are therefore required in order to validate this assumption. The second hypothesis states that different types of spatial appropriation might relate to different types of naming principles. The evidence from this study supports this idea, although caution must be applied here, too, because of the small data set and the rather simplistic assignment of the aims to the various nations applied here for analytic reasons. Further research using more data and a more fine-grained assignment is thus needed in order to enhance our understanding of colonial toponymy and its characteristics.

Acknowledgments: This study has been conducted within the scope of the Creative Unit *Koloniallinguistik – Language in Colonial Contexts* at the University of Bremen funded by the Initiative for Excellence through the federal and state governments of Germany. I wish to thank Prof. Dr. Thomas Stolz, Prof. Dr. Ingo H. Warnke and my fellow members of the Creative Unit for many inspiring discussions and helpful comments. Special thanks go to Nina Abo Alatta for correcting my English (any mistakes that remain are mine).

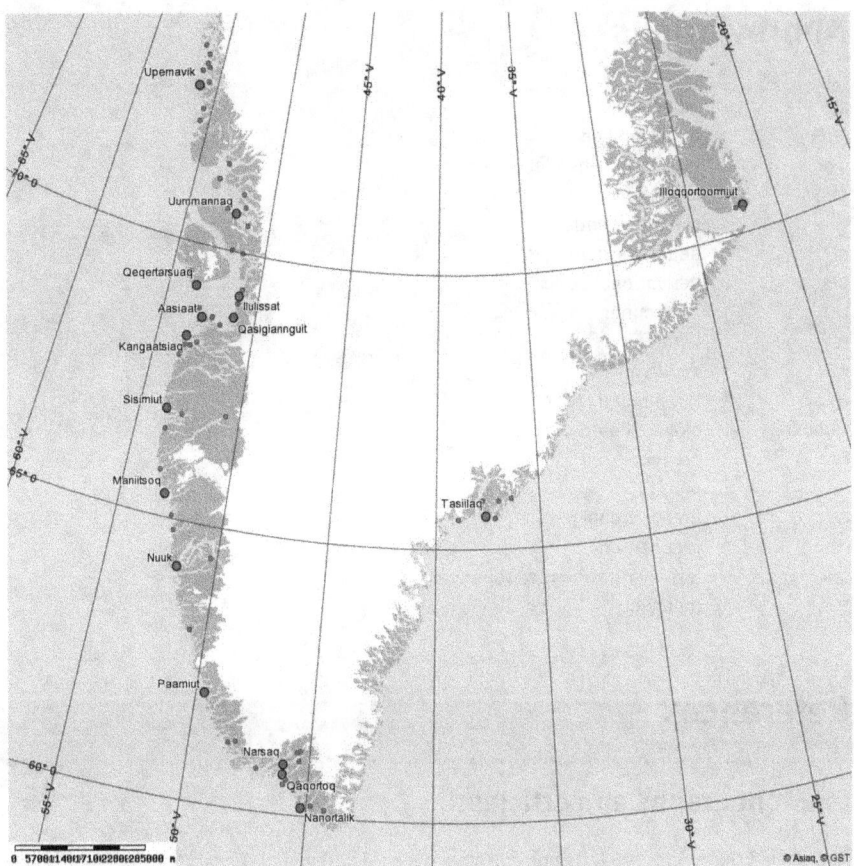

Map 1: NunaGIS Map of Greenland 1:250.000.

Abbreviations

ADJ	adjective
ANTH	anthroponym
BRH	binary right-headed toponym
CLASS	classifier
C	common gender
DEF	definite article
DER	derivational suffix
DET	determiner
FEM	feminine
GEN	genitive
LH	left-headed toponym
MONOSYL	monosyllabic
N	neuter
PL	plural
PP	prepositional phrase
PREP	preposition
TRH	ternary right-headed toponym
TOP	toponym

References

(a) Monographs and articles

Andersen, Erik Langer. 1982. De norrøne stednavne i Østerbygden. *Tidskriftet Grønland* 30(5–7). 163–176.

Anderson, John M. 2007. *The grammar of names*. Oxford: Oxford University Press.

Bobé, Louis. 1929. History of the trade and colonization until 1870. In Martin Vahl, Georg Carl Amdrup & Adolf Severin Jensen (eds.), *Greenland*. Vol. 3: *The colonization of Greenland and its history until 1929*, 77–165. Copenhagen: Reitzel.

Busse, Beatrix & Ingo H. Warnke. 2014. Ortsherstellung als sprachliche Praxis. In Ingo H. Warnke & Beatrix Busse (eds.), *Place-Making in urbanen Diskursen*, 1–7. Berlin & Boston: De Gruyter Mouton.

Carter, Paul. 1987. *The road to Botany Bay. An exploration of landscape and history*. London: Faber and Faber.

Cavell, Janic. 2008. Historical evidence and the Eastern Greenland case. *Arctic* 61(4). 433–441.

Crampton, Jeremy W. 2001. Maps as social constructions: Power, communication and visualization. *Progress in Human Geography* 2. 235–252.

Dewein, Barbara, Stefan Engelberg, Susanne Hackmack, Wolfram Karg, Birte Kellermeier-Rehbein, Peter Muhlhäusler, Daniel Schmidt-Brücken, Christina Schneemann, Doris Stolberg, Thomas Stolz, Ingo H. Warnke. 2012. Forschungsgruppe Koloniallinguistik:

Profil – Programmatik – Projekte. *Zeitschrift für Germanistische Linguistik* 40(2). 242–249.

Garde, Thomas Vilhelm. 1929. The navigation of Greenland. In Martin Vahl, Georg Carl Amdrup & Adolf Severin Jensen (eds.), *Greenland*. Vol. 3: *The colonization of Greenland and its history until 1929*, 215–243. Copenhagen: Reitzel.

Genft, Christof Ernst. 1820. *Nachrichten aus der Brüder-Gemeinde*. Vol. 2, Issues 1–5. Magdeburg: Gnadau.

Grant, Shelagh. 2010. *Polar imperative. A history of Arctic Sovereignty in North Amerika*. Vancouver: Douglas & McIntyre.

Helander, Kaisa Rautio. 2009. Toponymic silence and Sámi place names during the growth of the Norwegian nation state. In Lawrence D. Berg & Jani Vuolteenaho (eds.), *Critical toponymies. The contested politics of place naming*, 253–267. Farnham: Ashgate.

Higgins, Anthony K. 2010. *Exploration history and place names of northern East Greenland*. Copenhagen: Rosendahls (www.geus.dk/publications/bull).

Jónsson, Finnur. 1899. *Grønlands gamle Topografi efter Kilderne. Østerbygden og Versterbygden*. (Meddelelser om Grønland 20). Copenhagen: B. Lunos kgl. hofbogtrykkeri.

Kleivan, Inge. 1977. Place names in Greenland: Cultural imperialism and cultural identity. In Carola Sandbacka (eds.), *Cultural imperialism and cultural identity. Proceedings of the 8th Conference of Nordic Ethnographers/Anthropologists*, 197–215. Helsinki: Suomen Antropologinen Seura.

Kleivan, Inge. 1996. European contacts with Greenland as reflected in place-names. In P. Sture Ureland & Iain Clarkson (eds.), *Language contact across the North Atlantic*, 125–152. Berlin & New York: De Gruyter.

Laursen, Dan. 1972. *The place names of North Greenland*. (Meddelelser om Grønland, udgivne af Kommissionen for Videnskabelige Undersögelser i Grönland 180(2)). Copenhagen: Reitzel.

Loomba, Ania. 2005. *Colonialism/postcolonialism*. London & New York: Routledge.

Lynnerup, Niels. 1998. *The Greenlandic Norse: A biological-anthropological study*. (Meddelelser om Grønland, Man & Society 24). Copenhagen: Commission for Scientific Research in Greenland.

Marcus, Geoffrey Jules. 1980. *The conquest of the North Atlantic*. Woodbridge: Boydell Press.

Markham, Albert H. 1969. *The voyages of William Baffin 1612–1622*. New York: Franklin

Markham, Albert H. 1970. *The voyages and works of John Davis the Navigator*. New York: Franklin.

Møller Kruse, Lisathe. 2012. Stednavne i Grønland. *Grønland* 2. 2–11.

Nicolaisen, Wilhelm. 1995. Name und Appellative. In Ernst Eichler, Gerold Hilty, Heinrich Löffler, Hugo Steger & Ladislav Zgusta (eds.), *Namenforschung. Ein internationals Handbuch zur Onomastik*, 384–393. Berlin & New York: De Gruyter.

Nübling, Damaris, Fabian Fahlbusch & Rita Heuser. 2012. *Namen. Eine Einführung in die Onomastik*. Tübingen: Gunther Narr.

Nuttall, Mark. 2005a. Greenland. In Mark Nuttall (ed.), *Encyclopedia of the Arctic*. Vol. 2. G–N, 778–785. New York: Routledge.

Nuttall, Mark. 2005b. Greenland Inuit. In Mark Nuttall (ed.), *Encyclopedia of the Arctic*. Vol. 2. G–N, 790–794. New York: Routledge.

Olsen, Carl Christian. 2008. Nunat Aqqinik Aalajangiisartut – Grønlands stednavnenævn. *Sprog i Norden*. 185–188.

Ostermann, H. 1929. The trade from 1870 to the present time. In Martin Vahl, Georg Carl Amdrup & Adolf Severin Jensen (eds.), *Greenland*. Vol. 3: *The colonization of Greenland and its history until 1929*, 165–215. Copenhagen: Reitzel.

Petersen, Robert. 1995. Colonialism as seen from a former colonized area. *Arctic Anthropology* 32(2). 118–126.

Stolz, Thomas, Christina Vossmann & Barbara Dewein. 2011. Kolonialzeitliche Sprachforschung und das Forschungsprogramm Koloniallinguistik: eine kurze Einführung. In Thomas Stolz, Christina Vossmann & Barbara Dewein (eds.), *Kolonialzeitliche Sprachforschung. Die Beschreibung afrikanischer und ozeanischer Sprachen zur Zeit der deutschen Kolonialherrschaft*, 7–30. Berlin & Boston: De Gruyter Mouton.

Stolz, Thomas & Ingo H. Warnke. 2015. Aspekte der kolonialen und postkolonialen Toponymie unter besonderer Berücksichtigung des deutschen Kolonialismus. In Daniel Schmidt-Brücken et al. (eds.), *Koloniallinguistik. Sprache in kolonialen Kontexten*, 107–176. Berlin & Boston: De Gruyter Mouton.

Stolz, Thomas & Ingo H. Warnke. 2016. When places change their names and when they do not. Selected aspects of colonial and postcolonial toponymy in former French and Spanish colonies in West Africa – the case of Saint Louis (Senegal) and the Western Sahara. *International Journal of the Sociology of Language* 239. 29–56.

Stolz, Thomas & Ingo H. Warnke. 2018a. Comparative colonial toponomastics. Evidence from German and Dutch colonial place names. In Rita Heuser & Mirjam Schmuck et al. (eds.), *Sonstige Namenarten – Stiefkinder der Onomastik, 45–68*. Berlin & Boston: De Gruyter Mouton.

Stolz, Thomas & Ingo H. Warnke. 2018b. Auf dem Weg zu einer vergleichenden Kolonialtoponomastik. Der Fall Deutsch-Südwestafrika. In Birte Kellermeier-Rehbein, Matthias Schulz & Doris Stolberg (eds.), *Sprache und (Post)-Kolonialismus. Linguistische und interdisziplinäre Aspekte*, 71–103. Berlin & Boston: De Gruyter Mouton.

Stolz, Thomas, Ingo H. Warnke & Nataliya Levkovych. 2016. Colonial place names in a comparative perspective. *Beiträge zur Namensforschung*. 51(3–4). 279–353.

Sturmfels, Wilhelm & Heinz Bischof. 1961. *Unsere Ortsnamen*. Bonn: Dümmler.

Vuolteenaho, Jani & Lawrence D. Berg. 2009. Towards critical toponymies. In Lawrence D. Berg & Jani Vuolteenaho (eds.), *Critical toponymies. The contested politics of place naming*, 1–18. Farnham: Ashgate.

Warnke, Ingo H. 2009. Deutsche Sprache und Kolonialismus. Umrisse eines Forschungsfeldes. In Ingo H. Warnke (ed.), *Deutsche Sprache und Kolonialismus. Aspekte der nationalen Kommunikation 1884–1919*, 3–62. Berlin & New York: De Gruyter.

Warnke, Ingo H., Thomas Stolz & Daniel Schmidt-Brücken. 2016. Perspektiven der Postcolonial Language Studies. In *Sprache und Kolonialismus, eine interdisziplinäre Einführung zu Sprache und Kommunikation in kolonialen Kontexten*, 1–25. Berlin & Boston: De Gruyter Mouton.

(b) Online sources

Danmarks Stednavne: Nordisk Forskningsinstitut, accessed 3 April 2016, <http://danmarksstednavne.navneforskning.ku.dk/>

Finlayson, Douglas: *Frobisher Bay*. The Canadian Encyclopedia, accessed 10 April 2016, <http://www.thecanadianencyclopedia.ca/en/article/frobisher-bay/>

Grønlandskort, Geologiske kort 1:2 500 000. Udsnit 7: Nuuk, Godthåb, Julianehåb, Sønder strømfjord, De nationale geologiske undersøgelser for Danmark og Grønland, accessed 3 April 2016, <http://www.geus.dk/DK/data-maps/greenland/Sider/kost_07-dk.aspx>
McCaskill Popini, Eloise: *John Davis*. Encyclopedia Arctica Vol. 15, Biographies, accessed 20 April 2016, < http://collections.dartmouth.edu/arctica-beta/html/EA15-20.html>
NunaGIS, Greenland Geographic Information System, accessed 10 April 2016, <http://www.nunagis.gl>
Nunaqarfiit illoqarfiillu aqqi akuerisat: Overview of the Greenlandic city- and settlement names and their abbreviations approved by the Greenland Place Names Committee. pdf available at: Oqaasilerifffik. The Greenland Language Secretariat, accessed 21 April 2016, http://www.oqaasileriffik.gl/en/resources/greenlandiccity_andsettlementnames
Oxford English Dictionary online. , accessed 10 April 2016, <https://en.oxforddictionaries.com/>
Politics in Greenland: Naalakkersuisut: Government of Greenland, accessed 21 April 2016, <http://naalakkersuisut.gl/en/About-government-of-greenland/About-Greenland/Politics-in-Greenland>
The Place Names Committee: Oqaasileriffik. The Greenland Language Secretariat, accessed 21 April 2016, http://www.oqaasileriffik.gl/en/oqaasileriffik/placenamescommittee

Paolo Miccoli
Colonial place-names in Italian East Africa (AOI) (with additional data from Tripoli)

The linguistic heritage of colonial practice

Abstract: This article deals with Italian colonial toponymy in the former African colonies of East Africa. The focus is on the naming practices of Italian colonizers as evidenced by the toponymical traces of the colonial period. Both pure exonymic macrotoponyms and microtoponyms (mostly urbanonyms or odonyms) are taken into account. The objective is to illustrate empirically that there were two different phases during the fascist regime of Mussolini: the first begins with his regime in 1922, and the second, shorter than the previous one, begins with the conquest of Ethiopia in 1936 and ends with the loss of colonies during the Second World War (1941–42). Both phases manifested themselves in the domain of colonial naming practices. The second phase specifically shows the emergence of the colonial toponyms which are formally and semantically distinguishable to some extent both from those of the 1882–1922 Liberal period and those of the first fascist phase. The general aim is to identify characteristic traits connected to Italian practices of naming places in the context of colonialism as compared to those of other European and non-European colonizers.

Keywords: Italian colonialism, Italian East Africa, exonyms, fascism

1 Introduction

When *Africa Orientale Italiana* (Italian Eastern Africa, henceforth: AOI) was created officially in May 1936, a new (albeit brief and mostly illusory) phase of colonialism began, which presented some elements of originality. This new phase distinguished itself not only from the Liberal period, but to some extent,

---

Paolo Miccoli, University of Bremen, FB 10: Linguistics/Language Sciences, Universitäts-Boulevard 13, 28359 Bremen, Germany. E-Mail: pmiccoli@uni-bremen.de

Università degli Studi di Napoli "L'Orientale", Dipartimento di Studi Letterari, Linguistici e Comparati, Linguistica italiana, Palazzo Santa Maria Porta Coeli, via Duomo 219, 80138 Napoli, Italy. E-Mail: pmiccoli@unior.it

https://doi.org/10.1515/9783110623710-004

also from the first fascist colonial phase. The purpose of this paper is to analyze the colonial toponymy in this phase of Italian colonialism in order to answer the following research questions:
(a) How did this phase of Italian colonialism influence Italian colonial toponymy?
(b) Do Italian colonial toponyms characterizing this phase differ from toponyms appeared in earlier phases as to formal and semantic properties?

To answer these questions a selection of cases concerning macrotoponyms and microtoponyms was analyzed using the theoretical framework elaborated for the research program of *Comparative Colonial Toponomastics* (CoCoTop) (Stolz et al. 2016). Stolz et al. (2016: 280–281) laid out the framework, starting from the analysis of German colonial toponymy, and suggesting that the place-making function of language during the colonial period can best be investigated by means of toponyms referring to typical place names. According to Warnke (2009: 49–50), these toponyms are the "symbolic building blocks" of the discourse on colonialisms which can help us better understand the relationship between the "textual and space positions of colonialisms".

Section 2 of this paper focuses on the pure exonymic macrotoponyms[1] which emerged in AOI in the final phase of Italian colonialism, in order to compare them with their equivalents in the Liberal period and the first fascist period. Section 3 deals with the examination of the pure exonymic microtoponyms of the city of Addis Abeba, based on the map produced in 1938 by the *Istituto Geografico Militare*[2] and precisely by the *Ufficio Topografico e Monografie del Comando Superiore delle Forze Armate dell'AOI* on a 1:5000 scale.[3] These microtoponyms are, in turn, compared with those found in the maps of Tripoli by Salussolia of 1914 and by Michelini of 1934.[4] They were chosen as examples of colonial microtoponyms of the liberal period and the first fascist period. The

---

[1] The terminologies of pure exonyms, hybrid exonyms and pure endonyms and the distinction between classifiers and modifiers are taken from Stolz & Warnke (2017: 206–207) and (2018).
[2] The *Istituto Geografico Militare* (IMGI) is still the Italian Army's geographical auxiliary branch and also the national cartographic authority. (cf. https://www.igmi.org/).
[3] It is a precious cartographic source for Italian colonial microtoponomy from 1936 to 1941, as it is one of the very few cartographic examples in which the pure exonymic microtoponyms and the hybrid exonymic microtoponyms found therein emerged after 1936.
[4] For a careful analysis of the pure exonymic microtoponyms and of the hybrid exonymic microtoponyms present in the two maps of the city of Tripoli mentioned above and for a comparison with the colonial toponyms present in the *Quartiere Africano* of Rome, please refer to Miccoli (in press).

classification in this study follows the Schulz & Ebert (2016 and 2017) framework of German microtoponymy and the Nübling et al. (2015: 206–265), and Marcato (2009: 105–190) framework of toponyms.

2 Pure exonymic macrotoponyms in AOI

At the beginning of Italy's operations in Ethiopia, cartography in AOI was incomplete and by October 1, 1935, only summarized in a few papers, according to the third volume of *La costruzione dell'Impero. L'Opera dell'Italia in A.O.I. dopo la conquista dell'Etiopia*[5] (cf. GADAI-3: 940). Apart from the strongly propagandistic tone of this work, it is true that Italian cartography in Ethiopia before the conquest of 1936 was limited. Moreover, starting with geodesic research and geophysics in 1936, the Government gave every impression that such research could lead to scientific and practical results as promptly as possible (cf. GADAI-3: 940). The beginning of an intense and dynamic period of Italian cartography in AOI (particularly in Ethiopia) is confirmed by Traversi (1964: 200) who wrote the most important work about the history of Italian cartography in the former colonies in 1964. Almost twenty years after the end of World War II, the selfsame Traversi was not entirely immune to nostalgia for the Fascist regime.[6]

Nevertheless, it is clear that the Italian cartographic production in AOI experienced a surge after the Ethiopian campaign. The most noticeable outcome was the *Guida dell'Africa Orientale Italiana* (henceforth GAOI)[7], published by the

---

[5] The collection of volumes entitled *La costruzione dell'impero. L'opera dell'Italia in A.O.I. dopo la conquista dell'Etiopia* [The construction of the Empire. The work of Italy in A.O.I. after the conquest of Ethiopia] is part of the *Annali dell'Africa Italiana* [Annals of Italian Africa]. The collection in question consists of four volumes (from here on, in order to exemplify, GADAI-1, GADAI-2, GADAI-3 and GADAI-4), all published between 1939 and 1940; although it is a work with strong propaganda tones, it represents a valuable source on the triennial history of the newly formed *Africa Orientale Italiana* (AOI) [Italian Eastern Africa] after the conquest of Ethiopia (1936–1939). As Attilio Teruzzi writes in the introduction, the book is the official account of the works carried out by Italy in A.O.I. in the first three years after the conquest of the Empire (cf. GADAI-1: XVII). When considering the entry into the war in 1940 and the factual loss of the colonies in 1941, the collection of the Annals is one of the very few encyclopedic works that focuses solely and exclusively on that precise historical period of Mussolini's Italy.
[6] On the complex and delayed process of historical and cultural decolonization in Italy, the works of Angelo Del Boca and Nicola Labanca, among others, will be considered.
[7] From here on, the *Guida dell'Africa Orientale Italiana* will be indicated by the abbreviation GAOI, in agreement with Stolz et al. (2016: 309).

Consociazione Turistica Italiana in 1938. The GAOI is described adequately in GADAI-3, and it was based on the findings and reports of the topocartographic offices of the Government, the *Istituto Geografico Militare*. It was basically a graphic synthesis of the current knowledge of these vast territories, then still imperfectly known, and already bore the signs of the roads and public works that testified to energetic efforts at development with predictably imperial priorities. (cf. GADAI-3: 943). Also in this case the strong propaganda tones do not prejudice the veracity of the positive benefits of the work. The GAOI was, in fact, a well-documented work and a very important source for Italian colonial toponymy. It can be employed to analyze diachronically the naming processes in AOI. It is no coincidence that Stolz et al. (2016: 309) consider it, along with the *Guida Breve dell'Italia Meridionale e Insulare e della Libia*[8], an exceptionally useful source for the second phase of Italian colonialism in the domain of colonial place-naming.

Whereas Stolz et al. only distinguish two phases of Italian colonialism, it has been strongly argued in this paper that two distinct phases of the fascist period existed. Thus, there were three phases, viz. liberalism, first fascist phase and second fascist phase. To test this argument the ACI (*Atlante delle Colonie Italiane*) of 1928, the PEC[9] of 1929 and the GAOI of 1938 are used as sources. The GAOI is the only guide to include Ethiopia since it was the only one to have been published after the conquest of 1936. In the alphabetical index of the GAOI, the Italian colonial toponyms of Ethiopia represent a very significant testimony of those colonial Italian toponyms that saw the light of day after the conquest of Ethiopia and the creation of the Empire. They will therefore be taken into particular consideration in the analysis that follows. The PEC and ACI, on the other hand, will be used for comparison with the GAOI to identify the diachronic development of Italian colonial toponyms in Eritrea, Somalia, and in some areas of Ethiopia already known to Italian explorers and missionaries in pre-conquest times.

The GAOI is characterized by a detailed alphabetical index of some 2,800 localities. Most of those are macrotoponyms. When analyzing the particularities of the macrotoponyms, 236 hybrid exonyms and 58 pure exonyms are identified, with solely the latter being of interest for this study. The identification of the

---

8 *La Guida Breve dell'Italia Meridionale e Insulare e della Libia*, henceforth GBL in agreement with Stolz et al. (2016: 309), is an important source for the Italian colonial toponymy in Libya.
9 PEC is the abbreviation used to indicate the *Guida del Touring Club Italiano* of 1929, edited by Luigi V. Bertarelli, entitled *Possedimenti E Colonie: Isole Egee, Tripolitania, Cirenaica, Eritrea e Somalia*.

Italian pure exonymic macrotoponyms in Ethiopia in the GAOI is easy, since, in most cases, toponyms are indicated with the bracketed initial letter of the governorate to which they belonged.[10] So A stands for Amára, AA for Addis Abeba Governorate, GS for Galla and Sidama, H for Harar, while E and S stand for Eritrea and Somalia, respectively. If only the first four regions that correspond roughly to the parts of Ethiopia conquered in 1936 are considered, the presence of the following exonym macrotoponyms is identified, listed according to the entry order in the index of the localities in the GAOI: *Bari d'Etiopia (H)*, *villaggio Bòttego (GS)*, *colonia Cavalieri di Neghelli (GS)*, *Pattuglie del Grano (GS)*, *Romagna d'Etiopia (A)*, *villaggio Torino (AA)*, *cascata Vannutelli e Citerni (GS)* and *villaggio Zappa (GS)*.

These pure exonymic Italian macrotoponyms are not the only ones on the list that refer to places in Ethiopia, but it is preferred to distinguish them from the others because the GAOI authors reported them with the initials of their region of reference in brackets. This choice could depend on the fact that the authors of the GAOI perceived these toponyms as having greater official character in contrast to the others. This hypothesis could explain why the authors did not make the same choice for other Italian colonial exonymic macrotoponyms in Ethiopia like *Passo delle Gazzelle* (Gazzelles Pass), *Valle delle Meraviglie* (Valley of Wonders), *Passo Mussolini* (Mussolini Pass), *Vetta Mussolini* (Mussolini Peak), *Salto del Gallo* (Rooster's Drop), *Passo Sella* (Saddle Pass), *Lago Stefania* (Lake Stephanie), etc. Perhaps these toponyms were considered to have less official character, such as Italian reinterpretation of local names or even simple translations into Italian. It is no coincidence that many of these toponyms were reported together with the corresponding aboriginal names. But the analysis of these toponyms will not be covered in this paper. Here, the focus is only on the analysis of the toponyms of the first group, i.e. those that presented the region of reference in brackets.

- *Bari d'Etiopia (H)*[11] < *Bari* (= city in the south of Italy) + *di* (= genitival preposition) + *Etiopia* (= Ethiopia).
- *Villaggio Bóttego (GS)*[12] < *villaggio* (= classifier 'village') + *Bóttego* (= anthroponymic modifier).[13]

---

[10] The alphabetic index of the localities of the GAOI is preceded by a short list of abbreviations, among which stand out both those referring to classifiers (*fiume* 'river', *lago* 'lake', *monte* 'mountain', *passo* 'pass' and *torrente* 'creek'), and those referring to the new governorship of the AOI.
[11] It is one of the first centers of demographic colonization in the empire that was emerging in the basin of Uacchus (cf. GAOI 1938: 457).
[12] It is a village in the locality Asciúra (cf. GAOI 1938: 549).

- *Colonia Cavalieri di Neghelli (GS)*[14] < *colonia* (= classifier 'colony') + *Cavalieri di Neghelli* (= modifier), which is made of the common noun *Cavalieri* 'Knights', the preposition *di* 'of' and the indigenous name of the city *Neghelli*.
- *Pattuglie del Grano (GS)*[15] < *Pattuglie* (= common noun 'patrols') + *del* (= articulated preposition 'of the') + *grano* (= common noun 'wheat'). It is the name of a rural area that includes the only instance of a modifier.
- *Romagna d'Ethiopia* (A)[16] < *Romagna* (= name of the Italian region) + *di* (= simple preposition 'of') + *Etiopia* (= Ethiopia). It is the name of a settlement consisting only of a modifier.
- *Villaggio Torino (AA)*[17] < *villaggio* (= classifier 'village') + *Torino* (= modifier, the proper name of the Italian city Turin in the north of Italy).
- *Cascata Vannutelli e Citerni (GS)*[18] < *cascata* (= classifier 'waterfall') + *Vannutelli e Citerni* (= binary anthroponymic modifier).
- *Villaggio Zappa (GS)*[19] < *villaggio* (= classifier 'village') + *Zappa* (= anthroponymic modifier).

2.1 Toponyms *villaggio Bóttego* and *cascata Vannutelli e Citerni* and the significant case of the three variants *lago Afreda ~ lago Afrera ~ lago Giulietti*

The naming processes which determined the origin of these toponyms sometimes followed those of the liberal past, and, mainly, the first fascist period, as in the case of the *villaggio Bottego* and *Cascata Vannutelli e Citerni*. In fact, the tendency to name places with toponyms consisting of a classifier and an anthroponymic modifier indicating the surname of an Italian explorer has al-

---

13 *Bóttego* is the surname of Vittorio Bottego, explorer and Italian officer famous for his explorations in the Horn of Africa.
14 The place was named after the *Cavalieri di Neghelli*, a platoon of soldiers who founded the colony in 1937. This colony is one of the first examples of national colonization in the Empire and was an important agricultural experimental center (cf. GAOI 1938: 528).
15 This refers to national agricultural colonies established by the *Federazione dei Fasci del Galla e Sidáma* for the food autocracy of the Empire (cf. GAOI 1938: 528).
16 The toponym refers to another planned center of demographic colonization in the empire (cf. GAOI 1938: 257).
17 Name of a settlement (GAOI 1938: 432).
18 These surnames refer to Lamberto Vannutelli and Carlo Citerni, two Italian explorers. The waterfall is formed by a tributary of *Lago Margherita* (Lake Margherita). (cf. GAOI 1938: 550).
19 *Zappa* is the surname of the journalist and fascist writer Paolo Zappa. The village was located near Mount Néggio (cf. GAOI 1938: 511).

ready been shown in the colonial maps of the earlier phases. However, it should be noted that in the above cases toponyms have a particular commemorative function, since the second element recalls explorers who carried out particularly significant exploration missions on Ethiopian territory. In fact, in the case above, Vittorio Bottego was a famous explorer who had lost his life during a mission of exploration and guerrilla warfare in southern Ethiopia, in which the explorers Vannutelli and Citerni[20] also took part.

The background of Bottego's mission was that of the war fought between the Kingdom of Italy and the Empire of Ethiopia from December 1895 to October 1896. The resounding Italian defeat at the Battle of Adua of March 1, 1896 took place when Bottego was still in Ethiopia. The tragic end of Bottego's expedition (after the war) was also the consequence of the state of isolation in which the explorer was left by the Italian state as a result of the defeat. For diplomatic/strategic reasons, the state did not inform the explorer of the outbreak of war or of its end, thus abandoning him and his mission to disaster. Bottego and his men were known to be hostile and unscrupulous toward the population of Ethiopia and toward local institutions. This would certainly not have helped the peace negotiations with the emperor Menelik. This explains the policy adopted in isolating Bottego and his men (Del Boca 2001 v.1: 427–428 and 746–749).

About forty years after Adua and the defeat in the war against Ethiopia, Mussolini mounted a powerful propaganda-campaign based on the theme of revenge. This campaign became intense after the victory in the second war against Ethiopia in 1936 with the proclamation of the Italian Empire and the creation of AOI (see Del Boca 2001 v.2). From a toponymical point of view, the most evident traces of this propaganda can be found precisely from 1936 onwards.

In this historical scenario, in relation to the naming processes which led to the coining of toponyms like *villaggio Bottego* and *cascata Vannutelli e Citerni*, two premises are posed. On the one hand, the formation of binary toponyms

---

20 The Bottego expedition left Naples on July 3, 1895; accompanied by naval Second Lieutenant of vessel Lamberto Vannutelli (1871–1966), Maurizio Sacchi (1864–1897) and the Sub-Lieutenant Carlo Citerni (1873–1918). The latter was commissioned as a photographer of the expedition and also to keep the diary. At Daga Roba, the expedition met disaster: on March 17, 1897, it was attacked by a local tribe and suffered many losses; Bottego was shot and killed, while Citerni and Vannutelli were taken prisoner and released only on 6 June, also thanks to the mediation of Menelik. They were the only Italian survivors of the expedition. The story of the mission until its sad end was narrated by Citerni and Vannutelli in the volume *L'Omo*, published under the auspices of the *Società Geografica Italiana*, in 1899 (cf. http://www.archiviofotografico.societageografica.it/index.php?en/240/second-Shipping-Bottego-1895-1897).

with an anthroponymic modifier referring to an Italian explorer had already been seen in the two previous phases of Italian colonialism. On the other hand, the commemorative function of these two toponyms must be distinguished from that of structurally similar toponyms which had appeared previously.

In this regard the story of the toponym *lago Giulietti*, which involves the classifier *lago* 'lake' and the anthroponymic modifier *Giulietti* (referring to the Italian explorer Giuseppe Maria Giulietti) is very interesting. The explorer had headed many expeditions to Africa and had lost his life during an expedition to the Tigrè. In fact, on May 25, 1881, Giulietti was killed in Beilul, probably by the Dancali of the Sultanate of Biru, together with other members of the expedition, whom were a dozen sailors from the warship *Ettore Fieramosca* (cf. Del Boca 2001 v.1: 115–121). The massacre, as it was long known in Italy, caused a stir which resonated for decades. Several decades later, another explorer, Raimondo Franchetti, led an exploratory expedition from Assab across the Dancalia plateau. The Italian expedition reached *lago Afreda* in March 1929, which had already been discovered nine years before by another Italian explorer, Paolo Vinassa de Regny, who named the lake on behalf of the *Società Mineraria dell'Africa Orientale Italiana*. However, Franchetti decided to rename the lake *lago Giulietti*, in memory of the explorer who had died so tragically at the end of the previous century (cf. Lupi 2009: 136–139).

This is a clear example of how research about the historical events around the explorers of landmarks allows a deep analysis of the presence of the toponyms in the sources. However, the choice of names in successive sources has been led by political inclinations. The ACI of 1928 presents the toponym *Lago Afreda*, while the PEC of 1929 reports all the variants of the toponym *lago Afredà ~ lago Afrerà ~ lago Giulietti* (PEC 1929: 831). Then, the GAOI of 1938 reports the three variants of the toponyms as three different toponyms, so that the variant *lago Giulietti* has a particular prominence.

The most interesting results are those that a comparison of PEC and GAOI yields. On the one hand, the ACI had to mention the toponym *lago Afreda*, because it was the only choice after the discovery and naming of the lake by Paolo Vinassa de Regny during the 1919–1920 expedition. On the other hand, both the PEC and the GAOI had the possibility to choose between the two names, since the publication of both guides happened after the renaming of *lago Afreda* in *lago Giulietti* by Raimondo Franchetti during the expedition of 1929. It is certainly true that the close temporal proximity of Franchetti's renaming of the lake and the publication of the PEC justifies the co-existence of the different variants of the toponym in the PEC. However, this is by no means the only explanation. In 1929, the year of the publication of the PEC, the fascist dictatorship was at the height of its power. Four years had passed since the famous speech of Mussolini in the national Chamber of Deputies, in which he assumed responsibility for the politically motivated murder of the socialist deputy Giacomo Matteotti. Not long afterwards, the so-called *leggi fascistissime*, i.e. the laws of 1925–1926, was passed, which definitively transformed the legal order of the Kingdom of Italy from a liberal state to a fascist regime. However, the events that would have changed the fascist colonial policy definitively, i.e. the Ethiopian Campaign and the proclamation of the Empire, were still distant. In this first phase of fascist colonialism, the tendency to Italianize the colonial space with the use of Italian colonial deanthroponymic toponyms was undoubtedly already present. However, this tendency was not as strong as after the conquest of Ethiopia, which marked the beginning of the second phase of fascist colonialism, during which the Italian colonial toponyms had a precise commemorative function. The choice of the GAOI to report the variant of the lake's place name, referring to the Italian explorer Giulietti in a separate voice of the alphabetical index, is a relevant piece of evidence of this particular commemorative function.

The above toponyms *villaggio Bottego* and *cascata Vannutelli e Citerni* are other examples. As they are mentioned only in the GAOI, they must have been coined after the Ethiopian Campaign and the proclamation of the Empire. Consequently, they confirm two phenomena: (a) Italian colonizers of the second fascist phase made exclusive use of toponyms consisting of a classifier and an anthroponymic modifier and (b) toponyms were preferred which had a strong combined commemorative and reclaiming function, the latter as a way of stressing the ownership of the region. This becomes clear only when taking into account that Bottego, Vannuttelli and Citerni were the protagonists of an expedition, the so-called second Bottego expedition of 1895–1897, which, in the eyes of the colonists of the second fascist period, had a specific value. This peculiarity is mainly due to two factors: 1) the second Bottego expedition being the most relevant Italian expedition to have been accomplished on Ethiopian territory during the Italian-Abyssinian war of 1895–1896, 2) Bottego being abandoned to his fate by the Italian state for diplomatic reasons. These two historical aspects were considered fundamental for the colonial propaganda of the second fascist phase, which needed any way to justify a war of conquest against one of the last independent states of the African continent. This war of conquest not only went against the fundamental principles of the League of Nations but also cost the Italian economy a very high price.

In the light of these considerations, it is clear that the naming processes of the second fascist phase, which led to the creation of the toponyms *villaggio Bottego* and *cascata Vannutelli e Citerni*, must be differentiated from (a) the renaming *lago Afreda/lago Afrera* in *lago Giulietti* by Franchetti and (b) the decision of the PEC to report all the toponymic variants; both in the first fascist phase. The function of the toponyms *villaggio Bottego* and *cascata Vannutelli e Citerni* cannot be described as a merely memorial, but must be marked with the commemorative-reclaiming function, thus underlining the particular function of claiming a territory, whose conquest had failed previously.

2.2 Toponyms *Bari d'Etiopia* and *Romagna d'Etiopia*

The *Bari d'Etiopia* and *Romagna d'Etiopia* toponyms should be seen as being part of the new demographic colonization the fascist regime planned for the newly conquered territory. As stated in the GAOI, the new provisions concerning demographic colonization did not concern Eritrea and Somalia, for which the norms prior to the creation of the Empire were already in force. It was a broader organic plan prepared by the *Ministero dell'Africa Italiana* in order to rationally start the demographic colonization, to create an agrarian demography able to meet the food needs of the Empire, and to start on a large scale the cultivation of the most useful products to the autarchy of the Motherland, thus encouraging cooperation of indigenous farmers for these purposes (cf. GAOI 1938: 98). The plan included four forms of colonization, of which the first is described, because it is closely linked to the coining of the toponyms in question. The first demographic colonization was directed by the large *Enti di Colonizzazione*. According to the GAOI, it is clear that the naming processes, which led to the introduction of the macrotoponyms *Romagna d'Etiopia* and *Bari d'Etiopia*, are to be ascribed only and exclusively to the second phase of fascist colonialism. Because of the new plan of demographic colonization of the Italian Empire, there was a strong desire to Italianize the spaces of the colony with reference to the regional origin of the new settlers who were expected to inhabit and cultivate the lands (cf. GAOI 1938: 98). Compared to the liberal phase and the first fascist phase, these toponyms, therefore, represent a novelty not only for their particular classifierless structure, but also for the specific commemorative function.

2.3 Toponyms *Colonia Cavalieri di Neghelli* and *Pattuglie del grano*

The place names *Colonia Cavalieri di Neghelli* and *Pattuglie del grano* are included in the discourse of the demographic colonization process that started after the Ethiopian campaign. As to the first toponym, in particular, it can be said that it was the result of the fourth form of colonization of the plan, that is, that which provided for the granting of modest plots of land (10–15 ha.) to veterans of the Ethiopian campaign and to the workers who had cooperated in the conquest of Ethiopia (cf. GAOI 1938: 98). The toponym, therefore, represents a novelty insofar as its commemorative function was intended to ascribe those lands to a division of the Italian army that was instrumental for the Italian victory. However, the structure of the toponym presents also elements of novelty, as the modifier *Cavalieri di Neghelli* consists of three elements: (i) a common noun *Cavalieri* 'knights', (ii) the preposition *di* 'of', and (iii) the proper name Neghelli, i.e. the Italianized rendering of the name of an Ethiopian town. Moreover, even the use of the classifier *colonia* 'colony' is not usual in the naming processes of the previous phases. With its binary modifier, the toponym *Pattuglie del grano* is also a toponym with a new classifierless structure which was not seen in the previous phases.

2.4 Toponyms *villaggio Zappa* and *villaggio Torino*

The tendency to rename macroplaces with macrotoponyms composed of a classifier and an anthroponymic modifier was already present in the previous phases.[21] The toponym *villaggio Zappa* shows that in the second fascist phase this tendency became more frequent (see Miccoli 2017).

Finally, even the toponym *villaggio Torino* is a symbol of a toponymic tendency typical of the second phase of fascist colonialism, albeit for different reasons. Section 3, devoted to microtoponyms, will show that the predisposition to employ Italian colonial toponyms consisting of a classifier and the name of an Italian city, region or river as modifier was already in existence in the liberal phase and, above all, in the first fascist phase (see Miccoli in press). At the same time, in the domain of macrotoponomy, this pattern is representative of a naming process that developed mainly in the second fascist phase (cf. *villaggio Torino*).

---

[21] Typical examples are *lago Margherita* and *Castel Benito* which were coined in the liberal phase and the first fascist phase, respectively.

3 Pure exonymic microtoponyms in Addis Abeba in 1938

The existence of a toponymically relevant second fascist phase must also be demonstrated for microtoponyms. The latter are distinguished from the macrotoponyms by the level of knowledge of the toponym. In the case of microtoponyms, the level of knowledge is limited to a specific place of knowledge. In the case of macrotoponyms, there is a wider spread of the knowledge. In many cases the knowledge is correlated with the size of the place the toponyms designate. However, in some cases a clear demarcation is not entirely simple, as for the names of watercourses or mountains that can be both macrotoponyms and microtoponyms according to the level of knowledge of the object to which they are correlated. Another important difference between macrotoponyms and microtoponyms is the sources. In the case of macrotoponyms, the sources are mostly guides, atlases, large-scale maps. In the case of microtoponyms, however, regulatory plans or city plans constitute the basis. Therefore, on a small scale, the macrotoponyms are mostly urbanonyms and odonyms. On the basis of these differences, it is understood that the quantity is very variable. Microtoponyms are generally much more numerous than macrotoponyms. On this premise, the Italian colonial pure exonymic microtoponyms reported for the city of Addis Abeba after the conquest of Ethiopia by the Italian army in May 1936 can be analyzed.

Like the Italian macrotoponyms in Ethiopia, identified in the GAOI of 1938, the microtoponyms of Addis Abeba too arose in the second fascist phase. The main source is the Addis Abeba city-map of 1938. However, important toponymic information is also obtained from the adjusted plan of Addis Abeba by the architect Ignazio Guidi and engineer Cesare Valle (1936–1938).[22]

The Italian toponyms in Addis Abeba found in the aforementioned sources will be compared with those present in two colonial maps of Tripoli, namely that of 1914 by Salussolia, and that of 1934 by Michelini. These are colonial maps of a Libyan city that did not belong to AOI. Nevertheless, they provide a substantial microtoponomastic source of the liberal phase and the first fascist phase. Therefore they are very useful for a diachronic linguistic analysis of Italian microtoponyms.

Microtoponyms will also be subjected to a descriptive-analytical analysis of structures and functions. On the colonial map of Addis Abeba there are 75 pure

---

[22] The main source of the detailed information on the regular plan of Addis Abeba is GADAI-4.

exonymic microtoponyms. When the structure of microtoponyms is analyzed, both similarities and differences are identified, in comparison to those of previous colonial phases.

As for the analogies, there are 18 toponyms which constitute the following internal structure:
- [via$_{CLASSIFIER}$ Belluno$_{MODIFIER}$]$_{TOPONYM}$,
- [via$_{CLASSIFIER}$ Campania$_{MODIFIER}$]$_{TOPONYM}$,
- [via$_{CLASSIFIER}$ Tevere$_{MODIFIER}$]$_{TOPONYM}$;

The three examples consist each of a classifier (*via* 'street') and a modifier that corresponds to the name of an Italian city (= *Belluno*), region (= *Campania*) or river (= *Tevere*). This pattern had already been common in the liberal period. However, its frequency increased substantially in the first fascist phase. As a matter of fact, in the map of Tripoli of 1934, there are 86 Italian colonial odonyms reflecting the above pattern with modifier of the following kinds in commemorative function (see Miccoli in press):
(a) city names: (*via Bari, via Firenze, via Lecce,* etc.),
(b) names of regions: (*via Basilicata, via Lazio, via Lombardia,* etc.),
(c) names of rivers: (*via Adige, via Piave, via Reno,* etc.).

In reference to the structure of the microtoponyms of the first and second fascist phases, there is an additional analogy, namely the presence of binary deanthroponymic toponyms. On the colonial map of Addis Abeba, there are 35 toponyms with the above structure. They account for almost half of the total. Similarly, on the colonial map of Tripoli of 1934, toponyms with an anthroponymic modifier were very common, appearing more than 50 % of the time. These important structural analogies show that the processes of naming must be understood as a diachronic continuum. It would be a mistake to conceive of the various phases as isolated monads. Yet, it is permissible to demarcate different phases of naming processes when, in accordance with the concept of diachronic continuity, there are substantial differences.

Some Italian microtoponyms identified on the map of Addis Abeba of 1938 are evidence of new toponymic fashions. As to the internal structure, the most striking example are binary toponyms whose modifier reflects the name of a division of the Italian army which participated in the Ethiopian Campaign. This pattern is absent from the previous phases. Therefore, it is a characteristic of the second fascist phase.

Further important differences emerge when analyzing the function of microtoponyms. In this case, all toponyms (including those already mentioned) consisting of a classifier and an anthroponymic modifier are taken into consideration. As Miccoli (in press) points out, the binary deanthroponymic microtoponyms are an innovation of the first fascist phase, as compared to the preceding liberal phase. On the Tripoli map of 1914, there is only one toponym with this structure (*Ospedale Vittorio Emanuele*), whereas on the Tripoli map of 1934, there are almost 120 cases reflecting the pattern under review. The microtoponyms of Addis Abeba can be understood as a continuation of those of Tripoli coined in the first fascist phase. However, the results are different when moving from the structural analysis to the functional analysis of Italian microtoponyms.

From a functional point of view, the striking discontinuity between the liberal period and the first fascist period becomes evident. On the map of Tripoli of 1914, most of the microtoponyms have an orientation function, while on the map of Tripoli of 1934 the ratio is reversed. There is now a clear preference for microtoponyms with a commemorative function. The Italian microtoponyms coined after the proclamation of the empire and used for Addis Abeba in 1938 continue the patterns of those of the first fascist phase. Except for a minority of cases, they all have a commemorative function. However, on closer inspection of their semantics, the commemorative function of these toponyms has a different value from those of the first fascist phase. In particular, they differ from those found in the Tripoli city map of 1934. In the latter case, the deanthroponymic microtoponyms with a commemorative function recall mostly illustrious men of culture, personalities linked to the period of the Italian Risorgimento, individuals who played an important role in colonial politics. Moreover, there is a minority of anthroponymic modifiers that refer to personalities of ancient Rome, "fascist martyrs", important agents of the fascist regime, military heroes of World War I, finally, some anthroponyms related to people associated with the monarchy. The 35 binary deanthroponymic toponyms which appear on the map of Addis Abeba refer, instead, to explorers and individuals who had the merit, in the perspective of fascist propaganda, of "civilizing" the regions of the AOI before the conquest of the Ethiopia and the proclamation of the Empire of 1936:

(a) explorers and "civilizers": *via Ammiraglio Caimi, via Roberto Brichetti, via G. Bianchi*, etc.,

(b) military of the Ethiopian Campaign of 1935/6: *via Carboni, via P. R. Giuliani, via Generale Saletta*, etc.,

(c) "Martyrs" of the first Italian-Abyssinian war: *via Arimondi, via Galiano*, and, finally,

(d) personalities linked to the monarchy: *via Principe di Napoli, Ospedale Regina Elena, Viale Regina Margherita*, etc.).

As must be evident, unlike anthroponymic modifiers present on the map of Tripoli of the first fascist period, those appearing on the Addis Abeba map refer, in most cases, to personalities who had a relationship with the colony in which the toponyms connected to the person appear, in this case AOI or, specifically, Ethiopia. This is an important trait of the Italian colonial exonymic microtoponyms of the second fascist phase. Those that are reported for Addis Abeba as of 1938 represent an important example. Via their toponymical choice, the Italian colonizers of the second fascist phase attributed a special memorial function to the deanthroponymic microtoponyms. From the point of view of propaganda, they intended to establish a common link among the first Italian explorers who had contributed to the knowledge of those territories, the Italian soldiers who had lost their lives in the first Italo-Abyssinian war and the Italian soldiers who had fallen in battle during the Campaign of Ethiopia. The tragic defeat at Adua was thus turned into a victory so that vengeance was achieved. The victory of 1936 opened to Italy the gates of a territory that it righteously claimed according to the fascist propaganda. For all these reasons, the commemorative function of the Italian microtoponyms of Addis Abeba of 1938 is distinct from that of the Italian microtoponyms of Tripoli in 1934.

In the latter case, Italian colonizers of the early fascist period did not feel the need to make binding toponymic choices with respect to the territory or to the colony in which the naming process took place. When analyzing the anthroponymic modifiers in Tripoli of 1934, it can be noticed that, in most cases, these do not belong to personalities who had a specific connection with the Libyan territory and with the history of Italian colonialism in that colony. The commemorative function, in this case, had the sole purpose of Italianizing those territories, without claiming a particular link between the personalities of the anthroponyms and the colony. However, there are also some exceptions. In the Michelini map of Tripoli in 1934, there are 117 Italian colonial deanthroponymic microtoponyms. Among those 16 refer to personalities that had a particular connection with the colonial history. When analyzing the 16 anthroponyms, it can be seen that 11 denoted personalities of Italian colonialism who played a role in the Italian-Turkish war or in the colonial history of Libya. So, in the first fascist phase, the naming processes gave rise to microtoponyms with a particular commemorative function linked to the colonial history of the territory to which they belong. However this need became much stronger in the second fascist phase. On the colonial map of Addis Abeba, there are 33 Italian colonial deanthroponymic microtoponyms, 19 of which refer to personalities who had a link with the colonial history of AOI or, in particular, Ethiopia. The remaining 14, however, refer all to representatives of the monarchy. The pronounced increase of anthroponyms that refer to the members of the monarchy in the second fascist phase must be understood as a further characteristic of the naming practices of this period. In 1936, Italy was officially proclaimed an empire, and the king of Italy, Vittorio Emanuele III, assumed the title of *Imperatore d'Etiopia*. The rhetoric and propaganda of the *"riapparizione dell'Impero sui colli fatali di Roma"*[23] had to play a decisive role in this sense.

4 Conclusions

On the basis of the cases analyzed, one can legitimately speak of a second fascist phase in connection with the processes of naming and renaming the toponymy in the Italian colonial period. Changes in colonial policies, following the conquest of Ethiopia and the proclamation of the Empire, had important consequences also on colonial toponymy. Both from a macrotoponomastic and a microtoponomastic point of view, the coinage of toponyms with new structures, which was not observed in the previous phases, is described. Moreover, always from 1936 onwards, toponyms that display a particular commemorative function are also identified, although they reflect a structure which is in line with that of the previous phases. In the case of Ethiopia and AOI in general, this characteristic trait consists in the strong link between the toponym and the territory to which it belongs. This trait is illustrated empirically by the anthroponymic modifiers that have been analyzed in the two previous sections and the associated meanings of revenge, claim and belonging that they evoke.

However, the identification of this further phase should not suggest total discontinuity with the previous phases and, in particular, with the first fascist phase. As has been repeatedly underlined, for macrotoponyms and microtoponyms, there are important structural and functional similarities that should not be neglected in any effort at determining precise boundaries between various toponymic phases.

---

23 The translation: "reappearance of the empire on the fatal hills of Rome". It is a famous expression of Mussolini in the speech of the proclamation of the empire of May 9, 1936. With that expression the Italian dictator claimed, with the rhetoric of the empire, the direct link between the ancient Roman Empire and the new Italian empire.

Acknowledgments: This contribution is associated with the project *Comparative Colonial Toponomastics* which is conducted at the University of Bremen by Thomas Stolz and Ingo H. Warnke and their associates. I would like to express my gratitude and appreciation to Thomas Stolz for his support. I would also like to thank Rita Librandi for her constant patience and her valuable advice, corrections, and useful observations. Finally, I cannot but thank Brigitte Weber for inviting me to the conference in Klagenfurt (30–31 March 2015) that yielded this publication, and for her sincere friendship. I assume the sole responsibility for whatever is written in this paper and the form in which my ideas are presented therein.

References

(a) Atlases/maps/gazettes

ACI = *Atlante delle colonie italiane*, a cura di Mario Baratta & Luigi Visintin. Roma, Novara, Parigi: Istituto Geografico De Agostini, 1928.
GADAI-1 = *Gli Annali dell'Africa Italiana*. Volume III. *La costruzione dell'impero. L'Opera dell'Italia in A.O.I. dopo la conquista dell'Etiopia*. Volume I. A cura del Ministero dell'A.I. Roma: Mondadori, 1939.
GADAI-2 = *Gli Annali dell'Africa Italiana*. Volume III. *La costruzione dell'impero. L'Opera dell'Italia in A.O.I. dopo la conquista dell'Etiopia*. Volume II. A cura del Ministero dell'A.I. Roma: Mondadori, 1939.
GADAI-3 = *Gli Annali dell'Africa Italiana*. Volume III. *La costruzione dell'impero. L'Opera dell'Italia in A.O.I. dopo la conquista dell'Etiopia*. Volume III. A cura del Ministero dell'A.I. Roma: Mondadori, 1940.
GADAI-4 = *Gli Annali dell'Africa Italiana*. Volume III. *La costruzione dell'impero. L'Opera dell'Italia in A.O.I. dopo la conquista dell'Etiopia*. Volume IV. A cura del Ministero dell'A.I. Roma: Mondadori, 1940.
GAOI = *Guida dell'Africa Orientale Italiana*, a cura della Consociazione Turistica Italiana. Milano: C.T.I., 1938.
GBL = *Guida breve. Italia meridionale e insulare – Libia*, a cura della Consociazione Turistica Italiana. Milano: C.T.I., 1940.
PEC = *Guida d'Italia del Touring Club Italiano, Possedimenti e colonie: isolee egee, Tripolitania, Cirenaica, Eritrea, Somalia*, a cura di L.V. Bertarelli. Milano: T.C.I., 1929.
Pianta di Addis Abeba, Maßstab 1:5000. Firenze: Istituto Geografico Militare, Comando Superiore delle Forze Armate dell'A.O.I. Ufficio Topografico e Cartografico, 1938.

(b) Monographs and articles

Del Boca, Angelo. 2001. *Gli italiani in Africa Orientale*. Vol. 1: *Dall'Unità alla marcia su Roma*. Vol. 2: *La conquista dell'Impero*. 2. edn. Milano: Mondadori.

Lupi, Luca. 2009. L'esplorazione della Dancalia. La contesa per il primato. *Bollettino della Società Geografica Italiana* 13(2). 827–875.
Marcato, Carla. 2009. *Nomi di persona, nomi di luogo. Introduzione all'onomastica italiana*. Bologna: Il Mulino.
Miccoli, Paolo. 2017. Italokoloniale Toponomastik zwischen Liberalismus und Faschismus. Namenkundliche Aspekte des italienischen Kolonialismus. In Thomas Stolz, Ingo H. Warnke & Axel Dunker (eds.), *Benennungspraktiken in Prozessen kolonialer Raumaneignung*, 187–204. Berlin & Boston: De Gruyter Mouton.
Miccoli, Paolo. in press. Italo-koloniale Urbanonyme im Vergleich. Tripolis und Rom während Liberalismus und Faschismus. In Maria Aleff, Verena Ebert, Tirza Mühlan-Meyer & Matthias Schulz (eds.), *Koloniale Urbanonyme. Forschungsperspektiven und interdisziplinäre Perspektiven*. Berlin & Boston: De Gruyter Mouton.
Nübling, Damaris, Fabian Fahlbusch & Rita Heuser. 2015. *Namen. Eine Einführung in die Onomastik*. Tübingen: Gunther Narr.
Schulz, Matthias & Verena Ebert. 2016. Wissmannstraße, Massaiweg, Berliner Straße. Kolonial intendierte Urbanonyme – Befunde, Perspektiven, Forschungsprogramm. *Beiträge zur Namenforschung* 51(3/4). 357–386.
Schulz, Matthias & Verena Ebert. 2017. Kaiser-Wilhelm-Ufer, Wissmannstraße, Stuhlmannstraße – Straßennamen im Kontext kolonialer Raumaneignung. In Thomas Stolz, Ingo H. Warnke & Axel Dunker (eds.), *Benennungspraktiken in Prozessen kolonialer Raumaneignung*, 161–186. Berlin & Boston: De Gruyter Mouton.
Stolz, Thomas, Ingo H. Warnke & Nataliya Levkovych. 2016. Colonial place names in a comparative perspective. *Beiträge zur Namenforschung* 51(3/4). 279–355.
Stolz, Thomas & Ingo H. Warnke. 2017. Anoikonyme and Oikonyme im Kontext der vergleichenden Kolonialtoponomastik. In Thomas Stolz, Ingo H. Warnke & Axel Dunker (eds.), *Benennungspraktiken in Prozessen kolonialer Raumaneignung*, 205–229. Berlin & Boston: De Gruyter Mouton.
Stolz, Thomas & Ingo H. Warnke. 2018. System- und diskurslinguistische Einblicke in die vergleichende Kolonialtoponomastik. Eine gemeinsame Einführung. In Thomas Stolz & Ingo H. Warnke (eds*.), Vergleichende Kolonialtoponomastik – Strukturen und Funktionen kolonialer Ortsbenennung*, 1–75. Berlin & Boston: De Gruyter Mouton.
Traversi, Carlo. 1964. *L'Italia in Africa. Storia della cartografia coloniale italiana*. Edita a cura del Comitato per la documentazione dell'opera dell'Italia in Africa, Ministero degli Affari Esteri. Roma: Istituto poligrafico dello Stato.
Warnke, Ingo H. 2009. Deutsche Sprache und Kolonialismus. Umrisse eines Forschungsfeldes. In Ingo H. Warnke (ed.), *Deutsche Sprache und Kolonialismus. Aspekte der nationalen Kommunikation 1884–1919*, 3–62. Berlin & New York: De Gruyter.

(c) Online sources

http://www.archiviofotografico.societageografica.it/index.php?it/240/second-spedizione-bottego-1895-1897 [Last accessed on 15 December 2017].
https://www.igmi.org/ [Last accessed on 15 December 2017].

Marina Wienberg
Linguistic missionary heritage

Capuchin missionary Father Laurentius and his unpublished German-Chuukese dictionary

Abstract: It was not uncommon for missionaries to be the only persons collecting and describing the languages spoken in the regions where they were ecclesiastically active. For various reasons, a great number of these collected materials have never been published. As an example I would like to mention an unpublished manuscript of the German-Chuukese dictionary which was written by Father Laurentius Bollig, a Catholic missionary of the Order of Capuchin, on the Chuuk Islands. As far as is known, this handwritten dictionary is still unpublished to this day. As a result, only very few people know of the existence of this document.

Keywords: Chuuk language, German colonies, missionary linguistics, unexplored handwritten archival material

1 Introduction

In colonial historiography it was not rare that missionaries of different missionary societies were active in the territories well before these were intended to be colonized. They went into foreign countries with the firm intention of spreading the Christian faith, of converting and proselytizing the believers of another religion. It is difficult to imagine that spreading the Word of God would have been possible without knowledge of the local languages. Missionaries were often the first to undertake an attempt to learn and to describe the local languages and to translate religious materials into them in order to reach large numbers of people. A large number of linguistically relevant materials resulted from religious translations. Many of these documents, ranging from occasional sentences to exercise books, grammars or dictionaries and the like, were already published either during the colonial period or later. Nevertheless, it remains an undeniable fact, that a considerable amount of linguistic material, whether written by

---

Marina Wienberg, University of Bremen, FB 10: Linguistics/Language Sciences, Universitäts-Boulevard 13, 28359 Bremen, Germany. E-Mail: mwienberg@uni-bremen.de

missionaries or not, is still undiscovered or has fallen into oblivion, and therefore has never been published.

One of the aims of the colonial linguistic projects embedded at the University of Bremen is to publish these partially forgotten and now (newly) discovered linguistically relevant materials. These were composed not only by missionaries but also by settlers, administrative personnel or amateur linguists. As part of the colonial linguistic project, Barbara Dewein made the unpublished dictionary of Chamorro known to the public. This dictionary was written by Hermann Costenoble, a German settler who lived in Guam for 8 years. Apart from an overview of the contents of Costenoble's dictionary, Dewein also gave additional information about the author's biography (Dewein 2013). Susanne Schuster wrote a contrastive description to the editions of the German-Chamorro dictionary written by Georg Fritz, who was the first district administrator in service of the German colony from 1899 until 1907 in Saipan (Schuster 2013). An example of an amateur linguist Ludwig Cohn, a travelling museum curator on behalf of the Übersee-Museum of Bremen, can be found in Wienberg (2016). She presented a short overview of Cohn's linguistic notes on one of the languages of the Manus Island and of his daring idea regarding supposed Arabic loanwords in the Melanesian languages.

Within the context of colonial linguistics there is newly published anthology which is dedicated to missionary linguistics that was published by Klaus Zimmermann & Birte Kellemeier-Rehbein (2015). This volume was edited within the frame of *Colonial and Postcolonial Linguistics* and includes contributions that are relevant to the relationship of missionaries, missionary linguistics and the colonial administration.

The topic of the present paper is likewise embedded in the colonial linguistic context and is a further contribution to colonial and missionary linguistics. This treatise deals with a handwritten manuscript that presents a German-Chuukese dictionary written by Father Laurentius Bollig in 1917. As far as is known, it has never been published.

The article is organized as follows: Section 2 gives a brief overview of the German protectoral territories in the South Sea and presents some German missionary societies that were active in these territories. Section 3 consists of biographical information on Father Laurentius Bollig and his missionary activities on the Chuuk Islands. Section 4 is dedicated to Bollig's dictionary and includes a description of the dictionary, some examples from the manuscript, and comparative examples from the reference dictionaries. Moreover, some orthographic differences in these reference Chuuk dictionaries will be incorporated into this section. Conclusion remarks are drawn in Section 5.

2 German missionary societies in the South Sea

In order to provide a better idea of where German missionaries were active in the South See, a small map (Map 1) is shown below. On this map Germany's protectorate territories in the South Sea at around 1914 are marked. The following German territories lie in this area: Kaiser-Wilhelmsland (Germ. *Kaiser-Wilhelms-Land*); the Bismarck Archipelago (Germ. *Bismarck-Archipel*); the Marshall Islands (Germ. *Marshallinseln*); the Caroline Islands (Germ. *Karolinen*) including the Chuuk Islands; the Mariana Islands (Germ. Marianen); the northern part of the Salomon Islands (Germ. *Nord-Salomonen*) and Samoa.

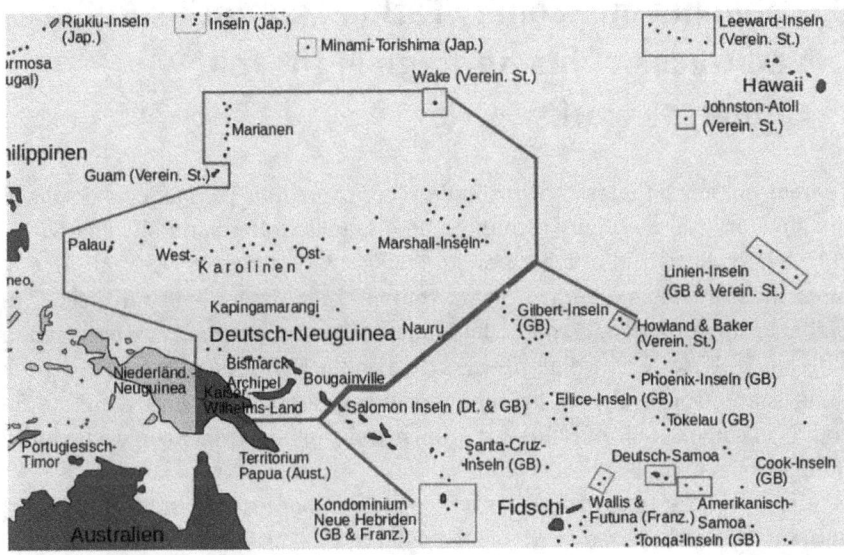

Map 1: Excerpt of the map *Kolonien und Einflusszonen in Ostasien und Ozeanien um 1914* – 'Colonies and zones of influence around 1914'.[1]

Long before the abovementioned territories were proclaimed to belong to the German protectorates, large numbers of missionary societies had begun their missionary work there. Examples of the many missionary societies that were ecclesiastically active are: the Protestant Rhenish Mission Society (Germ. *Rheinische Mission*, which today is combined with the Bethel Mission into the

---

1 https://de.wikipedia.org/wiki/Datei:East_Asia_and_Oceania_1914-de.svg (24.02.2016).

Vereinte Evangelische Mission – United Protestant Mission), the Protestant Mission One World (Germ. *Mission Eine Welt*, formely the Neuendettelsauer Mission) and the Catholic Divine World Missionaries[2] also known as the Steyler Missionaries (Germ. *Steyler Mission*) who were ecclesiastically active in Kaiser-Wilhelmsland.

The missionaries of the Liebenzell Mission (Germ. *Liebenzeller Mission*) were active in the Caroline and in the Mariana Islands. The territory of missionary activity for the Order of Capuchin (Germ. *Kapuzinerorden*) was in the region of the East- and West Caroline Islands, in Palau and on the Mariana Islands.

3 Capuchin missionary Father Laurentius Bollig and traces of his heritage in the following Chuukese works

There is not much that is known about Father Laurentius Bollig. Some details of his life story can be briefly recounted here thanks to Hermann Mückler (2010: 70f.) who collected information about active missionaries in Oceania. Among other missionaries mentioned in his volume, there is one entry dedicated to Bollig. Further information on Bollig followed from my personal communication with Lothar Käser. Käser himself was active on the Chuuk Islands on exactly the same island Tol as Father Laurentius several years before and therefore he could get some details of Bollig's life and activity on-site from people who knew Bollig personally.

Now to Bollig himself: He was born on November 19, 1883 in Wittlich (Eifel) in Germany and baptized as Nikolaus Bollig. In 1903 he joined the Order of Capuchin and was consecrated priest in 1909, using his religious name Laurentius from then on. In 1912 Father Laurentius was a missionary in Pohnpei (formerly known as Ponape), an island belonging to the Carolines. From 1913 to 1919 he practiced his missionary activity on the Chuuk Islands from where he was expelled by the Japanese Mandate in 1919. In 1922 Father Laurentius continued his missionary work in China. He died in Mettlach, Saarland on April 14, 1961.

---

2 This Missionary Society was founded in Steyl in the Netherlands, but a large number of German priests were active there and in the German branches of this society.

P. Laurentius Bollig, von Wittlich.

Figure 1: Father Laurentius Bollig.³

Nothing is known of Bollig's (linguistic) education. Most probably, he absolved some kind of training to become a missionary of the Order of Capuchin. These trainings were usually not exclusively held for Capuchin missionaries but also for others who intended to do missionary work in the colonies or in the overseas territories. Whether Bollig learned some of the Micronesian languages during this training remains unknown. But in his correspondence with Father Valentin there is a short note that refers to language acquisition. Bollig wrote to Fr. Valentin: "Augenblicklich bin ich hier in Porajap bei P. Crescenz um Sprache zu lernen und ein wenig Schule zu halten".⁴ Porajap is a place on Pohnpei Island where Bollig took language lessons, probably in Pohnpeian, a Micronesian language related to Chuukese, during his sojourn there in July 1912.

While he was in the Chuuk Islands, Bollig was active on the island Tol, the largest and the most populous island of the Chuuk Lagoon, in a district called Iluk. He described his experiences in Iluk in the text under the initial title *Allein auf der Insel Iluk*.⁵ At this point, it is striking that Bollig had wrongly transferred

---

3 http://marshall.csu.edu.au/CNMI/CNMIBIB/Photos/CapAnnRep1912_11R.html (24.02.2016).
4 My translation [Presently, I am here in Porajap with Fr. Crescenz in order to learn language and to teach a little] (ULB Münster, Kapuzinermission_021,005).
5 My translation [Alone on the Iluk Island] (ULB Münster, Kapuzinermission_034,142).

the name Iluk to the whole island Tol. The correct place name of the district of Iluk is probably Sapou.

This recount of the Iluk period became a part of Bollig's work describing the inhabitants of the Chuuk Islands. This ethnographical work was published in 1927 and is regarded as the first extensive work concerning this island group. In addition to a description of the religion and the life of the islanders, it included the first Chuuk grammar which was meritorious and significant reference work for coming missionaries, ethnologists and linguists.

In the course of my work on Bollig's dictionary, I could observe an interesting fact concerning publications that followed which were relevant to Chuukese. In almost all of them we find direct or indirect references to Bollig's grammar of 1927 but not a word of his dictionary. Thus Samuel H. Elbert, who was a linguist, wrote in the preface to his *Trukese-English and English-Trukese dictionary* published in 1947 that: "The value of the dictionary was greatly helped by Richard Neumaier[6], of the Liebenzell Mission, who checked nearly all the Trukese-English entries" (Elbert 1947: 1). In 2011 Lothar Käser (2011: 267f.) mentions more details on this point:

> Seine [Bolligs] Grammatik ergab den Ausgangspunkt für spätere Arbeiten, unter anderem für ein erstes Lehrbuch der Chuuksprache von Richard Neumaier, [...]. Spuren von Bolligs Ausführungen in Neumaiers Lehrbuch[7] sind offensichtlich. Eine Quelle gibt der Autor aber nicht an. Neumaier war im Übrigen auch am Zustandekommen des ersten größeren Wörterbuchs der Chuuksprache beteiligt, das Elbert 1947 veröffentlichte.[8]

Apparently Neumaier had used Bollig's grammar to write his own textbook. In this way Elbert consequentially took Bollig's grammar as a corner stone for his dictionary. In any case, we can identify a certain orthographic similarity in Bollig's and Elbert's entries as will be shown in Sections 4.3 and 4.4 below. Goodenough & Sugita (1980: ix), for their part, wrote in the preface to their Trukese-English dictionary that "[their] work builds on the dictionary by Samuel H. Elbert, [...]". This evidence leads us to assume that Bollig had an indirect influence on Goodenough & Sugita's dictionaries as well.

---

6 Richard Neumaier was a missionary of the Liebenzell Mission on Chuuk from 1935 until 1947 (Käser 2011: 267).
7 This textbook exists only in copy. It has not been published until today.
8 My translation [His [Bollig's] grammar gave a starting point for the works that followed, among others for Richard Neumaier's first textbook, [...] Traces of Bollig's implementations are obvious in Neumaier's textbook. However, the author does not mention the source. Furthermore, Neumaier was also involved in the formation of the first substantial Chuukese dictionary that Elbert published in 1947].

4 The unpublished German-Chuukese dictionary

Bollig's German-Chuukese dictionary is a handwritten manuscript. It is stored in the manuscripts section of the library of the University of Münster, where the Archive of the Order of Capuchin has been deposited since 2010/2011. This manuscript is accessible in coordination with the employees responsible for the manuscript section.[9]

The dictionary was written by Bollig sometime between 1913 and 1917, 1913 being the year he came to Chuuk as a missionary and 1917 the year Bollig recorded at the end of the manuscript. A short typewritten entry on the inside of the manuscript's cover shows the date 1916 to 1919. This incorrect entry might have been made later in the Archive of the Order of Capuchin where the manuscript was stored after Bollig had been expelled from the Chuuk Islands.

Many questions remain open regarding the manner in which this dictionary was written. There is no introductory text in the dictionary and we do not have any kind of information regarding the method Bollig used to collect the words. We do not know whether there was a draft version, whether he made word lists or took notes. We do not know who his informants were. There are no references to this dictionary: neither to the work on it nor in Bollig's correspondence[10] nor in any texts regarding his activity on Chuuk.[11] Only one trace leads to the one person who knew about the existence of this dictionary: Prof. Dr. Augustin Krämer. On the inside of the manuscript's cover there is a very finely penciled note. This note is difficult to read and discloses the name Prof. Dr. Augustin Krämer, a German anthropologist and ethnologist. Krämer took part in the *Hamburger Südsee-Expedition* (i.e. Hamburg South Seas Expedition) and published the results in the publication series *Ergebnisse der Südsee-Expedition 1908–1910*. Krämer himself wrote that "mir auch ein Wörterbuch im Manuskript von ihm [Bollig] vorliegt, Deutsch-Truk, ca. 10 000 Wörter"[12] (Krämer 1932: 29). Apparently Krämer had examined Bollig's dictionary as he also mentioned:

---

[9] http://www.ulb.uni-muenster.de/sammlungen/nachlaesse/sammlung-kapuzinermission.html (24.02.2016).
[10] Although we cannot with all certainty say that all of Bollig's correspondence is known.
[11] *Allein auf der Insel Iluk* – Alone on the Iluk Island (Kapuzinermission_034,142).
[12] My translation [I also have his (Bollig) dictionary as a manuscript, German-Chuukese, approx. 10.000 words].

> Natürlich habe ich auch ein solches [Wörterbuch?] angefertigt. Insbesondere wenn noch neues Material zuströmt, wird es am besten sein, alles zusammen zu verarbeiten, mit den übrigen zentralkarolinischen Sprachen zusammen, [...].[13] (Krämer 1932: 29)

It remains unclear whether Krämer had already published a Chuuk dictionary (if so, this is unknown to me) or if he had intended to publish one. But one thing is certain: Krämer had Bollig's dictionary manuscript in his hands and he did not publish it.

4.1 Structure of the dictionary

With regard to structure, it becomes immediately apparent that this bilingual dictionary consists only of the German-Chuukese part. Bollig apparently addressed it to native speakers of German such as missionaries or settlers who followed him. The German part was written in the old German Kurrent script, the Chuukese transcription was written in the Latin style. The entries in the dictionary are organized as follows: the German lemma, i.e., the headword, is entered on the left side. The Chuukese translation of the German headword and related expressions, supplements and comments are recorded on the right hand side.

The manuscript contains approximately 7.300 German lemmas on 282 pages. It should be noted here that only the hyperonyms are counted and not the equivalent expressions and supplements to the German lemma (see example in Section 4.2).

The lemmas are mainly arranged in alphabetical order. Nevertheless, it should be noted that inconsistencies cannot be avoided in a handwritten document. And thus the very first lemma *Aas* 'carion' is incorrectly recorded ahead of *Aal* 'eel' directly on the first page of Bollig's manuscript (cf. ULB Münster, S. Kapuzinermission B, 1 p. 1). But such minor imperfections are very rare.

Bollig tried to order the morphologically related items alphabetically. However, the additional expressions and word combinations related to the headwords do not always have an alphabetical classification. Furthermore, both kinds of entries – morphologically related items and expressions – are grouped on the right together as shown by the reproduced example 1:

---

13 My translation [Of course, I have also made such one (dictionary?). Especially if more new material comes, it will be best to process it together with the other Central Caroline languages, (...)].

(1) Abend, -s, *lekunion, lefäf*; früh *lefäfsit*; spät *lefäfmau*; gestern *lekunionwe*; heute *lekunionei*;
morgen *lekunion en nau*; es wird [Abend M.W.]- *a kunionediu*; zu [Abend M.W.]
- essen *fäf*.
- dämmerung *leosoumele, lekunionepuin*
- kühle *badd en lefäf, lebadd en akar*
- land *hanuen nodau*
- mahl *Komunio fadanap mi [p]bin*
letzte -mahl *lefäf kasop mi [p]bin*
- rot *dubisö, murisö*
es ist schönes [Abendrot M.W.] - *a söot*
nach dem [Abendrot M.W.] *murin man du[p]b*
- stern *enewenmöñer*
- tau *enewenmöñer* [ULB Münster, S. Kapuzinermission B, 1 p. 2f.]

In this example we see that some entries, such as "-mahl *Komunio fadanap mi [p]bin*"or "letzte -mahl *lefäf kasop mi [p]bin*" where <p> was replaced by <b>, have been corrected. In reference to this, it should be pointed out that Bollig generally changed voiceless consonants into voiced consonants in his corrections. Some examples of this are illustrated very well in Table 4 in Section 4.4 where Bollig's entries are compared with the relevant entries of the other dictionaries. Additionally, some entries in the dictionary have been crossed out completely[14] by Bollig without any corrections. The viewing of some corrections and supplements suggests that they could have been made by Augustin Krämer (Section 4 above). This assumption could be supported by the penciled abbreviation *Kr.* put in some places in the round brackets. This kind of correction was only done for a few entries but without any explanation. Moreover, these corrections were penciled in and, unfortunately, in some cases they are illegible. In some places, it is unclear to which of Bollig's entries Krämer's corrections actually refer. By and large, it can be said that Krämer's corrections did not help a great deal in the analysis of this dictionary.

The following kind of lexical items which occur as lemma can be found in the dictionary: nouns, pronouns, articles, quantifiers, adjectives, prepositions, verbs, conjunctions, interjections, cardinals and ordinals. The complete sentences and inflected forms of the verbs are found in the imperative (2):

---

14 These dropped entries will be taken over into the dictionary's publication.

(2)   Steh auf! (Schlaf) *Puädä*!
      [Wake up (sleep)]   [ULB Münster, S. Kapuzinermission B, 1 p. 23]

There are some, but not many, German nouns which are translated into Chuukese with grammatical elements. Thus, for example, some entries are translated either with the possessive suffix 1SG -*ei* (3a) or with the possessive pronoun 1SG *ai* (3b):

(3)   a.   Abdruck mein *rasei*
           ras   ei
           trace   POSS SUFF 1SG
           [trace my]
           'my trace'   [ULB Münster, S. Kapuzinermission B, 1 p. 2]
      b.   Armut m. *ai molene*
           ai   molene
           POSS PRON 1SG   poverty
           [poverty my]
           'my poverty'   [ULB Münster, S. Kapuzinermission B, 1 p. 29]

With regard to the Bollig's Chuukese writing approach, it can only be presumed that Bollig used a transcription system which he had possibly developed himself and which is mainly based on the German writing system (with the exception of <ñ>).[15]

On the subject of the German spelling style there are several cases of different spellings of the same lexeme. Thus there are two items for the lexeme 'cigarette' with different initial consonants: as "Cigarette" *suwa*[16] with <c> and as "Zigarette, m." *ulumei suwa*[17] 'my cigarette' with <z>. A similar instance of different spellings can also be seen for the word "Caffee" *kofi ulumei; föri kofi*[18] with <c> and "Kaffee, m." *ulumei kofi (engl.), ulumei tönepiut*[19] 'my coffee' written with <k>.

---

15   This writing approach of Chuukese refers to the writing in the manuscript. It changes in Bollig's grammar of 1927.
16   ULB Münster, S. Kapuzinermission B, 1 p. 78.
17   ULB Münster, S. Kapuzinermission B, 1 p. 275.
18   ULB Münster, S. Kapuzinermission B, 1 p. 78.
19   ULB Münster, S. Kapuzinermission B, 1 p. 142.

4.2 One headword – 45 expressions. The semantic field of *Kanoe*[20]

Not for every entry, but, nevertheless, for many entries Bollig tried to describe an extensive semantic field and to group the words into relevant categories. An example which allows a closer look at the internal structure according to which Bollig grouped the semantically relevant expressions of a headword, is given further below in this section. In Table 1 below the semantic field of the headword *Kanoe* is reproduced and translated with all the entries done by Bollig. As we can see he grouped the sub-lemmas, additive expressions and word combinations in the following categories: *Art* 'type of canoe'; *Bestandteile* 'component parts'; *Arbeiten auf Kanoe* 'kinds of work on canoe' and *weitere Ausdrücke* 'other expressions'.

Table 1: Bollig's entries for the semantic field *Kanoe*.

Bollig's entries in manuscript	English translation
m. *efot uai*	my canoe *efot uai*
Art: Ruder-k. *uafadil*; Segel-k. *melik*; Spiel-k. *lulu*.	**Type:** c. with oars *uafadil*; sailing c. *melik*; toy c. *lulu*.
Bestandteile: Ausleger *dam*; Brücke *kiön*; Schnabel [von Kanu? M.W.] *sopun*; Haus *im en ua*; Inneres [des Hauses oder des Kanus? M.W.] *lefön ua*; Kiel *epin ua*; Mast *oun, efot*; Mitte *nuganapan ua*; Segel *amara*; Segelstange *tutun amara*; Schöpfer *num, en ai* –; Ruder *fadil, efotai; tutu*; Unterlage [Was ist genau gemeint? M.W.] *noñum ua*	**Components:** outrigger *dam*; bridge *kiön*; prow [of c.? M.W.][21] *sopun*; house *im en ua*; interior [of house or of canoe?M.W.] *lefön ua*; keel *epin ua*; mast *oun, efot*; middle, center *nuganapan ua*; sail *amara*; yard, spreader *tutun amara*; bail *num, en ai* –; rudder/oar/puddle *fadil, efotai; tutu*; underlay/pad [What does it refer to? M.W.] *noñum ua*
Arbeiten auf Kanoe: d. K. tragen *kegi ua*; K. ausschöpfen *numei ua*; K. unterlegen *nañuni ua*; K. machen *fala ua*; ein Kanoebauer *sou falafal*; K. probieren *apuñu ton*; Segel hochziehen *urada amara*; Segel einziehen *uradiu*; [Segel?] kreuzen *on, ät*; hin u. her kreuzen *önfedal ätofedal*; [Segel?] Kanu? M.W.] drehen *kun*; mit dem Wind fahren *äsä*; in d. Wind *fañ*; etwas [mit dem Wind fahren? M.W.] *emen* z.B. *äsä emen, fañ emen*; Kanoe festbinden *emisini*	**Works on canoe:** to carry c. *kegi ua*; to bail out c. *numei ua*; to underlay c. *nañuni ua*; to build c. *fala ua*; a c. builder *sou falafal*; to try the c. *apuñu ton*; to raise the sail *urada amara*; to lower the sail *uradiu*; to tack [the sail?] *on, ät*; to tack back and forth *önfedal ätofedal*; to turn [the sail? the canoe M.W.] *kun*; to sail with the wind *äsä*; into the wind *fañ*; a bit [to sail with the wind? M.W.] *emen* e.g. *äsä emen, fañ emen*; to tie up the canoe *emisini*

---

20 *Kanoe* – original spelling in Bollig's manuscript!
21 Supplements to unclear entries are made by the author (M.W.) and enclosed in square brackets.

(**Table 1** continued)

Bollig's entries in manuscript	English translation
Weitere Ausdrücke: Kanoefahrt *sei*; Essen auf d. Kanoe *pau*; das K. läuft gut – *a mutir*; läuft schlecht – *a mañ*; segelt schlecht *äteñau*; läuft gut in dem Wind *a döof*; schlecht i. d. W. *döñau*; Woher kommt ihr? *Emi sein ia*? Wir kommen von P. – *Em sein P.*; von irgendwoher sein *sein* – *egis*; Wir kommen heute nicht mehr an – *si sap dori ikeneie*; Wir wollen P. anlaufen – *si bue ileidi P.*; Wettfahrt machen *kitir tr. kitiridi mt.*	**Other expressions**: c. trip *sei*; eating on a c. *pau*; the c. runs/sails well – *a mutir*; c. runs badly – *a mañ*; c. sails badly *äteñau*; runs well in the wind *döof*; badly i.t.w. *döñau*; Where do you come from? *Emi sein ia*? We come from P. – *Em sein P.*; to be from somewhere *sein* – *egis*; We will not arrive anymore today – *si sap dori ikeneie*; We want to dock in P. – *si bue ileidi P.*; to compete in the regatta *kitir tr. kitiridi mt.*

As mentioned above, there is neither an introductory text to this dictionary nor a list of abbreviations. This fact complicates the transcription of the manuscript and leaves many questions open regarding certain expressions. In some entries we can only guess at what Bollig intended to say. Some expressions from the same semantic field *Kanoe* can be taken to illustrate this point: "Inneres [des Hauses oder des Kanus?] *lefön ua*" 'interior [of house or of canoe?]' or "[Segel? Kanu? M.W.] drehen *kun*" '[the sail? the canoe M.W.] 'turn *kun*'. In these expressions we cannot explicitly see what he had intended to be understood: what does "Inneres" refer to for example? For this reason, unclear expressions still need to be analyzed and compared with the entries of other relevant dictionaries.

4.3 Work with Chuukese reference dictionaries

Figure 2 below is an excerpt of Bollig's manuscript which shows lemmas and expressions relating to the lexeme *Haar* 'hair'. As already indicated above, translation of the German nouns with grammatical elements in Chuukese can be repeatedly noted, as example (4) shows:

(4) Haar   m. *magureii*
     magur   ei
     hair   POSS SUFF 1SG
     [hair my]
     'my hair'   [ULB Münster, S. Kapuzinermission B, 1 p. 137]

Furthermore, in "H.-schopf – *nugudoda, pitidoda, pitar, pitinu[k]g*" 'shock of hair' where the grapheme <k> is replaced by <g> we can see a further example of Bollig's corrections replacing a voiceless consonant by a voiced consonant.

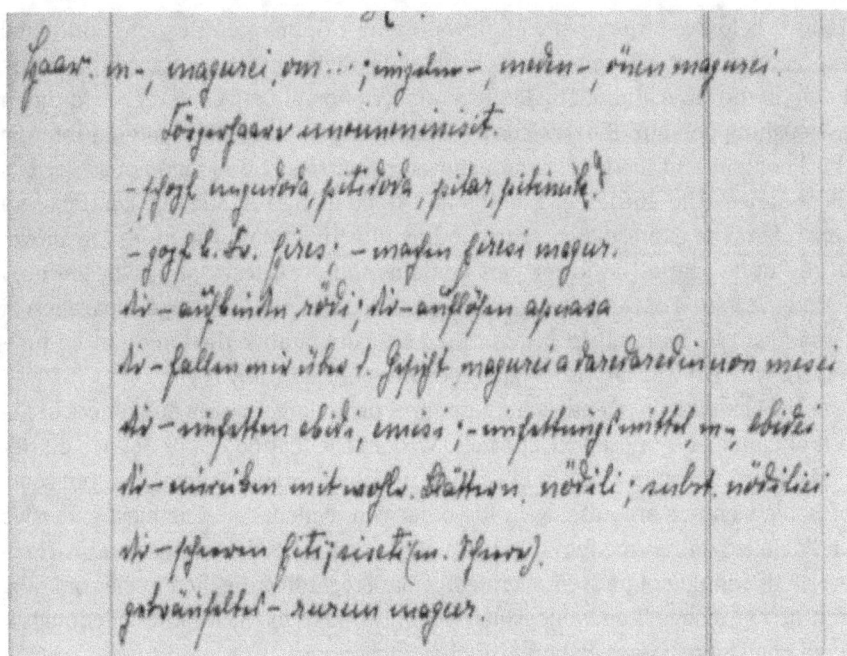

Figure 2: Excerpt of Bollig's manuscript with entries to lexeme *Haar* 'hair'.[22]

The entries and additional expressions of the headword *Haar* 'hair' are compared with the entries of the reference dictionaries and shown in Table 2. For this purpose two dictionaries have been consulted:
- Trukese-English and English-Trukese dictionary of Samuel Hoyt Elbert (that was published in 1947) and
- two parts of Trukese-English dictionaries compiled by Ward Hunt Goodenough and Hiroshi Sugita. The first volume of the dictionary was published in 1980. The second volume is a companion volume with an English-Chuukese index and root forms of morphemes and was published in 1990. The entries of both dictionaries by Goodenough & Sugita will be presented together in one column and not separated because they complement one another.

---

22 ULB Münster, S. Kapuzinermission B, 1 p. 137.

Table 2 below is structured as follows: Bollig's German entries and additional expressions of the lexeme *Haar* 'hair' with their Chuukese transcription are found in the left column. The English transcription of Bollig's entries is found in the ensuing column. Elbert's corresponding entries have been entered into the third column and the last column shows the entries of Goodenough & Sugita's dictionaries. The entries in Elbert's and Goodenough & Sugita's columns are separated. The expressions corresponding directly to Bollig's entries are shown in the upper part. The lower part contains those expressions which are only found in Elbert's or Goodenough & Sugita's dictionaries. The same separation of entries will be maintained in the Chuukese comparative dictionary to be published, where it will serve to augment expressions listed by Bollig.

The comparison of entries in these three dictionaries shows differences in the orthographic and in the lexical levels. We can see that not all of Bollig's entries find equivalent expressions in Elbert and in Goodenough & Sugita, and that some of Bollig's entries are missing in the other two dictionaries. The most extensive and detailed entries are found in the dictionaries of Goodenough & Sugita. However, this should not be seen as critical remark regarding the dictionaries of Bollig or Elbert or reduce their value, since it is only due to the fact that Goodenough & Sugita had more time to elaborate on their dictionaries.

Table 2: Compilation of Bollig's lexeme *Haar* 'hair' with the relevant entries and other expressions which occurred in the reference dictionaries.

Bollig 1917 (Germ.)	Bollig 1917 (Engl.)[i]	Elbert 1947	Goodenough & Sugita (1980, 1990)[iii]
Haar, m – *magurei, om...*; einzelne – *meden-, önen magurei*; Körperhaare – *inouneninisit*; H.-schopf – *nugudoda, pitidoda, pitar, pitinu[k]g**; H.-zopf b. Fr. – *fires*; H.-zopf machen – *firesi magur*; die H. aufbinden – *rödi*; die H. auflösen – *apuasa*; die H. fallen mir über d. Gesicht – *magurei a daredaredin non mesei*; die H. einfetten – *ebidi, emisi*; H.-einfettungsmittel, m – *ebidei*; die H. einreiben mit wohlr. Blättern subst. – *nödili*; subst. *nödiliei*; die H. scheren – *fiti*; *siseti* (mit Schere); gekräuseltes H. – *rurun magur*; weißhaarig – *uwan* * *k* is crossed-out by Bollig in the original	**hair** – my h. – *magurei*, *om...*; single hairs – *meden-*, *önen magurei*; body h. – *inouneninisit*; shock of h. – *nugudoda, pitidoda, pitar, pitinu[k]g*; pigtail, plait, braid – *fires*; to make pigtail – *firesi magur*; to put up the h. – *rödi*; to undo the plait – *apuasa*; the hair falling into my face – *magurei a daredaredin non mesei*; to grease the h. – *ebidi, emisi*; my product to grease the h., -*ebidei*; rub the h. w. aromatic leaves – *nödili*; (subst.) *nödiliei*; to shear/cut the h. – *fiti*; *siseti* (w. scissors); curly h. – *rurun magur*; white haired – *uwa* [i] Translation by M. W.	**hair** – (h. in their entirety) *metenmōkur, mōkur*; (a single h.) *met*; body h. or animal h. – *ūn-, mōrōun*; gray or white h. – *ūwan, pwōch*; old style of tying h. in knot in back part of head, of both men and women – *rōt*; braid – *fires – n* and *v.* (*firesi*). curly – *rūrū*. **Other expressions:**[ii] gray or white h. – Mort* *mōkūre mōi, mōi*; closely clipped h.- *nipōōnimōng*, Jap** – *pochū*; shedded hairs -*moren mūkūr*; short h. in front part of forehead – *kochokoch*; old style of tying h. in front part of head – *fittin nūk* * Mort – expression from island Mortlok ** Jap – expression from island Jap [ii] Other expressions to item 'hair' in Elbert's dictionary	**hair** – *téréwún* (n.):[iv] scales (of fish), feathers (of bird), hair (of animals and people). [...]*wúún*₁ (n.): hair (of head or body, of person or animal), fur, feather, scale (of fish). *méréwún* (nu.): body or animal hair (as a whole), fur, scales (of fish), feathers. *pwoochú* (nu.): closely clipped hair, crew cut. *pitinnúk* (vi.): wear the hair bound on top of the head or in a knot on the front of the head, held by means of a braded head band (traditionally of men only). *fires, fúres* (nu.), *firesini* (vo.), *ffiresi* (vo.): braid. *ppit* (va.): braid, twist, twine. *piti* (vo.): braid, twist (hair, rope, leis). *epitiyo* (vi.): anoint the hair with coconut cream and not wash it out afterwards (formerly tabu because it would result in the death of a kinsman). *fichiiy*₁ (vo.): snip, cut (with scissors). *rúúrú*₁ (vi.): be curl, wavy (of hair). *érúúrúúw* (vo.): curl (hair), make curly or wavy. *wúwan* (n.): grey hair, white hair. *pweech* (ni.): white hair, grey hair.

(Table 2 continued)

Bollig 1917 (Germ.)	Bollig 1917 (Engl.)	Elbert 1947	Goodenough & Sugita (1980, 1990)[iii]
			Other expressions: *éwúchimw* (n.): strand of hair. *één₂* (nu.): strand of hair. *meetekúkkún* (vi., adj.): have fine hair. *meetekkiis* (vi., adj.): have fine hair. *mékúr₁* (n.): (fig.) hair. -*é* (suf.): thread, hair (in counting). *kochokoch* (nu.): short hairs on top of forehead (especially of women). *kkor* (n., Tb1.): underarm hair, pubic hair. *fisikkor* (vi., Tb1.): have an abundance of pubic hair. *túwékkor* (vi., Tb1.): be plentifully endowed with pubic hair (of a woman). *pitimékúr* (nu.): hair braided on either side (formerly worn by both sexes). *épúngúmóng* (vi.): wear one's hair long and loosely down the back. *pwoochú* (vi.): have closely cropped hair. *michiyapwúra* (nu.): hair oil. *fichiiy₁* (vo.): snip, cut (with scissors). *rúúrú₁* (vi.): be curl, wavy (of hair). *mékúromoy* (vi., adj.): (be) gray-haired, white-haired. *mékúrotopw* (nu.): be gray-haired.

[iii] For the comparison, the entries from both dictionaries, 1980 and 1990, have been combined and complement each other.
[iv] The abbreviations to the items of Goodenough and Sugita are explained at the end of this paper.
[v] Other expressions to the item 'hair' from Goodenough and Sugita's dictionaries.

4.4 Orthographic differences in Chuukese dictionaries

The graphemes combined in Table 3 below show that the authors described the phonetic material of Chuukese differently. The orthography in all three dictionaries differs from each other. Let us start with the orthography used by Bollig. The vowels and the consonants that are shown in the table below are extracted from his dictionary manuscript and from his Chuukese grammar (cf. Bollig 1927). It should be noted that the orthography used by Bollig in his dictionary manuscript (1917) differs from the orthography in his Chuukese grammar (1927).

Table 3: Graphemes describing phonetic material of Chuukese occur in the dictionaries of Bollig, Elbert and Goodenough & Sugita.

	Bollig		Elbert	Goodenough & Sugita (1980)
	1917	1927		
vowels	<a>	<a>	<a>	<a>
	<ä>		<ä>	<á>
	<e>	<e>	<e>	<e>
				<é>
	<i>	<i>	<i>	<i>
	<o>	<o>	<o>	<o>
	<ö>		<ö>	<ó>
			<ò>	
	<u>	<u>	<u>	<u>
	<ü>		<ü>	<ú>
consonants	<b>	<b>		
	<d>	<d>		
	<f>	<f>	<f>	<f>
	<g>	<g>		
	<k>	<k>	<k>	<k>
	<l>	<l>		
	<m>	<m>	<m>	<m>
			<mw>	<mw>
	<n>	<n>	<n>	<n>
	<ñ>	<ng>	<ng>	<ng>
	<p>	<p>	<p>	<p>
			<pw>	<pw>
	<r>	<r>	<r>	<r>
			<ch>	<ch>
	<s>	<s>	<s>	<s>
	<t>	<t>	<t>	<t>
	<w>	<w>	<w>	<w>
				<y>

Other graphemes can be found in the grammar than in the dictionary manuscript, which was written ten years before the grammar. Additional vowels that he used in his dictionary such as the graphemes <ä>, <ö> and <ü> are omitted in the grammar (Bollig 1927: 259). In the dictionary he used for a velar nasal [ŋ] grapheme <ñ>. This grapheme was replaced by <ng> in the grammar (Bollig 1927: 259). Against the background of the Chuukese phonetic material, it seems that Bollig tried to show a specific quality of long and short vowels by choosing graphemes such as <ä>, <ö> and <ü> in his manuscript. However, he seemed to have abandoned them in his grammar. Moreover, as can be gathered from the examples and tables above, he used the voiced consonants which are not shown in the dictionaries of Elbert and of Goodenough & Sugita. Thus, for example, we do not find graphemes for the following phonemes: voiced bilabial plosive [b], voiced dental plosive [d] and voiced velar plosive [g] in other dictionaries. Regarding the phonemes Bollig was uncertain of how to describe, he wrote:

> Die Konsonanten *l* und *n* werden oft miteinander vertauscht, weil die Trukleute einen Zwischenlaut haben, der, je nach dem Zusammentreffen mit anderen Lauten, bald wie *l*, bald wie *n* gehört wird. Auch *w* und *m*, *s* und *t* werden von manchen Eingeborenen vertauscht.[23] (Bollig 1927: 259)

In the dictionaries of Elbert and of Goodenough & Sugita a grapheme for the alveolar approximant [l] does not occur. They consistently used a grapheme <n> in cases where Bollig wrote <l> instead. We can also see that the grapheme <ch> for the affricate consonant [tʃ] does not exist in Bollig's orthography, whereas it is present in the orthographies of the other two dictionaries. Instead of <ch> Bollig used <t> like in "*tai, tan* – Blut" (see Table 4).

Other corrections in Bollig's manuscript show his uncertainty related to the usage of graphemes <u> and <w>. We can see an example of this in the entry "abnötigen *pötakulñeni e ren mt., etimaseni e mt. m[w]uaseni e mt.*"[24], 'to wring sth. out of/from sb.' where he replaced <w> by <u>. However, he did not make this kind of correction consistently. Furthermore, the other two dictionaries show the labialized sounds for the graphemes <mw> und <pw>, while Bollig recorded them as two separated graphemes <m> and <u>, <p>/<b> and <u> (see Table 4).

---

23 My translation [The consonants *l* and *n* are often interchanged because the Chuuks have an intermediate sound that, depending on the overlapping with other sounds, is heard either as *l* or as *n*. Also *w* and *m*, *s* and *t* are interchanged by some indigenous people].
24 ULB Münster, S. Kapuzinermission B, 1 p. 21.

Table 4: Orthographic differences in the dictionaries of Bollig, Elbert and Goodenough & Sugita.

	Bollig (1917)		Elbert (1947)		Goodenough & Sugita (1980)	
	Chuukese	German	Chuukese	English	Chuukese	English
b	baddekid	kalt	patekkich	very cold	patúkkich	be very cold
	boda	weshalb?	pweta	why?	pwata	why?
ch	matañ	Vogel	matchang	bird	machchang	bird
	tai, tan	Blut	cha, -l, -n	blood	chcha	blood
d	dö	kriechen	tötö	to creep	té	to creep/crawl
	obud	Abneigung	oput	dislike	opwut	dislike
g	gogon	Dialekt	koko	voice	kkúúkú	dialekt
	magurei	Kopfhaar	mökür	hair	mékúr	hair
l	bölu	einheimischer Kapitän[25]	pönü	sea captain and expert in all phases of sailing and seamanship	ø	ø
	lulu	kauen	nünü	chew	núúnú	chew, eat
mw	muetun uet	springen = laufen	mwöt	to jump, bounce	mwet	to spring, jump
	omotu	halten (fest)	amwöchü	to hold, retain, hold fast to	émwéchú	to grasp, retain, hold fast to
pw	pupuu	münden	pupu	to flow	pwuupwu	to flow
	puto	Huhn	pucho	chicken	pwuchóó	chicken
y	ø	ø	ø	ø	yi	-y 1SG.POSS. PRON: my

It can be presumed that Elbert's orthography may be partly based on Neumaier's texts and, in this way, indirectly on Bollig's spelling (see Section 3). Furthermore, according to Goodenough & Sugita, the Chuukese alphabet, as it was written up to 1972, was adapted to the English alphabet. It was hardly influenced by the missionaries who came from the Mortlock Islands and who "mortlockized" the Chuukese language (Goodenough & Sugita 1980: xiii). The

---

25 Indigenous captain.

present alphabet that is found in the dictionaries of Goodenough & Sugita, is based on decisions made at two conferences on orthography held in Chuuk in 1972 and 1975 (Goodenough & Sugita 1980: xiv).

5 Closing remarks

The newly-discovered dictionary of Father Laurentius Bollig is not the work of a professional linguist. Nonetheless, it can surely be named as the first dictionary which was written for the Chuukese language, even though it remained hidden for nearly 100 years.

The quick glimpse into the manuscript presented in this paper cannot deliver a comprehensive analysis of this dictionary. As we have seen, on the one hand, it shows many discrepancies and insufficiencies in comparison with the dictionaries of Elbert (1947) and Goodenough & Sugita (1980, 1990). Thus we saw on the basis of the examples shown here that there are many differences in the orthographic and lexical levels between Bollig's entries and those of Elbert and of Goodenough and Sugita. This suggests that these differences still need a further and more thorough analysis. On the other hand, the exhaustive description of many lemmas done by Bollig is an exceptional contribution to the (re-)discovery of previously unknown Chuukese expressions. Bollig's manuscript can be considered as a valuable source for rediscovery or revitalization of obsolete words. Thanks to his dictionary, a gap in the lexicology of Chuukese can be filled.

At the moment, the work on the publication of the Chuukese comparative dictionary is still in progress. In this dictionary it is intended to maintain Bollig's original entries in German and to complement them with an English translation. Additionally, Bollig's entries will be contrasted to the entries of the reference dictionaries on the principle that was outlined in this paper (Table 2). The compared entries of all three dictionaries will complement one another and that will offer the users of the dictionary a wider range of Chuukese lexemes.

Acknowledgments: I would like to sincerely thank the colleagues of the manuscripts section of the library of the University of Münster who helped me in my work with the manuscripts. Furthermore, I would like to thank Professor Dr. Lothar Käser for his fruitful information concerning Father Laurentius Bollig which he was kind enough to provide me. All remaining errors are mine.

Abbreviations

1, 2, 3	1st, 2nd, 3rd person
POSS	possession
PRON	pronoun
SUFF	suffix
SG	singular

Abbreviations in dictionaries of Goodenough & Sugita

adj.	adjectival
fig.	figurative; figuratively
n.	noun
nu.	noun, uninflected
suf.	suffix
v.	verb
va.	verb, active and subject focused; when transitive it is indefinite or unspecific as to its object
vi.	verb, inactive and intransitive; it is descriptive of the condition (which may be active) of the subject
vo.	verb, active and object focused (transitive); it is definite and specific as to its object

References

(a) Manuscripts

Bollig. *Correspondence with Father Valentin*. Universitäts- und Landesbibliothek Münster, Kapuzinermission_021,005.

Bollig. *Allein auf der Insel Iluk*. Universitäts- und Landesbibliothek Münster, Kapuzinermission_034,142.

Bollig, P. Laurentius. *Ungedrucktes Wörterbuch der Truksprache 1916–1919.* Universitäts- und Landesbibliothek Münster, S. Kapuzinermission B,1.

(b) Dictionaries

Elbert, Samuel. 1947. *Trukese-English and English-Trukese dictionary. With notes on pronunciation, grammar, vocabularies, phrases.* Pearl Harbor: T.H, U.S. Naval Military Government.
Goodenough, Ward H. & Hiroshi Sugita. 1980. *Trukese-English dictionary – Pwpwuken tettenin fóós: Chuuk-Ingenes.* Philadelphia: American Philosophical Society.
Goodenough, Ward H. & Hiroshi Sugita. 1990. *Trukese-English dictionary. Supplementary volume: English-Trukese and index of Trukese word roots.* Philadelphia: American Philosophical Society.

(c) Monographs and articles

Bollig, P. Laurentius. 1927. *Die Bewohner der Truk Inseln.* (Anthropos ethnologische Bibliothek 3/1). Münster i. W.: Aschendorffsche Verlagsbuchhandlung.
Dewein, Barbara. 2013. H. Costenoble's work on Chamorro (re-)edited. In Steven Roger Fischer (ed.), *Oceanic voices – European quills. The early documents on and in Chamorro and Rapanui,* 177–199. Berlin: Akademie Verlag.
Käser, Lothar. 2011. 'Den Buchstaben *h* können die Eingeborenen nicht aussprechen' Pater Laurentius Bollig und die Sprache von Chuuk. In Thomas Stolz, Christina Vossmann & Barbara Dewein (eds.), *Kolonialzeitliche Sprachforschung. Die Beschreibung afrikanischer und ozeanischer Sprachen zur Zeit der deutschen Kolonialherrschaft,* 263–285. Berlin: Akademie Verlag.
Krämer, Augustin. 1932. Truk. *Ergebnisse der Südsee-Expedition, 1908–1910.* (Ethnographie, Mikronesien, 5). Hamburg: Friederichsen, de Gruyter.
Mückler, Hermann. 2010. *Mission in Ozeanien.* Bd. 2. Wien: facultas.wuv.
Schuster, Susanne. 2013. The *Chamorro-Wörterbuch* by Georg Fritz – a contrastive description of the editions 1904 and 1908. In Steven Roger Fischer (ed.), *Oceanic voices – European quills. The early documents on and in Chamorro and Rapanui,* 83–102. Berlin: Akademie Verlag.
Wienberg, Marina. 2016. Moanus or Titan? On Ludwig Cohn's amateur linguistics. In Schmidt-Brücken, Daniel, Susanne Schuster & Marina Wienberg (eds.). *Aspects of (post-)colonial linguistics. Current perspectives and new approaches.* Berlin & Boston: De Gruyter Mouton.
Zimmermann, Klaus & Birte Kellermeier-Rehbein (eds.). 2015. *Colonialism and missionary linguistics.* Berlin & Boston: De Gruyter Mouton.

Doris Stolberg
Positioning by naming: Constructing group affiliation in a colonial setting

Abstract: Defining groups and affiliating the self and the other with specific social categories is an important part of constructing a colonial conceptualization of societies. Many written documents from the colonial period attest to this practice. The current paper focuses on missionaries' ways of positioning themselves and others within the colonial context. The German speaking Rheinische Missionsgesellschaft (RMG, Rhenish Mission Society) established mission stations in the Astrolabe Bay area of New Guinea, an area that was under German domination between 1884 and 1914. The paper analyzes how RMG missionaries, by means of language, construct, define, and position different population groups, and it investigates what patterns emerge from these language practices.

Keywords: colonial group construction, positioning of self and other, genericity, stereotyping, mission societies

1 Introduction

Colonialism[1] is founded, in large parts, on the construction of ideology-based borders between humans (cf. Anderson 1983). As a result, colonized people are not only geographically located outside of the colonial metropole[2] but also, from a colonial viewpoint, positioned in specific spaces of a constructed socio-cultural landscape (cf. Spivak 1985). Such spaces, and the borders separating them, are crucially established through language and patterns of language use.

Conceptualizing people as inherently divided into groups that colonize and those that are (to be) colonized is an important part of justifying imperial colonialism (Said 1978). This conception is documented historically on a general level as well as with respect to specific local and small-scale interactions. It is reflected,

---

[1] Colonialism, as a term, is used here to refer to the modern imperial colonialism of the European colonial period, starting with the 15th century, and more specifically to German colonialism of the 19th and 20th century.
[2] The term metropole refers to the homeland of the colonizing power.

Doris Stolberg, Institut für Deutsche Sprache, Abt. Lexik, R 5, 6–13, 68161 Mannheim, Germany. E-Mail: stolberg@ids-mannheim.de

https://doi.org/10.1515/9783110623710-006

for example, in the communication of expatriate missionaries working in colonized areas and in the way groups are constructed in the missionaries' writings.

The current paper is based on historical documents from the Rheinische Missionsgesellschaft (RMG, Rhenish Mission Society), a German mission society that was active in colonial New Guinea between 1887 and 1932. Special attention is paid to documents from the period of German colonial rule, that is, 1887 to 1914. The paper investigates what groups are identified in these documents, and how they are addressed, referred to, or positioned.

The following section offers information on the relevant historical background. Next, the data are presented, framed theoretically, and analyzed. The paper ends with a summary of the findings and some considerations on discursive group construction in a colonial setting.

2 The colonial setting

During the second half of the 19th century, Germany assumed colonial dominance over several areas in Africa and Oceania. This paper centers on the South Pacific. Between 1884 and 1900, the northeastern part of New Guinea, the Bismarck Archipelago, the northern Solomon Islands, the Marshall Islands, Nauru, the Mariana Islands (except for Guam), the Caroline and Palau Islands, and (Western) Samoa became colonies of the German Empire. German colonial rule lasted until 1914 (*de iure* until 1919) when, with the beginning of WW I, the colonies were taken over by Australia, Japan, or New Zealand.

Christianizing the colonized population, and transmitting values of European culture, was considered an important part of exerting colonial power and carrying out the so-called 'mission civilisatrice'[3], the civilizing mission the colonizers claimed to pursue within the colonial scheme of power. Therefore, the German government arranged for, or permitted, various mission societies to become active in the colonies. One of them was the RMG, a mission society already active in southern Africa since 1829. In 1885, the German government asked the RMG to set up the Protestant mission work in German New Guinea (Bade 1987: 62). The first RMG missionaries arrived in the Astrolabe Bay area (New Guinea) in 1887, and the RMG remained active in this region until 1932 when their mission area was transferred to the American Protestant mission.

---

[3] This term is originally linked to French colonialism (cf. Conklin 1998, Costantini 2008), but as a concept, it is applicable to other colonial powers as well.

Until 1900, the German Empire was represented in New Guinea by a German trading company, the New Guinea Company (N.G.C.). Since the RMG had been sent out by the German government, they were obligated to cooperate to a certain extent with the agents of the N.G.C. and to provide services as interpreters and mediators between the German staff (of the N.G.C. and, later, of the German government) and the local population (cf. Bade 1987). Several of the early mission stations were located in the vicinity of N.G.C. stations, a result of the requirement to have mission station locations approved by the N.G.C. (Bade 1987: 64). Especially Friedrich-Wilhelmshafen (Madang) is mentioned as a harbor town in close vicinity to several of the early RMG stations where not only missionaries but also the local population came into contact with a life style that the missionaries did not approve of (e.g., RMG 3.002-1 Nobonob; RMG 3.003-1 Ragetta).

Besides German officials and staff (N.G.C. and governmental), two other groups of expatriates were located close to the RMG mission area in New Guinea. These are the Societas Verbi Divini (SVD, Divine Word Society), a Catholic mission society, and the Neuendettelsauer Mission (NM, Neuendettelsau Mission Society), a Protestant mission society. The SVD had their mission area northwest of the RMG, bordering on the RMG area in the north of the Astrolabe Bay (cf. Loeffen 1991). The NM was located further east around the Huon Bay, so they had no shared border with the RMG but, as another Protestant mission, interacted and cooperated with the RMG to some degree.

During the colonial period, conflicts arose from the differing understanding the government and the missions had of the missions' role in the colonial setting. From the missions' perspective, it was their role to Christianize the local population, to spread European and Christian values and education, and to do so in the addressees' native languages, if possible. The government's expectation, in contrast, was that the mission societies provided education to the local population at low cost (for the government), to produce trained and acculturated local workers (by spreading European values and acceptance of the colonial order), and to disseminate knowledge of the German language by teaching it in school (cf. Adick & Mehnert 2001). While there were some parallels in these goals, there were also obvious areas of tension.

Mission societies were thus colonial agents who contributed to the shaping of social structures under colonial conditions. One way of doing so was the missionaries' constructing groups and group membership in their writings that reflected preconceived notions of a colonial socio-cultural landscape.

3 Theoretical aspects of group reference

This paper investigates different patterns of group reference from a formal and functional perspective, analyzing the linguistic means of group conceptualization and their applications in positioning the self and the other in a hierarchized structure of center and periphery. Among the linguistic options for constructing groups and group membership are exogenous group naming, that is, the introduction and application of exonyms (cf., e.g., Harder 2008), person stereotypes and their linguistic expressions (cf. Pümpel-Mader 2010), the use of genericity to assert group-defining characteristics, at the morphological-lexical and the syntactic level (cf. Schmidt-Brücken 2018), and discursive group characterizations by means of discursive descriptions of events (related to textual genericity, cf. Schmidt-Brücken 2018: 47). All of these strategies can be found in the analyzed data.

One of the functions of conceptualizing group membership is identity work by positioning the self relative to others. While positioning theory is usually applied in conversational analysis and to face-to-face interactions, it can also offer some insights regarding (historical) written group reference. In the following, some central aspects of positioning theory are outlined. Further, two types of generalizing language use, namely genericity and stereotyping, are delineated, and it is indicated what linguistic forms and patterns can be applied to these ends.

3.1 Positioning theory

Positioning theory is an approach to interactive identity work that is originally based in social and cognitive psychology (Harré & van Langenhove 1999, Harré et al. 2009). It refers to discourse strategies that participants of an interaction use in order to mark identity aspects they wish to present or enact. Lucius-Hoene & Deppermann (2004: 171) note that positionings are not performed by one specific class of speech acts only.[4] Positioning is a function of interactive language-based practices; it is not tied to a specific form (Lucius-Hoene & Deppermann 2004: 171). This theoretical approach has been applied in linguistics research to such areas as discourse studies, conversation analysis, and language and identity studies (cf. Harré & Moghaddam 2003, Lucius-Hoene & Deppermann 2004, Schulze et al. 2008) as well as to postcolonial studies (for example, Aberdeen 2003).

---

4 "Positionierungen werden nicht mit einer bestimmten Klasse von sprachlichen Akten vollzogen" (Lucius-Hoene & Deppermann 2004: 171).

Harré et al. (2009) emphasize that with positioning the self and the other within a social space "a framework of rights and duties" (Harré et al. 2009: 6) is called up. This connection is obvious in the missionaries' writings, and the interaction between self-positioning and assuming certain duties becomes clear when seen from the perspective of positioning theory: Missionaries are convinced of their Christian-European duties and their being responsible for the bettering of the situation of those who are perceived to be not at the same level of understanding and 'development' as they themselves are. That is, from positioning themselves as 'saviors of souls', as doctors, artisans, helpers in various ways (cf. Helmich 1905) and as owners of material goods that are difficult or costly to acquire, they derive the duty to help and support the local population in achieving presumably higher levels of moral standing, and to provide (or withhold, for assumed educational purposes) material goods. They are convinced of these duties and of their ability to shoulder them; as a prerequisite and as a result, they position themselves in a dominant and superior position.

Positioning theory has been applied to narrative identity work and to spoken language interaction, among other things. In this paper, I probe its applicability to written data. The missionaries' texts can be seen as one part of an interaction, where the other side is only implicitly present. Accordingly, there is no information on whether the missionaries' positionings of the self and others were accepted by the intended addressees (usually in-group members) or by third parties that are referred to in these texts (such as other expatriate groups or the local population). While there is no direct evidence of negotiating positions, some texts indicate selective re-positionings that are likely to have been triggered by such negotiations (e.g., Helmich 1905).

It should be noted that this paper does not attempt to discuss the different roles and positions the agents took and negotiated. It is concerned with naming and group reference as a mechanism for constructing a social reality from a certain perspective, and it looks at specific linguistic means that are employed in this process.

3.2 Linguistic means of constructing groups and group membership

Different linguistic strategies can be employed to express the concept of specific groups and to place group boundaries within the constructed socio-cultural landscape. Among these strategies are genericity, stereotyping, and the use of exonyms.

3.2.1 Genericity

Generic language use makes implicit assertions about people, conditions, concepts, etc. (cf. Schmidt-Brücken 2015, 2018). Genericity can be invoked by different linguistic means, that is, there is no stable correlation between specific linguistic forms and the expression of genericity. From a functional perspective, generic language use is often employed to affirm shared attitudes and perceived certainties.

Generic language use in colonial contexts can be localized in three different linguistic areas: textual genericity, syntactic genericity, and morphological-lexical genericity (Schmidt-Brücken 2018: 66). Textual genericity is created within the narrative or discursive treatment of a topic, an event, or an activity. Different syntactic means can be used to establish genericity, such as generic noun phrases, the assignment of specific semantic roles (e.g., patient), the use of adverbials, or, as a strategy to reclassify entities, the use of predicative constructions. Morphological-lexical genericity includes two aspects, namely, the use of collective derivational morphemes, and the pragmatic contribution to meaning via the usage of specific words. In addition, part of speech, number and the semantic category of a chosen word all interact with world knowledge (Schmidt-Brücken 2018). For example, the difference between the specific use of *der Bezirksamtmann* ('the county commissioner') and the generic use of *der Papua* ('the Papuan') in the missionaries' writings does not rest on a morphological differentiation but on contextual and world knowledge.

3.2.2 Stereotyping

The cognitive purpose of stereotyping can be summarized as providing an efficient way of handling information by reducing complexity. Similar to the encoding of genericity, stereotyping does not depend on specific linguistic means. There are, however, characteristic ways of encoding stereotypes, such as the use of main clauses or of the generic present, representing generalization and atemporality (Pümpel-Mader 2010). While there are differences between generic language use and stereotyping, both imply the general validity of the summarizing, and often simplifying, propositions that are made. According to Pümpel-Mader (2010: 424), stereotypes include two constituting elements: a social category (the carrier of a stereotype), and a quality or behavior (the feature) that is identified as typically belonging to or being part of the carrier.[5] Terminologically, a distinction has to be made between the stereotype expression, that is, the verbal, figurative, or visual form of the sign, and the conceptual structure of stereotype that is represented by the stereotype expression (Pümpel-Mader 2010: 423). Four patterns of textualizing stereotypes can be identified: a descriptive, narrative, explicative, and argumentative pattern (Pümpel-Mader 2010: 329ff.). In addition, cognitive strategies (e.g., metonymy and synecdoche, such as naming the living environment instead of the persons) are frequent in stereotype expressions (Pümpel-Mader 2010: 425). These patterns show some overlap with the ways genericity is expressed. Both ways of generalizing language use depend on contextual cues that, in sum, contribute to the production of generalizations.

3.2.3 Exonyms

In the colonial context, place names/toponyms are often exonyms assigned by members of the colonial powers, and they are employed to demonstrate colonial dominance toward the colonized population as well as to other colonial powers (cf., for example, Stolz & Warnke 2015, 2018; Engelberg & Stolz 2016; Iturrioz Leza 2008; Schöner 2018). Exonyms, that is, names given from an external perspective, by a non-group member or an exogenous person, are frequently place names (Harder 2008) but there are also exonyms of people(s) or languages. In the current paper, the main attention is on group designations that are intended to structure and stratify communities into entities in accordance with exogenous cultural perceptions and expectations that is, not on exonyms in a narrower sense. One example of such conceptual structuring is that only with the advent of missionaries and the beginning of Christianization in New Guinea, it became meaningful to speak of pagans and to contrast them with Christians. The example also hints at the social repercussions of exogenous group conceptualizations. In this respect, exogenous group reference, especially in colonial settings, contains parallels to the application of exonyms; in both cases, exogenous concepts (social, geographical, etc.) are imposed on local groups and conditions.

---

5 "Die Festlegung des Stereotyps auf die beiden Elemente 'soziale Kategorie' (Träger) und 'Eigenschaft' bzw. 'Verhaltensweise' (Merkmal) sollte zur Präzisierung des Begriffs Stereotyp einen Beitrag leisten" (Pümpel-Mader 2010: 424).

4 The data and their contextualization

The materials discussed in this paper are kept by the archives of the Vereinte Evangelische Mission (VEM = UEM/United Evangelical Mission), the successor organization of the RMG in Wuppertal (Germany).[6] They consist of station reports from the early 1930s, reporting on the previous development and the contemporary situation of different mission stations; letters between missionaries (1912–1914); and a small number of other texts, mainly manuscripts relating to language matters and to the interaction with the local population. The large majority of these texts are written in German.[7] While the main focus is on data from the German colonial period, a number of more recent texts, in particular station reports, were included because they contain information relevant for the colonial period.

The documents record the main activities of the RMG in the Astrolabe Bay, such as the foundation of new mission stations, staff decisions, interactions with other mission societies, and with the N.G.C. Beyond this factual information, the texts express attitudes towards different groups of colonial agents.

None of the analyzed texts were (intended to be) published or otherwise circulated outside of the mission society. They were part of the discourse within the mission society, and they were aimed at members of this community. Non-missionary expatriates and the local population in the mission area in New Guinea are unlikely to have been part of the intended audience. The documents testify to the effort of coping with a previously unencountered social structure and linguistic diversity. Social categorizations are employed to structure this new social environment conceptually; these conceptualizations from an exogenous perspective, in turn, shape the way the environment is perceived.

5 Group references in RMG documents

At the level of discourse, different groups are distinguished that can again be grouped together into higher-level categories. The conceptualization of these

---

[6] The RMG and another evangelical mission society, the Bethel Mission, merged in 1971 to form the Vereinte Evangelische Mission (VEM). – I wish to thank the archive of the Vereinte Evangelische Mission (VEM) in Wuppertal (Germany) and especially Wolfgang Apelt for his generous help in making these documents available to me.
[7] There is only one exception: Hannemann-1 is in English. A complete list of the materials used can be found in the reference section.

higher categories is implicit in the texts but their understanding is crucial for assessing where the missionaries positioned themselves and others in the colonial social landscape. The data indicate further, explicitly and implicitly, that these higher-level divisions are linked to values of membership and moral acceptability. The higher-level categories include expatriate groups, subdivided into mission societies and other expatriate groups, and the local population.

Expatriate groups
Mission societies:
– the Rhenish Mission Society (RMG) (Protestant; G[8])
– other Protestant missions: Neuendettelsauer Mission (G), Methodists (E[9])
– Catholic mission: Societas Verbi Divini (SVD) (G)
Other expatriate groups:
– New Guinea Company
– German colonial government
– traders, planters

Local population
– Papuans, Melanesians
– Christians vs. non-Christians

A differentiating treatment can be observed within the category of mission societies, namely, with respect to denomination: While the Protestant missions are mentioned and named in a neutral manner, the Catholic mission is constructed as a rival or competitor, and interactions with the Catholics are described as being conflict-ridden (cf. below).

In the data, a number of strategies and linguistic means are employed to express group distinctions. In the following sections, examples of group reference are given to provide an overview of the range of usages.[10]

The first section includes expressions that are used to refer to the RMG and its members. These expressions can be pronominal, possessive (indicating a strong identification with the RMG), or referring to the position or rank of individuals.

---

8 G = German speaking.
9 E = English speaking.
10 All translations from German originals are mine (D.S.). They are intended to reflect the German originals as closely as possible and are therefore not always idiomatic English translations. – Please note that Hannemann-1 is written in English, so there are no German versions for quotes from this source.

Reference to *self*
- *die Rheinische Mission* 'the Rhenish Mission [Society]'

pronominal (1st person):
- *wir* 'we'

possessive (1st person):
- *unsere Mission* 'our mission [society]'

rank/function (in increasing specificity):
- *Missionare/der Missionar* 'missionaries/the missionary'
- *Bruder/Schwester* 'brother/sister' (a common way of referring to members of a religious order)
- *Laienbruder, Baubruder, Pflanzungsbruder* etc. 'lay brother, building brother, plantation brother' (referring to lay members of the mission who fulfil special functions)
- *der Präses* 'the president [of the RMG]'

The options for self-reference demonstrate a well-differentiated range of expressions, including a general reference to the institution as well as the specification of a singular function. Morphologically, generic singular or plural forms are rarely used (only with *der Missionar* 'the missionary'). Overall, there is little genericity or stereotyping to be found in the expressions referring to (members of) the RMG.

Other mission societies
- Protestant mission societies
    - *die Neuendettelsauer* 'the Neuendettelsau [people/missionaries]'
    - *die Methodisten im Archipel* 'the Methodists in the [Bismarck] Archipelago'

Other Protestant mission societies are only referred to as groups, with generic plural marking, characterized by their affiliation (and location). No individual reference is made to members of these groups.
- The Catholic mission society

    All of these expressions refer primarily to the SVD, the Catholic mission society whose area bordered on that of the RMG. Some neutral expressions are used, denoting the institution rather than individuals:
    - *die katholische Mission* 'the Catholic mission'
    - *die römische Mission* 'the Roman mission'

Already the reference *römisch*, however, includes a stereotypical expression that hints at a more conflict-laden relationship by referring to a place instead of a denomination. The next examples indicate the competition that was felt between the two denominations. Expressions such as *Römlinge* and *Rom* point towards the conflicts of the 1870s Kulturkampf[11] between the Catholic Church and the German nation state.

- *die römische Konkurrenz* 'the Roman competition'
- *Römlinge* 'Rome-lings' (a derogatory term for Catholics that originated in the 18th century[12] and was also employed in connection with the Kulturkampf)
- *Rom* 'Rome' (a doubly-metonymic reference, to the place where the head of the Catholic church (i.e., the Pope) resides, the place and the Pope both being metonyms for the Catholic mission society in this case)

In a discursive description, the two groups are depicted as hostile parties fighting over a shared border:
- *[D]ie (wohl im Jahre 1915) zwischen Br. Hanke/Blum und dem Pater Präfekt vereinbarte Grenze (S.W.Linie) wurde nie inne gehalten und das Protokoll von den Kath. nie unterschrieben. Sie bestanden auf der S.S.W. Linie, die aber von uns niemals zugestanden wurde.* (RMG 3.002-1 Nobonob) 'The border line that was agreed upon (apparently in 1915) between Br[others] Hanke/Blum and the Pater Prefect (S[outh].W[est]. line) was never kept and the protocol was never signed [i.e., ratified] by the Catholics. They insisted on the S[outh].S[outh].W[est]. line which, however, was never accepted by us.'

In addition, it is implied that turning to the Catholics may be even worse than forsaking Christian values. This attitude highlights once more the strongly felt rivalry between the RMG missionaries and the Catholic mission.
- *manche sind in der Versuchung nicht bestanden, etliche neigen gar zu den Katholiken* (RMG 3.003-1 Ragetta) 'some have not resisted the temptation, several even tend towards the Catholics'

Hannemann-1, in the early 1930s, strikes a more conciliatory note. While still using a generic plural, he emphasizes the connecting rather than the dividing aspects by using a possessive (1st person) pronoun and emphasizing the regional vicinity of the Catholic mission. This may well have to do with the

---

11 Kulturkampf (with respect to Prussia and Germany) refers to the period of strong political conflict between the rising nation state and the Catholic Church (cf. Orosz 2011 for repercussions of the Kulturkampf in the German colonial area in Cameroon between 1885 and 1914).
12 Cf. Deutsches Wörterbuch von Jacob Grimm und Wilhelm Grimm, vol. 14, col. 1161 (http://www.woerterbuchnetz.de/DWB?bookref=14,1161,1).

changed political climate after WW I and the end of German colonialism, and also with the increased temporal distance to Kulturkampf-related conflicts.
– *our neighbors, the Romanists*
– *the Catholics*

Other expatriate groups: N.G.C., government, traders/planters
Non-missionary expatriates are referred to in more neutral terms. There is some indication of hostile attitudes (missionsfeindlich 'hostile towards the mission(s)') but it is not as prevalent as with respect to the Catholic mission. Social stratification within this group is marked by naming the function or rank of individuals, something that is also found regarding the RMG (the self) while it is not done with respect to the Catholic mission.
– *Europäer* 'the Europeans'
– *die Weissen* 'the white'
officials:
– *die Beamten der N.G.C.* 'the officials of the N.G.C.'
– *Vertreter der N.G.C. und sonstige Herren* 'representatives/officials of the N.G.C. and other gentlemen'
– *missionsfeindliche Pflanzer und (einz.) Regierungsbeamte* 'planters and (few) government officials who are against (the) missions'
– *some planters and officials of the government*
– *die Herren der Deputation* 'the gentlemen of the deputation'
– *Die Nähe der Pflanzungsstationen der Neu Guinea Comp. in Stephansort und Erima übte keine guten Einflüsse aus und brachte die Christen in Gefahr* (RMG 2.997-1 Bogadjim) 'The close vicinity of the New Guinea Company's plantation stations in Stephansort and Erima [sc. to the RMG mission stations] did not exert a positive influence [sc. on the mission's Christians] and endangered the Christians'

rank/function (individuals):
– *der Admiral mit seinem Offiziercorps* 'the admiral with his officer corps'
– *der Bezirksamtmann* 'the county commissioner'
– *der Gouverneur/Exzellenz* 'the governor/Excellency'

Within stereotype expressions, features can be linked implicitly to their carriers: The areal adjacency to the *Pflanzungsstationen* ('plantation stations', as a synecdoche for the N.G.C. representatives and their staff) – the syntactic subject of the clause – is blamed for a negative impact on local Christians. The (implied) actual carrier of this feature is, of course, the members of the N.G.C. and their lifestyle.

Local population
- generic reference
  plural nouns
    - *die Leute* 'the people'
    - *die Eingeborenen* 'the natives/the indigenous [people]'
    - *die Bergleute* 'the mountain people'
    - *die Papua* 'the Papuans'
    - *unsere Papua* 'our Papuans'
    - *die Christen* 'the Christians'
    - *die heid. Bergbewohner* 'the pagan mountain dwellers'
  singular nouns
    - *der Eingeborene* 'the native/the indigenous [person]'
    - *der Papua* 'the Papuan'
    - *der Bergchrist* 'the mountain Christian' [i.e., the Christian living in the mountain area]
    - *der erwachsene Tamol* 'the adult Tamol' (Helmich 1905)
    - (*Tamol* is the Bel/Gedaged word for 'person/human being' or 'man/male'; cf. ABVD word list for Gedaged, entries no. 53, 54 and Stolberg 2017: 76)

When discussing translation problems, Helmich (1907) emphasizes that social and economic structures in New Guinea are quite different from those described in Biblical texts. He maintains that these differences pose a problem for translating the texts in a comprehensible way.[13] The examples he offers contain generic propositions such as:
- *Der Papua pflanzt, aber er säet nicht.* (Helmich 1907: 124) 'The Papuan plants [crops], but he does not sow.'
- *Die Eingeb. flicken weder Kleider, noch bringen sie ihr Geld in die Wechselbank. Er (der Eingeb.) kann auch das Licht nicht unter den Scheffel stellen.* (Helmich 1907: 124) 'The natives neither mend their clothes nor do they take their money to a bank. He (the native) cannot hide his light under a bushel, either.'
- *Wenn man hier an der Küste einen als dumm und unerfahren, ungeschickt bezeichnen will, dann sagt man: du bist wohl aus den Bergen, aus dem Hinterlande [...]* (Helmich 1907: 133) 'If you want to refer to someone as stu-

---

13 What is curiously absent from his remarks is any expression of awareness that the Biblical texts also had to be adapted culturally when they were translated into German from the original Hebrew resp. Greek.

pid and unexperienced, clumsy, down here at the coast you say: you seem to be from the mountains, from the back country [...]'
- *[...] daß man diese Bezeichnung für die Nichtchristen nehmen solle [...] ist [...] aber nicht gut möglich – wie soll dann der Bergchrist die heid. Bergbewohner benennen. Außerdem muß es für die Bergleute verletzend sein.* (Helmich 1907: 133 cont.) 'to take this label to identify non-Christians is not feasible – how should the mountain Christian refer to the heathen mountain dwellers. In addition, it must be offensive for the mountain people.'

These remarks, while referring to groups of local people in a generic manner, indicate a more differentiated view, including a reflection on sensitive language use. Comments as these converge with Engelberg's (2014: 322) observations regarding an increasing recognition of the complexities of local languages among those expatriates who acquired them. Similarly, missionaries who worked locally developed awareness for the social structures around them.
- specific reference
  With respect to the local population in the Astrolabe Bay, individual recognition (by name and rank/function) is reserved for Christians only.
    - *4 samoanische Gehülfenpaare (eingetroffen* [named individually]*) [...] alle vier Paare* '4 Samoan helper couples (arrived [names are listed]) [...] all four couples'
    - *Häuptling Mul [...] Ältester (treuer Christ und Führer)* 'Chief Mul [...] Elder (faithful Christian and leader)'
    - *Samoaner Taeao (mit Frau und einem Kind)* 'the Samoan, Taeao (with wife and one child)'
    - *Lehrer Madom* 'the teacher Madom'
    - *Gemeindeleiter Madoi* 'the congregation leader Madoi'

Local population: Stereotype constructions with carrier + feature
For a number of group and generic references, the pattern Pümpel-Mader (2010: 424) identified can be observed. The carrier + feature construction appears in attributive constructions as well as in predicative ones in the data. The following examples show how it is employed to assign intellectual and psychological features to different groups (mental feature stereotypes) as well as to position local Christians within a paternalistically defined caretaking relationship ((im)maturity stereotypes).
Mental feature stereotypes:
- *die schwerfälligen Bongu* 'the cumbersome Bongu [people]'
- *die trägen stolzen Bodadjim* 'the lazy, haughty Bogadjim [people]'
- *die unzuverlässigen Keku-Inländer* 'the unreliable Keku inland people'

- *the supposed superiority of the inland people over against the lethargic and lazy Melanesians has been overemphasized*
- *the Papuan – a bit more sequacious and lively than the Melanesian on account of the cooler climate in the hills*
- *the coastal man – more grave, more deliberating, and intellectually a little bit above the inlander*

(Im)maturity stereotypes:
- *die Eingeborenen arbeiten* **schon ziemlich selbständig** *darin* [i.e., in the mission station's store] 'the natives **already** work **fairly independently** [in the mission station's store]'
- *Gemeinde von Br. Schütz gut* **erzogen** 'congregation well **trained** by Br[other] Schütz'
- **selbständige** *Reisen von Christen unter* **Führung** *der Ältesten* '**independent** travels of Christians under the **guidance** of the elders'
- *bisher* **unberührte** *Heiden* 'heathens who were **untouched** [by Christianity] until now'
- *die Christen (zumeist standhaft, einige* **ließen sich** *ins Garn* **locken***)* 'the Christians (mostly steadfast, some **let themselves be lured** into temptation)'

The latter descriptions, in particular, construct the stereotype that local/converted Christians are in a (possibly vulnerable) state of development – they have to be trained, they are susceptible to temptations, and they are not expected to act without guidance.

Metaphor: 'natives are children'

In Helmich (1905), the extensive use of educational vocabulary is noteworthy (e.g., *erziehen* 'educate', *groß ziehen* 'raise', *verziehen* 'spoil', *verwöhnen* 'pamper', *strafen* 'punish'). Here, local people, adults and children alike, are implicitly and also explicitly equated with children, indicating a strong conceptual asymmetry between the locals and the missionaries from the perspective of this missionary.
- *Unsere Eingb. sind Kinder, und zwar nicht Kinder an der Bosheit, wohl aber am Verständnis. Es sind somit meist recht ungezogene Kinder, die einer straffen, aber doch auch wieder liebevollen Erziehung bedürfen.* 'Our natives are children, not children in terms of maliciousness but in understanding. Thus, they are mostly rather naughty children who need a strict but also loving education/upbringing.'
- *Allein es gilt auch hier die Erziehung der Leute im Auge zu behalten. Wir dürfen kein Bettelvolk groß ziehen.* 'However, also here it is important to keep an eye on the education/upbringing of the people. We must not raise a people of peddlers.'

- *Nun habe ich schon oben darauf hingewiesen, daß wir es im allgemeinen mit ungezogenen und unverständigen Kindern zu tun haben, die erzogen werden müssen.* 'I mentioned above already that, in general, we are dealing with naughty and ignorant children who have to be educated.'

A similar asymmetry is reflected in the depiction of spiritual relationships where the relationship between God and the missionaries is compared with that between the missionary and the local people:
- *Der Missionar tritt als ein Zeuge des Heilandes und als ein Träger des Christentums unter die Heiden* 'The missionary steps forward among the heathens as a witness of the Savior and as a carrier of Christianity'
- *Je demütiger wir erkennen, welch unaussprechliche Geduld der Herr doch auch mit uns noch Tag um Tag haben muß, desto besser werden wir auch an unsern Eingeb. Geduld üben können.* 'The more we humbly recognize how inexpressibly patient the Lord has to be even with us every day the better we will be able to exercise patience towards our natives.'

With a generic singular noun as the carrier, adjectives work as features in stereotypical descriptions of local people. In some cases, such descriptions are contrasted with similarly stereotypical ones of the in-group, referred to as 'we' or 'we Europeans'. While such contrasts function well as positioning devices, the examples also show that there is no clear-cut correlation between positive and negative evaluations as relating to either the in-group or the out-group.
- *Der Eingeb., schlau und pfiffig, wo es sich um seinen Vorteil handelt* 'the native, clever and smart when his own advantage is concerned'
- *Im allgemeinen hat der erwachsene Tamol ein würdiges Auftreten.* 'In general, the adult tamol has a dignified appearance.'
- *Der Eingeb. ist träge, oft bodenlos gleichgültig und zuweilen schwer von Begriff. Wir unserseits [sic] sind meist nervös, und infolgedessen schnell aufgeregt und leicht gereizt.* 'The native is lethargic, often infinitely indifferent, and occasionally slow-witted. We, on our part, are often nervous and consequently quickly excited and easily irritated.'
- *Wir Europäer sind im allgemeinen an rasches Entschließen und Handeln gewöhnt. [...] Anders ist es mit unserm Papua.* 'We Europeans are, in general, used to decide and act quickly. [...] This is different with respect to our Papuan.'

This last example illustrates well what Schmidt-Brücken (2018) refers to as effects of syntactic genericity. While *wir Europäer* constitutes the subject in the nominative at the beginning of the clause, *unser[...] Papua* is not only referred to in (generic) singular and used with a possessive pronoun, but it also appears at the end of the clause (in a contrastive chiasm position to *wir Europäer*) and is embedded syntactically as the dative noun phrase within a prepositional phrase. The contrastive positioning and the stereotypically framed differences in agentivity are thus underpinned by the syntactic structure.

Narrative group characterization
As a final example, the narrative, or textual (Schmidt-Brücken 2018), construction of groups and group membership is represented below. The excerpt from a letter (of 1913) by the missionary Hanke to superintendent (*Missionsinspektor*) Kriele contains not only explicit group references but shows how in a contrastively structured narrative these group references are contextualized from a colonial viewpoint (line and page breaks as in the original; emphasis added, D.S.).

> *Am 12. JULI hatte ich ganz ungesucht Gelegenheit vor dem Offizier-*
> *corps und einem Teil der Mannschaft Zeugnis abzulegen. Es starb ein*
> *Oberheizer evgl. Konfession. Da bat mich dann der Kommandant des Sch.*
> *Die [sic] Beerdigung zu übernehmen, was ich natürlich mit Freuden tat. Das Be-*
> *gräbnis war für die vielen Eingeborenen, die in Fr.W.H. waren, ein ein-*
> *drucksvoller* **Anschauungsunterricht**. *Am Nachmittage dieses Tages war*
> *Parade. Es wurden 400 Mann Infanterie und von der Artillerie und den*
> *Maschinengewehrabteilungen 200 Mann ausgeschifft. Auf einem großen Ron-*
> *dell* **hatten an 1500 Eingeborene, die der Bezirksamtmann zu der Feier zu-**
> **sammengeholt hatte,** *Aufstellung gefunden. Auf dem das Rondell umgeben-*
> *den Wege rückten dann die Kolonnen an. An der Spitze die Infanterie*
> *mit klingendem Spiel und aufgepflanztem Seitengewehr. Hinter ihr Artil-*
> *lerie und Maschinengewehrabteilungen. Was* **machten da unsere Papua für**
> **Augen**! *Das schien ja als wollte es gar kein Ende nehmen [sic]. Das ganze*
> *Rondell war schließlich umgeben* **von einer Mauer in Waffen starrender**
> **weißer Menschen. Die braunen Leutchen meinten, ihr letztes Stündlein**
> **sei gekommen.** *Endlich kam der Admiral, die Parade abzunehmen. Als nun*
> *die Kolonnen sich im Paradmarsch in Bewegung setzten und die* **Umklam-**
> **merung** [page break]
> *allmählig [sic] sich löste,* **atmete alles auf**. *Ihr Leben lang werden die Papua*
> *dies Schauspiel nicht vergessen.* (RMG 2.149-006 Hanke an Kriele, 1913-9-23)
> 'On the 12th of July I had the unexpected chance to testify [sc. my Christian faith] in front of the officer corps and part of the crew. An *Oberheizer* [a nautical rank] of Protestant faith had died. So the commander of the ship asked me to hold the funeral service, which I gladly agreed to do. The funeral was

an impressive **demonstrative object lesson** for the many natives who were in Fr[iedrich-]W[ilhelms]h[afen]. In the afternoon of the same day, there was a parade. 400 infantrymen and 200 men from the artillery and the machine gun sections were disembarked. On a great rondel, **around 1,500 natives whom the district officer had brought together** had assembled for the ceremony. Along the way around the rondel, the troops advanced. They were headed by the infantry, approaching with ringing music and bayonet fixed. It was followed by the artillery and the machine gun sections. How **our Papuans grew wide-eyed**! This [parade] seemed to take no end. Eventually, all of the rondel was surrounded by **a wall of white people bristling with weapons. The brown people** [*Leutchen,* diminutive of *Leute* 'people', lit. 'little people'] **were convinced that they should die**. Finally, the admiral came to take the salute. As the troops began their march in review and the **stranglehold** slowly started to loosen, everybody **breathed a sigh of relief**. Never in their lives will the Papuans forget this spectacle.'

In this passage, several features can be identified that position different groups of agents within the reported setting. Early on, the term *Anschauungsunterricht* 'demonstrative object lesson' links to the child metaphor already mentioned above. Further, syntactic means are used to place the involved agents in different hierarchical positions: The district officer (*Bezirksamtmann*) is described as acting while the local population is the syntactic object (of the relative clause referring to the people's location on the rondel). In addition, reference is made to skin color (white vs. brown). While the colonizers are depicted almost as machinery (with detailed descriptions of weapons, no indication of emotions, and in possession of control: *Umklammerung* 'stranglehold'), the local population is termed in the diminutive (*Leutchen*) and described as expressing strong emotions of bewilderment (*machten [...] Augen* 'grew wide-eyed') and great fear (*meinten, ihr letztes Stündlein sei gekommen* 'were convinced that they should die') that are finally resolved in a 'sigh of relief' (*atmete alles auf*).

Interestingly, there is a change of perspective at one point, after *Was machten da unsere Papua für Augen!* 'How our Papuas grew wide-eyed!'. While this sentence still describes the situation from the viewpoint of the missionary-observer, the following clause, *Das schien ja als wollte es gar kein Ende nehmen*, seems to intend to take the perspective of the Papuan people present, almost as if speaking for someone who cannot speak for himself (cf. Spivak 1988). This new perspective offers an interpretation of the (assumed) emotions of the Papuan participants. It is an interpretation, however, that cannot be checked against the Papuans' own perspective and experience. This constructed perspective is then framed as an instructional context (*Ihr Leben lang [...] nicht vergessen* 'never in their lives [...] forget'), not only contrastively highlighting the power asymmetry between the colonizing power (here presented as military power) but also tying in with the metaphor of the local people as children that lack understanding and education.

6 Results and discussion

The examples from the data show how different language-based strategies are employed to construct group membership and to demarcate positions of the self and the other. Some of the social patterns that emerge from the implicit and explicit attributions made in the texts are considered here more closely.

The main division line between groups of people runs along the lines of local vs. expatriate. Group-internally, expatriates are distinguished according to rank level, with respect to denomination (Protestant/Catholic), and whether they are mission members or not. This last group (non-mission members) is heterogeneous, being defined *ex negativo* and including traders, administrative staff, sailors, etc.

The two groups (local vs. expatriate) are assigned different values, and the level of detail in reference to individuals diverges. The data indicate, however, that there is not just a line between the colonizers and the colonized: The RMG also positions itself with respect to other religious denominations and to non-church agents of the colonial metropole. Thus, these divisions result in a three-way group distinction: the in-group (self), the close out-group (other expatriates), and the distant out-group (the autochthonous population). While hierarchies of rank are named in both groups, the local as well as the expatriate population, the distinctions are more fine-grained for members of expatriate groups. Another difference is that positioning within the in-group is done by societal rank but not by local origin. The geographic origin of expatriates is never mentioned; in contrast, for the local population, explicit distinctions regarding regional provenance are made and linked with (stereotypical) personal characteristics (cf. the section on "Local population: Stereotype constructions with carrier + feature").

Within the group of local people, a crucial divide appears between Christians and non-Christians. Becoming Christian seems to offer the opportunity for the local, colonized population to cross borders and become, to a certain degree, in-group members of the RMG. This is reflected linguistically by a changed way of reference, that is, these persons are named individually (a form of reference usually reserved for expatriates) instead of generically or as groups.

In sum, the societal patterns that emerge from the group references in the documents are as follows:
- Regarding **expatriates**, differentiated reference is made to the in-group as a whole (governmental as well as missionary) as well as to individual members of this group.
- Within the **local population** (i.e., the out-group), **non-Christians** are never referenced individually but always in generic and stereotypical terms.
- **Local individuals** are referred to only if they are **Christians** and are members of or cooperate with the RMG, but Christian out-group members are often referred to in a generalized way as well.

An aspect that is worth mentioning with regard to group conceptualization is the use of possessive adjectives in the data. It is also an example of one grammatical form serving different discursive functions. In general, possessive marking can be understood as being linked to identity and identification. The authors of the investigated texts position themselves as members of the RMG but also as Europeans and as 'whites'. The use of a 1st person plural possessive adjective can mark either one or all of these positionings as a point of reference.

There are two groups with whom the 1st person plural possessive adjective is used: the local population and the Catholic mission. From the context, it is clear that these two cases must be understood differently. In the case of *unsere Papua* 'our Papuans'/*unsere Eingeborenen* 'our natives', the possessive does not express in-group affiliation at eye level but on a hierarchical scale of assumed responsibility that is linked to superiority on the side of the writers, almost pointing in the direction of an actual possession. This type of in-group membership is marked by appropriation in the sense that the colonized people are not considered independent agents within the colonial structure. As the context indicates, they are rather seen as dependent and in need of guidance. In contrast, the use of the possessive adjective in *our neighbors, the Romanists* is, though formally the same, quite different in meaning. The RMG's relationship with the Catholic mission society changes over time from competition to affiliation, finally emphasizing geographical vicinity as a common ground. Thus, here the possessive adjective appears to reflect the assumption of (more or less) equal standing, expressing shared group membership rather than subjected group membership.

In general, the colonizers are depicted as dominant agents, and they figure as the point of reference for any judgment on the local population. It is not surprising, of course that documents from a mission archive, produced by members of this mission society, focus on expatriate mission members specifically and also on other expatriates (from the same homeland). By identifying different groups that are distinct from the in-group, an in-group identity is constructed and shaped through language use. This strategic use of language for creating group distinctions was probably not fully intentional. It resulted, however, in a stronger specification of the mission members' own group identity and in the creation of mental borderlines between group formations that were newly defined in this process.

7 Concluding remarks

The examples of group reference from the colonial missionary data indicate how human society can be structured conceptually by language means. The data also show, however, that the ability to exert this structuring power is not available to all agents. Being able to introduce and spread a new terminology is one example of agency in this respect. Missionaries are among the agents who had this power, for example when they translated Biblical texts that became reference points for the Christianized population. Another aspect of the assertive application of new (group) concepts is the matter of written vs. spoken language and the question of who documents their (own) language use. Again, missionaries were among those who recorded their language use and their considerations regarding language, translation, how to integrate foreign concepts into their own language use, and how to impose loanwords on other group's languages, denoting, for example, Christian concepts and values.

In a setting of power asymmetry such as colonialism, language use may have even more social consequences than in other contexts. Its influence is mediated by the function of specific language users (e.g., missionaries) and their ranking in the relevant social hierarchies. That is, societal position makes a difference for whose conceptualizations are preserved and may become dominant. Stereotyping, genericity, and exogenous attributions are used to position not only the language users themselves but also those they place within the colonial sociocultural landscape. Their group categorizations had broad repercussions in the colonial areas as well as in the homeland. Schmidt-Brücken (2018: 65) notes that the non-negated use of a word forces the presupposition that its denotatum actually exists.[14] In this sense, referring to groups in specific ways is a claim to the existence of such groups and to their dividing characteristics.

---

14 "[...] dass unnegierter Wortgebrauch eine Existenzpräsupposition über das Denotat des Wortes erzwingt" (Schmidt-Brücken 2018: 65).

References

(a) Primary sources

Archival material (Archive of the United Evangelical Mission (VEM), Wuppertal):

Letters:
- Hanke-2 = RMG 2.149-2 Hanke an Kriele, 1912-6-21 (letter)
- Hanke-4 = RMG 2.149-4 Hanke an Kriele, 1914-1-19 (letter)
- Hanke-5 = RMG 2.149-5 Hanke an Kriele, 1913-1-19 (letter)
- Hanke-6 = RMG 2.149-6 Hanke an Kriele, 1913-9-23 (letter)
- Hanke-7 = RMG 2.149-7 Hanke an Kriele, 1913-2-8 (letter)
- Hanke-8 = RMG 2.149-8 Hanke an Spiecker, 1914-1-13 (letter)
- Diehl-1 = RMG 2.154-1 Diehl, 1913-2-17 (letter)

Information on RMG mission stations:
- RMG 2.997-1 Bogadjim
- RMG 2.998-1 Bongu
- RMG 3.001-8 Neuguinea
- RMG 3.002-1 Nobonob
- RMG 3.003-1 Ragetta

Other documents:
- Sprachkonferenz = RMG 3.008-28: Anon. 1898. "Die 3. Sprachkonferenz/Sprachkonferenz in Bogadjim" [records of the mission language conference of 1898], pp. 98–102.
- Helmich 1905 = RMG 3.014a G/b 2 a: Heinrich Helmich. 1905. "Die Behandlung unserer Eingeborenen durch den Missionar im alltäglichen und persönlichen Verkehr/Konferenzreferat" [manuscript of a presentation held at a missionaries' meeting], pp. 67–80.
- Helmich 1907 = RMG 3.014a-9: Heinrich Helmich. 1907. "Die Bildung einer christlichen Terminologie in der Siar Sprache und die damit verbundenen Schwierigkeiten" [on developing a Christian terminology in Siar; manuscript of a presentation held at a missionaries' meeting], pp. 111–134
- Hannemann-1 = RMG 3.013-1: E[mil] F[riedrich] Hannemann [no date]. "A few statements in regard to the introduction of Ragetta as the universal language in our mission at Madang." [arguing for the introduction of Ragetta as the "universal" Lutheran mission language in the Astrolabe Bay area].
- Kleintitschen, [P.] August. 1906. Die Küstenbewohner der Gazellehalbinsel (Neupommern – deutsche Südsee) ihre Sitten und Gebräuche. Hiltrup: Herz-Jesu-Missionshaus.

(b) Monographs and articles

Aberdeen, Lucinda. 2003. Positioning and postcolonial apologizing in Australia. In Rom Harré & Fathali M. Moghaddam (eds.), *The self and others: Positioning individuals and groups in personal, political, and cultural contexts*, 189–196. Westport, CT: Praeger.

ABVD. Austronesian Basic Vocabulary Data base. Language: Gedaged. Source/Author: Robert Blust, from J. F. Mager. 1952. Gedaged-English Dictionary. Columbus, OH: Board of Foreign Missions of the American Lutheran Church, https://abvd.shh.mpg.de/austronesian/language.php?id=7&sort=word_id (accessed 05 May 2018).

Adick, Christel & Wolfgang Mehnert (unter Mitarbeit von Thea Christiani). 2001. *Deutsche Missions- und Kolonialpädagogik in Dokumenten. Eine kommentierte Quellensammlung aus den Afrikabeständen deutschsprachiger Archive 1884–1914*. Frankfurt a. M. u.a.: IKO-Verl. für Interkulturelle Kommunikation.

Anderson, Benedict. 1983. *Imagined communities: reflections on the origin and spread of nationalism*. London: Verso.

Bade, Klaus J. 1987. Culture, cash and Christianity: The German colonial experience and the case of the Rhenish Mission in New Guinea. *Pacific Studies* 10(3). 53–71.

Conklin, Alice L. 1998. *A Mission to Civilize: The Republican Idea of Empire in France and West Africa 1895-1930*. Stanford: Stanford University Press.

Costantini, Dino. 2008. *Mission civilisatrice. Le rôle de l'histoire coloniale dans la construction de l'identité politique française*. Paris: La Découverte.

Deutsches Wörterbuch von Jacob Grimm und Wilhelm Grimm. http://dwb.uni-trier.de/de/.

Engelberg, Stefan. 2014. Die deutsche Sprache und der Kolonialismus. In Heidrun Kämper, Peter Haslinger & Thomas Raithel (eds.), *Demokratiegeschichte als Zäsurgeschichte*, 307–332. Berlin & Boston: De Gruyter Mouton.

Engelberg, Stefan & Thomas Stolz. 2016. Einleitung: Namen und Kolonialismus. *Beiträge zur Namenforschung* 51(3/4). 269–277.

Harder, Kelsey B. 2008. Names in language contact: Exonyms. In Ernst Eichler, Gerold Hilty, Heinrich Löffler, Hugo Steger & Ladislav Zgusta (eds.), *Name studies. An international handbook of onomastics*, vol. 2, 1012. Berlin & New York: De Gruyter.

Harré, Rom & Fathali M. Moghaddam (eds.). 2003. *The self and others: Positioning individuals and groups in personal, political, and cultural contexts*. Westport, CT: Praeger.

Harré, Rom, Fathali M. Moghaddam, Tracey Pilkerton Cairnie, Daniel Rothbart & Steven R. Sabat. 2009. Recent advances in positioning theory. *Theory & Psychology* 19(1). 5–31.

Harré, Rom & Luk van Langenhove (eds.). 1999. *Positioning theory*. Oxford: Blackwell.

Iturrioz Leza, Jose-Luis. 2008. Namen in kolonialen und postkolonialen Verhältnissen: Mesoamerika. In Ernst Eichler, Gerold Hilty, Heinrich Löffler, Hugo Steger & Ladislav Zgusta (eds.), *Name studies. An international handbook of onomastics*, vol. 2, 1058–1064. Berlin & New York: De Gruyter.

Loeffen, Volker. 1991. *Die Rheinische Mission in Neu-Guinea 1886–1914*. Unpublished M.A. Thesis. University of Duisburg.

Lucius-Hoene, Gabriele & Arnulf Deppermann. 2004. Narrative Identität und Positionierung. *Gesprächsforschung – Online-Zeitschrift zur verbalen Interaktion* 5. 166–183. www.gespraechsforschung-ozs.de.

Orosz, Kenneth J. 2011. An African Kulturkampf: Religious conflict and language policy in German Cameroon, 1885–1914. *Sociolinguistica* 25. 81–93.

Pümpel-Mader, Maria. 2010. *Personenstereotype. Eine linguistische Untersuchung zu Form und Funktion von Stereotypen*. Heidelberg: Winter.
Said, Edward W. 1978. *Orientalism*. New York, NY: Pantheon Books.
Schmidt-Brücken, Daniel. 2015. *Verallgemeinerung im Diskurs: Generische Wissensindizierung in kolonialem Sprachgebrauch*. München, Berlin & Boston: De Gruyter Mouton.
Schmidt-Brücken, Daniel. 2018. Generizität. Sprachgebrauchsgeschichtliche und diskurslinguistische Aspekte kolonialer Kommunikation. In Birte Kellermeier-Rehbein, Matthias Schulz & Doris Stolberg (eds.), *Sprache und (Post)Kolonialismus. Linguistische und interdisziplinäre Aspekte*, 41–69. Berlin & Boston: De Gruyter Mouton.
Schöner, Mathias. 2018. Kulturmission oder Herrschaftssymbolik? Zur Verbreitung deutscher Zeichensysteme in der „Musterkolonie" Tsingtau. In Birte Kellermeier-Rehbein, Matthias Schulz & Doris Stolberg (eds.), *Sprache und (Post)Kolonialismus*, 205–234. Berlin & Boston: De Gruyter Mouton.
Schulze, Mathias, James M. Skidmore, David G. John, Grit Liebscher & Sebastian Siebel-Achenbach (eds.). 2008. *German diasporic experiences: Identity, migration, and loss*. Waterloo, ON: Waterloo Centre for German Studies and Wilfrid Laurier University Press.
Spivak, Gayatri Chakravorty. 1985. The Rani of Sirmur: An essay in reading the archives. *History and Theory* 24(3). 247–272.
Spivak, Gayatri Chakravorty. 1988. Can the subaltern speak? In Cary Nelson & Lawrence Grossberg (eds.), *Marxism and the interpretation of culture*, 271–313. Chicago: University of Illinois Press.
Stolberg, Doris. 2017. Historical sociolinguistics in colonial New Guinea: The Rhenish Mission Society in the Astrolabe Bay. *Journal of Historical Sociolinguistics* 3(1). 55–92.
Stolz, Thomas & Ingo H. Warnke. 2015. Aspekte der kolonialen und postkolonialen Toponymie unter besonderer Berücksichtigung des deutschen Kolonialismus. In Daniel Schmidt-Brücken, Susanne Schuster, Thomas Stolz & Ingo H. Warnke (eds.), *Koloniallinguistik. Sprache in kolonialen Kontexten*, 107–173. Berlin & Boston: De Gruyter Mouton.
Stolz, Thomas & Ingo H. Warnke (eds.). 2018. *Vergleichende Kolonialtoponomastik. Strukturen und Funktionen kolonialer Ortsbenennung*. Berlin & Boston: De Gruyter Mouton.

Philipp Krämer
Third-hand colonial linguistics: Adolphe Dietrich's comparative study of Indian Ocean Creoles

Abstract: This article gives an overview of the work of Austrian creolist Adolphe Dietrich, his academic background and the epistemological foundations of his research. Dietrich's comparative analysis of Indian Ocean Creoles differs from the work of most of his contemporaries: While most 19th century creolists describe creole languages on the basis of a racialist framework, Dietrich and his teacher Hugo Schuchardt avoid such a determinist colonial logic. Based on these observations, the article raises the question whether Dietrich can be seen as a 'colonial' linguist at all and what degree of 'coloniality' we can attribute to his research.

Keywords: creole languages, Indian Ocean, history of linguistics and philology, racism, 19th century

1 Racial theory and independent thinkers in 19th century creolistics

Adolphe Dietrich is probably one of the lesser-known names among 19th century researchers that published on the topic of creole languages.[1] As Hugo Schuchardt's student, he is overshadowed by the professor's ground-breaking work in early creolistics. However, Dietrich himself also made an important contribution to the development of the study of creole languages as an academic field with his 1891 article "Les parlers créoles des Mascareignes" which was published in the renowned journal *Romania*.

---

[1] I would like to thank the organizers and participants of the 9th workshop of the Colonial Linguistics Research Group in Klagenfurt and the colleagues from Bremen University for their comments and feedback to the paper I presented and to the drafts of this article. I am also grateful to the archives of the University of Graz for providing me with digital copies of the documents in Adolphe Dietrich's student and dissertation files from the 1890s.

Philipp Krämer, Free University of Berlin, Institute of German and Dutch Languages and Literatures, Habelschwerdter Allee 45, 14195 Berlin, Germany. E-Mail: philipp.kraemer@fu-berlin.de

https://doi.org/10.1515/9783110623710-007

The description and examination of creoles was a thriving area in philological and linguistic erudition in the last decades of the 19th century and the beginning of the 20th century. The emergence of creolistics as an academic discipline gained momentum as the creole languages were no longer an exclusive object of study for missionaries. Up until the mid-19th century, documents in and about creole languages were important tools for the Christian mission in the colonies in order to be able to communicate with the local population and to spread the faith. When academic scholars took an interest in creoles, the focus shifted from a rather practical use of linguistic knowledge towards a genuinely scientific inquisitiveness. Such a shift can also be observed in the study of other languages and certainly is not a specificity of creolistics (Stolz & Warnke 2015).

What is striking, however, is the widespread participation of the emerging discipline in a discourse of supposed racial hierarchies that serve as an explanation for the structures and history of creole languages. Many early creolists, especially in France and its colonies, attributed the process of creolization to the alleged difference between 'Blacks' and 'Whites' since the 'inferior' race was believed to be unable to fully acquire the sophisticated and complex European languages.

In Chicago, the young scholar René de Poyen-Bellisle from Guadeloupe stresses the idea of inferiority on a physical level:

> L'esclave n'essaie pas pour un seul instant d'assimiler les nouveaux sons qu'il entend à ceux qu'il connaît déjà [...]. Ce qu'il a à faire c'est d'essayer de parler comme son maître. Et il essaie. Mais il n'appartient pas à la même race, son appareil vocal n'est pas le même, ses lèvres sont différentes. De là les sons articulés par le Blanc subiront certaines transformations quand ils sont répétés par le nègre. (Poyen-Bellisle 1894: 14–15)
> [The slave doesn't even try to bring together the new sounds that he hears with those that he knows already [...]. What he needs to do is to try and speak like his master. And he does try. But he does not belong to the same race, his vowel tract is not the same, his lips are different. That's why the sounds as articulated by the White man will undergo certain transformations when they are repeated by the negro]. My translation.

Poyen-Bellisle links the process of creolization, more precisely the process of sound-change from French to Antillean Creole, to differences in physiognomy and anatomy. Very much in accordance with the theory of 'thick lips' that was widespread also in other branches of the language sciences, first and foremost in the United States, creole phonology was supposed to be due to the physical incapacity of 'Blacks' to pronounce the unfamiliar sounds of French (Holm 2000: 23).

Unlike Poyen-Bellisle, the Mauritian Charles Baissac, one of the most influential early creolists in the French sphere, stresses cognitive rather than physical differences:

> [...] brusquement placés par l'esclavage en présence du monde d'idées nouvelles pour eux que portait en elle la langue française, nos noirs se bouchèrent résolument les yeux et les oreilles, et, en dehors du cercle étroit de la vie matérielle, ils voulurent tout ignorer, se sentant incapables de rien comprendre. (Baissac 1880: VIII)
> [Our blacks, that slavery had suddenly placed before a world of new ideas which the French language brought along, resolutely plugged their eyes and ears and they wanted to ignore anything outside the narrow circle of material life as they felt incapable of understanding anything]. My translation.

As Baissac puts it, racial predisposition allegedly restricts the mental capacities of 'Blacks' so that abstract concepts are impossible for them to grasp. Consequently, Baissac's grammar of Mauritian Creole explains the lack of the copula verb *être* with the argument that the notion of *being* or *existence* is inconceivable for 'Blacks' and hence cannot be transported from French into the restricted system of creole that can only express material concepts (Baissac 1880: 31–32). Beyond the physical and cognitive level, some creolists also refer to moral categories in order to explain creolization. Jean Turiault's account of the development of creole in Martinique is a good example as he states that 'Blacks' have "une certaine paresse d'esprit les portant à dire les mots de la manière la plus facile [...]" (Turiault 1877: 407), [a certain intellectual laziness which makes them pronounce the words in the easiest possible way [...], my translation].

Taken together, these ideas paint a picture of an absolute racial hierarchy that culminates in the words of the renowned French philologist Julien Vinson who defines a creole language as an

> adaptation du français, de l'anglais, de l'espagnol, au génie pour ainsi dire phonétique et grammatical d'une race linguistiquement inférieure. (Vinson 1884: 416)
> [adaptation of French, English, Spanish to what can be called the phonetic and grammatical genius of a linguistically inferior race]. My translation.

This general idea is omnipresent in 19th century creolistics, though certainly most prominent in the works of numerous French creolists and much less so in Portuguese creolistics or in the works of Hugo Schuchardt in Austria (Krämer & de Sousa 2017). Despite the predominance of this racialized discourse, not all creolists share this view on the emergence and grammars of creole languages. One of the creolists that show a certain resistance to the predominant discourse is Adolphe Dietrich in his article. Therefore, his personal background and the particularities of his contribution to the field deserve a closer look.

2 A young creolist's legacy: Adolphe Dietrich's life and work

Little was known about the biography of Adolphe Dietrich but new information was made available by the archives of the University of Graz. His personal file (*Rigorosenbuch* No. 353, 1890) shows that he was born on January 20th, 1867 as a German national in Graz, Austria. He went to school in his home town and graduated from the University of Graz in 1889 before starting his PhD project under the supervision of the renowned professors Hugo Schuchardt and Gustav Meyer. During his undergraduate studies, he concentrated on Romance and German philology, comparative linguistics and philosophy. He then chose Romance philology as his major (*Hauptfach*) and classical philology as a minor (*Nebenfach*) for his postgraduate studies and his PhD exams (*Rigorosum*). Interestingly, Dietrich passed the exam in his major with distinction, but failed in the first attempt at the exam in his minor subject (*Philosophicum*) as all three examiners marked his performance as *unsatisfactory*. After a three months' suspension, Dietrich was allowed to take a second attempt at which he passed with the relatively low and unanimous mark *satisfactory*. One can speculate if this discrepancy between the excellent result of the first exam as compared to the second one might be the sign of a growing separation between the canonical background of classical philology or philosophy on the one hand, and the growing emancipation of the study of modern languages on the other. Alternatively it is also possible that Dietrich saw his focus in the second area and put all his efforts into the study of the Indian Ocean Creoles while he did not take the study of classical disciplines as seriously. Nevertheless, the formal documentation of Dietrich's career as a student and young scholar at the University of Graz shows that his research on creole languages, as exotic as the field may have been to many of his contemporary colleagues, was very much anchored in the traditional academic structures and canonical disciplines of European philology. This is not at all the case for many other creolists at the time who were basically laymen in linguistics or philology and published their research on creoles even though they had very different academic backgrounds as physicians, lawyers, or teachers for example (Krämer 2014: 188).

The university files also prove that Dietrich's official first name is *Adolf* and not *Adolphe* as it appears both under the article in *Romania* and in his letter to Hugo Schuchardt that he sent from Paris shortly after the publication of the article when he decided to spend some time in France in order to improve his French.[2] In his evaluation of Dietrich's dissertation, Schuchardt had criticized the linguistic "clumsiness" (*Unbeholfenheit*) of the text that was due less to grammatical mistakes than to a somewhat unidiomatic style. As the dissertation had the exact same subject as the article in *Romania*, that is, a comparative study of the creole languages of Réunion and Mauritius, and both were written in French, the published form was probably a corrected version of the original dissertation.

The documents from the university archives confirm the impression that all of Dietrich's work in creolistics was more or less a result of Schuchardt's support. The dissertation and, consequently, the article were based upon the materials that the professor had collected through his excellent network of contacts all over the world. Schuchardt himself concentrated predominantly on Portuguese-based creoles (Stein 2005), but he also published extensively on English-based and Dutch-based creole languages. He left his materials on and in Indian Ocean Creoles to his student because he deemed them insufficient for an in-depth analysis and besides that, he did not have the time to conduct the research himself (Dietrich 1891: 217). As a result, Dietrich's work is the first comparative study ever published on the creole languages of the Mascarene Islands (La Réunion, Mauritius, and Rodrigues). Dietrich made thorough use of Schuchardt's collection not only in terms of primary sources – Schuchardt had asked his local contacts to send him anything they had in creole, mostly songs, poems, tales and translated fables – but also in terms of the relevant literature that was available at the time.

The comparative perspective of Dietrich's work is what makes it unique in 19th century French creolistics as most other studies described only one single creole language.[3] Furthermore, Dietrich's approach is radically different from that of other French creolists in this period as he does not focus on racial difference as a core principle of creolization but rather on the structure of early colonial societies. As a result, he also takes into account social groups that would usually be subsumed with the wide and generalized categories of "Blacks" and "Whites". In this sense, Dietrich's analysis is much more fine-grained in terms of speaker groups and their influence on the process of creolization than most other works.

---

2 See Dietrich's letter to Schuchardt from October 18th–20th, 1891, ed. in Krämer (2013).
3 Adam (1883) is one of the few other examples as he compares creole languages from the Caribbean with those from the Indian Ocean. Outside French creolistics, comparative studies are much more widespread in the works of Portuguese creolists.

Dietrich makes a clear distinction between groups of slaves that were brought to the colonies from different places. To give but one example, he tries to understand why the nasalized French phoneme [õ] turns into [un] (spelled *oun*) in the pronunciation of one particular speaker group:

> Les bM ont-ils gardé plus de particularités des premiers colonisateurs que les autres, parce que, vivant dans les champs, ils n'avaient pas tant de rapports avec les nouveau-venus ? ou ces *oun* sont-ils d'origine mozambique? (Dietrich 1891: 224)
> [Did the bM keep more particularities from the first colonizers than the others because, as they lived in the fields, they didn't have as much contact with the newly arrived? Or are these *oun* of Mozambican origin?] My translation.

Dietrich uses abbreviations such as *bM* throughout the text in order to classify sociolinguistic groups with their particular historical backgrounds. In this code, *b* stands for *bourbonnais*, i.e. inhabitants of Réunion that was historically called île Bourbon, so that the speakers from this island can be told apart from speakers in Mauritius with a code beginning with *m*. The *M* in *bM*, then, is to indicate speakers with a background in Mozambique as they constitute a different social group and have a different linguistic background from slaves that were brought to the islands from Madagascar.

Following this methodology, Dietrich did not conceive the creole languages as uniform or homogenous, as most other creolists do at the time. He learned from his teacher Schuchardt that the inner variation of a language is not only interesting to study but crucial to the understanding of language change. Both variation and the very emergence of creole languages can be explained, according to Dietrich and Schuchardt, with the specific conditions and qualities of interaction in a colonial society, particularly during the formative period. The idea of racial predispositions of a speaker group due to their biological or genealogical background is not a part of Dietrich's reasoning. Hence, speakers that would be considered members of the same race within the racialist paradigm of creolistics can now be told apart and studied in great detail so that also microvariational features can be documented:

> On a donc [...] sur chacune de deux îles, un madécasso-créole qui a commencé à être influencé depuis 1820 par le mozambique et par d'autres langues, un mozambique-créole basé sur un madécasso-créole, et à Bourbon (en serait-il de même à Maurice ?) le parler des créoles des bois ou petits créoles. Ceux-ci descendent [...] des premier colonisateurs de Bourbon, et comme ils avaient moins de rapports avec les noirs parce qu'ils s'étaient retirés sur les hauteurs, ils ont pu garder une réminiscence du français [...]. (Dietrich 1891: 219)
> [Hence we have, in both islands, a Malagasy-Creole that began to be influenced by Mozambique and other languages from 1820 on, and a Mozambique-Creole based on a Malagasy-Creole, and in Bourbon (maybe also in Mauritius?) the dialect of the *créoles des*

bois or *petits créoles*. The latter are descendants of the first colonizers of Bourbon, and as they had less dealings with the Blacks because they had retreated to the heights, they were able to keep a reminiscence of French]. My translation.

This paragraph is so dense and rich in information that we can use it to analyze Dietrich's metalinguistic way of thought. To begin with, he refrains from calling the creole variety of the *petits créoles* any of the depreciative names that most other creolists accepted, such as *jargon* or *patois* (Mufwene 2002: 18–19, Boyer 2013). As a matter of fact, the English translation as *dialect* is somewhat inaccurate as the term *parler* is the least marked expression for a form of speech. Dietrich refrains from any classification of the creole languages or their subvarieties. Charles Baissac, for example, extensively discusses the terms *dialecte* and *patois* in the light of their supposed genealogical significance and finally rejects both in favor of the term *jargon*. He even goes as far as to deny Mauritian Creole the status of *language* altogether (Baissac 1880: xlvi–xlvii, Krämer 2014: 47). Dietrich avoids such debates and refrains from any term that carries the long-standing connotations of creoles as backwards, underdeveloped or ahistorical forms of speech.

Another important point in this paragraph is the reference to the variety spoken by the *petits créoles* (often called *petits blancs*). These inhabitants of Réunion form a particular social group as they used to be underprivileged inhabitants of the island's interior that, despite their European background, did not profit from the exploitation in the colonial system but lived in precarious autarchy in the less accessible parts of the island (Bourquin 2005). Even though they were visibly 'White' and would have been classified as such in the contemporary racial terminology, they spoke (and, as far as the group can still be distinguished as a separate part of La Réunion's society today, still speak) creole like the majority of the island's population. Consequently, speaking creole cannot be immediately associated to racial categories. In so far as other creolists mention 'white' creole speakers at all, they usually need to explain away this phenomenon, e.g. by saying that using creole is needed in order to be understood by 'black' speakers. Dietrich does not need to construct such artificial explanations as he generally conceives the languages independently from constructs of racial entities. It would have been easy for him to tie the proximity of the *petits blancs'* creole with French to their genealogical background. However, he exclusively deduces his findings from the fact that this part of the population rarely came into contact with speakers whose creole was more heavily influenced by non-European languages and hence did not pick up many of their particular basilectal features.

This does not mean that the category of *race* is completely absent from Dietrich's work. The overall structure of a colonial society was obviously shaped by the hierarchies of a racist system of exploitation in mass slavery. Therefore, the types of interaction that lead to the emergence and variation of creoles indirectly depend on *race* as a category that is socially constructed. It is not, however, a valid scientific category that would come to bear in Dietrich's work. In present-day terms, as a somewhat drastic and ahistorical interpretation of Dietrich's article, we might say that creolization in the colonial context is not due to *race* but to *racism*. The social sub-groups that the colonial system brought about give rise to specific types of interaction and communication, which can explain the internal variation of creoles as Dietrich described it.

While this independence from the predominant discourse on creole languages is certainly impressive, one important nuance must not be overlooked: Dietrich may not have taken into account any of the racialist arguments that most of his contemporaries use, but this did not immediately make him an antiracist. At no point in his publication did he openly contradict or condemn the prevailing racialist discourse in his field. This might have been due to his position as a young scholar in the rather hierarchical surroundings of an academic system where openly speaking out against established views and convictions could have seriously harmed one's career. Moreover, we have to take into account that the validity of *race* as a scientific category was not a matter of open debate in creolistics anyway. Much the contrary, Schuchardt's works – even though renouncing to a racialist overtone – were widely recognized and Schuchardt's respect was sought after by many creolists, including those that openly relied on racialist arguments. The paradoxical effects of hoping for Schuchardt's approval while at the same time conducting research that is heavily influenced by a racialist colonial discourse is only obvious today due to the increased awareness for such discursive discrepancies.[4] For creolists in the 19th century, this question simply did not seem a relevant subject to raise in a discussion among peers – a fact that clearly shows how deeply rooted the racialist discourse about creole languages must have been.

With these foundations in mind, we can turn to some more general observations in Dietrich's text. It does not only differ from the 'mainstream' of 19th century creolistics in that it avoids a racialist epistemology, but also in the fact that Dietrich applies a completely different style of writing and composing his article. Whenever he discusses individual features of the languages he is studying,

---

[4] Schuchardt's correspondence with René de Poyen-Bellisle is a striking example, see Krämer (2012: 146–148, 153).

he does not trace them back to any inherent characteristics of the speakers but merely to grammatical features in their heritage languages. In doing so, he still attains a certain level of generalization, for example in his classification of *Mozambique* as one linguistic category even though the area is multilingual and slaves from the coastal regions of Southeast Africa did not necessarily form a homogenous linguistic group. Despite this imprecision, Dietrich is much less categorical in his assertions. While the majority of creolists who drew on racialist arguments present their findings as basically irrefutable due to the tautological structure of a racial logic, Dietrich could not rely on such truisms and therefore often rather raises questions or expresses doubts instead of presenting a seemingly definite solution.

Dietrich also manages to avoid some of the encrusted stereotypes that can be found in many texts of late 19th century creolistics. One of the widespread ideas was that of creole languages as *child languages* – an idea that is linked to the colonialist attitude towards 'Blacks' as child-like beings that either need support in their development or that are limited in their understanding of the world (Krämer 2014: 46, 133–137). Dietrich also refrains from judgments such as the common interpretation of creolization as a sign of linguistic decay or the idea that the grammatical transformations supposedly are deformations or the result of damages to the French language. Much more so than most of creolists contemporary with him, Dietrich succeeds in his effort to look at language and its structures in an objective way so that his article is considerably closer to present-day scientific standards than for example the influential works by Charles Baissac or René de Poyen-Bellisle.

3 Is Adolphe Dietrich a 'colonial' linguist?

The particular position of Adolphe Dietrich's work within the field of 19th century creolistics allows us to deduce some general reflections for present-day research in colonial linguistics. To start with, we have to ask ourselves whether or not the historical sources we are dealing with – as far as scientific publications are concerned – are part of colonial *linguistics* or rather part of colonial *philology*. The term *philology* might be misleading at this point, due to the fact that it is used with very different meanings and connotations in different academic traditions. In this case, I am leaning towards the idea of *Philologie* in a German sense, that is the long-standing practice of studying both languages and texts in a common framework that allows to examine the intertwined meanings and characteristics of these two levels of expression (Krämer 2014: 9–10, Messling

2012, Trabant 2006: 186). Many descriptions of French-based creole languages from the late 19th century can be characterized as *philological*, rather than *linguistic*, studies. They would typically establish a close connection between the way creole languages emerged or were spoken and the narrative traditions in creole-speaking societies. Again, racial thinking played a key role in these reflections as both the structures of traditional creole oral literature and the structures of creole languages were deduced from alleged genealogical predispositions. Creole tales and stories were supposed to mirror the 'Black mind' just as much as the language was its product. In a form of triangular conditioning, language, text, and mind were used as tautological explanations for each other's characteristics (Krämer 2014: 167–185). Dietrich in contrast conceived language as an independent object of study without any interpretations of narrative traditions. Just like in Schuchardt's works, any text he dealt with was only a source of data for his structural analysis of creole grammar. Literary texts, like any other, were manifestations of language embedded in societal contexts that allow for a grammatical and variational examination of the material they provided.

Within this strictly limited scope, Dietrich is representative of the (then) spreading phenomenon of division of philology into what we today know to be linguistics and literary studies. Hence, it is absolutely admissible to classify Dietrich as a *linguist* whereas many of his contemporary colleagues have to be described more appropriately as *philologists*.

Dietrich's position as a linguist, then, seems unambiguous – but was he a 'colonial' linguist? There are three important factors that have a bearing on this question. Firstly, Dietrich was not a colonial agent in any way. He was neither a missionary nor a member of a colonial administration. Unlike many other French-creolists, he probably never even visited a colony and it seems unlikely that he even met a native speaker of a creole language. Austria, his home country, was much less involved in colonial activities than other European powers – even though this does not mean that Austria did not indirectly profit from the other countries' colonial projects through commerce or political cooperation. These facts certainly do not automatically exclude the possibility that an Austrian linguist would nevertheless perpetuate the hierarchical logic of a colonialist discourse.

Secondly, Dietrich himself did not directly communicate with other colonial agents. He made productive use of the material that Schuchardt collected through his own contacts and that he actively requested from his correspondents in the colonies. Often enough, the correspondents themselves did not directly provide the information that Schuchardt asked for but they used their own local networks to find the documents or testimonies that they subsequently sent to Graz. With this complex chain of testimony and data transfer in mind, Dietrich's work is definitely a result of 'third-hand' colonial linguistics since any piece of information passed through several hands from its source in the colony until it reached Dietrich's desk. Dietrich himself was not at all involved in the colonial societies or the local speech communities.

Thirdly, the most important factor lies in the fact that Dietrich's work does not carry the hierarchical conception of language and its speakers as found in other creolists' publications. He avoids any type of argument that would make his analysis of language accessible as a means of legitimization of a colonial regime. As a matter of fact, colonial linguistics is anything but uniform (see Errington 2008, Calvet 2002 [1974] for a thorough account of the implications of the study and use of language in a context colonial rule). Not all linguistic or philological works that were carried out in the historical frame of colonialism were necessarily 'colonial' in the sense that they confirmed the patterns of colonial thinking that ultimately supported the colonial system as such. This is not only an important nuance that has to be observed in the study of the history of creolistics, but it is a valid reservation in any metascientific study about this period of time. One emblematic example is Edward W. Said's influential work on European orientalism in the 19th century (Said 2003 [1978]) and the following criticism that helped nuance Said's view of a seemingly inevitable colonialist discourse about the languages and cultures of the so-called 'Orient' (Messling 2011: 364, Harpham 2009: 41). Dietrich's work, then, does not correspond to any of the typical patterns of 'coloniality' that we would find in other texts of the time (Mignolo 2012 [2000]: 13–17, Osterhammel & Jansen 2012: 19). A description influenced by colonial ideology would deny the colonial 'others' the potential to develop independently from European influence, therefore advocating the maintenance of European-dominated administrative, military or commercial structures. It would, furthermore, deny the potential and necessity of mutual cultural understanding or exchange and would instead construct the European language or culture as superior. None of these patterns can be found in Dietrich's text.

Yet, it seems insufficient to simply list Dietrich's article among the numerous examples of what has been called "kolonialzeitliche Sprachforschung" [linguistics in colonial times] (cf. Stolz et al. 2011). This term obscures the fact that Dietrich's work is epistemologically independent of a colonialist logic despite the fact that it was not only published during the colonial era but also with a subject that was intrinsically linked to the colonial past: The creole languages that Dietrich describes emerged as a direct consequence of colonialism, so any study of these languages is unthinkable without taking into account this historical background. This is why Dietrich's article is *potentially*, but not *acutely* colonial. In fact, Dietrich's work could just as easily have been published in the 1960s or 1970s after the main wave of decolonization. The state of affairs in creolistics was not yet advanced to an extent that would have allowed Dietrich to come to considerably different results. In that case, his work would have been difficult to classify as part of "kolonialzeitliche Sprachforschung" while it would have remained on the same (relatively low) level of 'coloniality' as it was at the time of publication in 1891. This is an important differentiation to make because the question whether or not Dietrich is a 'colonial linguist' is an epistemological rather than purely chronological one. This is not to say, of course, that the historical frame of his work is unimportant – it is merely not the exclusively decisive factor for determining the epistemological orientation of Dietrich's contribution to creolistics. Due to the historical link between Dietrich's object of study with colonialism and his epistemological distance to colonial thinking, we might rather classify him as part of *para-colonial linguistics*. This seems to be a more appropriate way to describe the study of a historically 'colonial' language (which emerged from the hierarchical and violent power structures of colonialism) from an outside perspective with little epistemological 'coloniality'.

In order to do fully understand the interplay of language and colonialism, it might be a productive approach to consider not only which part a linguist or philologist played in the legitimization of the colonial regime, but also which part they *did not play*. For today's colonial linguistics, such an analysis can give us important impulses for self-reflection about manner in which language in a (post-)colonial context can be scientifically studied without at the same time taking a colonialist stance towards either a language or its speakers. Dietrich teaches us how to avoid essentialisms and hierarchical thinking and his work is a stunning example of how linguistics can succeed in balancing both universalist and relativist views on cultural or social phenomena. Even though Dietrich did not become a widely known figure in the history of linguistics, neither in creolistics nor outside, his particular epistemological position is what makes his short and dense article valuable to both the historiography of creolistics and to postcolonial linguistics in general.

References

Adam, Lucien. 1883. *Les idiomes négro-aryen et maléo-aryen. Essai d'hybridologie linguistique.* Paris: Maisonneuve et Cie.
Baissac, Charles. 1880. *Etude sur le patois créole mauricien.* Nancy: Berger-Levrault.
Bourquin, Alexandre. 2005. *Histoire des Petits-Blancs de La Réunion.* Paris: Karthala.
Boyer, Henri. 2013. 'Patois': le déni français de glossonyme. In Georg Kremnitz (ed.), *Histoire sociale des langues de France*, 169–177. Rennes: Presses Universitaires de Rennes.
Calvet, Louis-Jean. 2002 [1974]. *Linguistique et colonialisme.* Paris: Payot & Rivages.
Dietrich, Adolphe. 1891. Les parlers créoles des Mascareignes. *Romania* 20. 216–277.
Errington, Joseph. 2008. *Linguistics in a colonial world. A story of language, meaning, and power.* Malden et al.: Blackwell.
Harpham, Geoffrey Galt. 2009. Roots, races and the return of philology. *Representations* 106. 34–63.
Holm, John. 2000. *An introduction to pidgins and creoles.* Cambridge: Cambridge University Press.
Krämer, Philipp. 2012. Hugo Schuchardt im Zentrum der frankophonen Kreolistik. Korrespondenzen mit Lucien Adam, Volcy Focard, Alfred Mercier, Alcée Fortier und René de Poyen-Bellisle. *Grazer Linguistische Studien* 78. 129–156.
Krämer, Philipp. 2013. Die Korrespondenz zwischen Adolphe Dietrich und Hugo Schuchardt. In Bernhard Hurch (ed.), *Hugo Schuchardt Archiv.* http://schuchardt.uni-graz.at/korrespondenz/briefe/korrespondenzpartner/1057 (last accessed November 6th, 2016)
Krämer, Philipp. 2014. *Die französische Kreolistik im 19. Jahrhundert. Rassismus und Determinismus in der kolonialen Philologie.* Hamburg: Buske.
Krämer, Philipp & Silvio Moreira de Sousa. 2017. Across the oceans and through the Alps: The intellectual networks of 19th century creolistics. *Grazer Linguistische Studien* 87. 107–132.
Messling, Markus. 2011. Text, Darstellung und Ethik: Jean-Pierre Abel-Rémusats kritische Philologie. *Romanistische Zeitschrift für Literaturgeschichte/Cahiers d'Histoire des Littératures Romanes* 35(3–4). 359–377.
Messling, Markus. 2012. Philologie et racisme. A propos de l'historicité dans les sciences des langues et des textes. *Annales. Histoire, Sciences Sociales* 67(1). 153–182.
Mignolo, Walter D. 2012 [2000]. *Local histories/global designs. Coloniality, subaltern knowledges, and border thinking.* 2nd edn. Princeton: Princeton University Press.
Mufwene, Salikoko. 2002. Typologie des définitions des créoles. In Claudine Bavoux & Didier de Robillard (eds.), *Linguistique et créolistique*, 17–34. Paris: Anthropos.
Osterhammel, Jürgen & Jan C. Jansen. 2012. *Kolonialismus. Geschichte, Formen, Folgen.* München: Beck.
Poyen-Bellisle, René de. 1894. *Les sons et les formes du créole dans les Antilles.* Baltimore: John Murphy & Co.
Said, Edward W. 2003 [1978]. *Orientalism. Western conceptions of the Orient.* 2nd edn. London: Penguin.
Stein, Peter. 2005. Hugo Schuchardt und die portugiesischen Kreolsprachen. In Annette Endruschat & Axel Schönberger (eds.), *Portugiesische Kreolsprachen: Entstehung, Entwicklung, Ausbau und Verwendung*, 201–215. Frankfurt a. M.: Domus Editoria Europea.

Stolz, Thomas, Christina Vossmann & Barbara Dewein. 2011. Kolonialzeitliche
    Sprachforschung und das Forschungsprogramm Koloniallinguistik: eine kurze Einführung.
    In Thomas Stolz, Christina Vossmann & Barbara Dewein (eds.), *Kolonialzeitliche
    Sprachforschung. Die Beschreibung ozeanischer und afrikanischer Sprachen zur Zeit der
    deutschen Kolonialherrschaft*, 7–27. Berlin: Akademie Verlag.
Stolz, Thomas & Ingo H. Warnke. 2015. From missionary linguistics to colonial linguistics.
    In Klaus Zimmermann & Birte Kellermeier-Rehbein (eds.), *Colonialism and Missionary
    Linguistics*. 3–25. Berlin & Boston: De Gruyter Mouton.
Trabant, Jürgen. 2006. *Europäisches Sprachdenken. Von Platon bis Wittgenstein*. München:
    Beck.
Turiault, Jean. 1877. Étude sur le langage créole de la Martinique. Deuxième partie. *Bulletin
    de la Société Académique de Brest* 2(3) (1875–1876). 1–111.
Vinson, Julien. 1884. Créoles (linguistique). In Louis-Adolphe Bertillon et al. (eds.), *Dictionnaire
    des Sciences Anthropologiques*, 345–347. Paris: Doin.

Yliana Rodríguez
Spanish-Guarani diglossia in colonial Paraguay: A language undertaking

Abstract: The colonial relationship during which the Guarani were reduced by the Jesuits – a religious venture that touched the deepest foundations of the Amerindian culture – led to a situation of diglossia. By reducing the Guarani language to writing, grammars, catechisms and sermons, the Jesuits orchestrated a standardization which would also serve them as a tool of manipulation. Guarani was not marginalized, let alone replaced by Spanish; Guarani was absorbed, and therefore altered. The preservation of the native language by the missionaries appears to have facilitated the religious conversion. The present chapter studies the diglossic relationship in which Guarani suffers a reorientation of some lexical semantic fields; focusing on the domain of religious language.

Keywords: colonialism, missionary linguistics, Guarani, Jesuits, language contact

1 Societal bilingualism and its consequences

In colonial Paraguay, both the colonial and republican power ranged from a policy of linguistic Europeanization of the Indians to the Indigenization of the officials directly engaged in the administration or evangelization of the Indigenous peoples. During the monarchy of Charles V, the strategic objective of the Spanish Crown was the rapid Hispanization of Indigenous elites and through them, the linguistic assimilation of Indigenous peoples. In practice, only the first stage of this program was attempted, without much success. Missionaries and other church officials, together with language conversion agents, preferred to preserve – especially in rural areas – the linguistic isolation of innocent peoples (Lienhard 1989). This preservation of the native language seems to have facilitated the religious conversion, since evangelizing the Indians in Spanish would have probably been less successful. In fact, once they had mastered the Indian's words, the Jesuits managed to effectively confront the shamans

---

Yliana Rodriguez, University of the Republic of Uruguay, Center for Foreign Languages, Montevideo, Uruguay. E-Mail: ylianarodriguez@gmail.com

https://doi.org/10.1515/9783110623710-008

(Ganson 2003). Therefore, it turned out more convenient for the missionaries to study the Prehispanic language.

1.1 The establishment of reductions

To protect the Guarani from colonists, authorities and *bandeirantes*[1], the Jesuits kept them in *reductions*, i.e. settlements for Indigenous people, where they would be evangelized and governed more efficiently.[2] More than 140.000 evangelized Indians lived in an area of 100.000 square meters (Merello 2015). These reductions were a closed system, with a very particular social, political and religious organization. The inauguration of the Jesuit reductions was set when the first provincial father – Diego de Torres – was invited by Hernando Arias de Saavedra to tackle the conversion of the many Indians present in the territory he governed. The missionaries were the only non-indigenous element of the reductions, and managed to make the Indians self-sufficient based on agriculture and livestock; in most cases with their own judicial and military systems (Santos 1992).

The reduction of the Guarani peoples of the province of Paraguay was a religious enterprise that would leave a serious imprint on their societies, affecting the most intimate fibers of their culture. Ruiz de Montoya, who was a missionary for twenty-five years in Paraguay, explains what his Order considered as reductions:

> Llamamos reducciones a los pueblos de indios, que viviendo a su antigua usanza en montes, sierras y valles, en escondidos arroyos, en tres, cuatro o seis casas solas, separados a legua, dos, tres y más, unos de otros, los redujo la diligencia de los Padres a poblaciones grandes y a vida política y humana, a beneficiar algodón con que se vistan. (Montoya 1989: 58)

1.2 Spanish-Guarani diglossia

In the linguistic domain, the colonial relationship derived into a diglossic situation, i.e. a form of social bilingualism, in which two linguistic systems with a functional distribution co-exist in a speech community, one with more prestige than the other one. In fact, one of the most profound colonial transformations that Guarani suffered was being ideologically situated in a relationship of de-

---

[1] 17th century Portuguese settlers in Brazil who raided the reductions in search for goods of all types and captive Indians that they would later sell as slaves.
[2] This system was introduced by the Franciscans (Curbelo 2014).

pendency towards Spanish (Meliá 1986). Despite this unbalanced relationship, the Amerindian language posed great resistance to being colonized.

In the present work, I use the term diglossia as Fishman does, i.e. extending Ferguson's (1959) original concept and rather strict definition of diglossia in 1967. Fishman understands that a diglossic speech community is not only characterized by the use of two language varieties but may also be characterized by more than two languages. Diglossia describes many sociolinguistic situations, from stylistic differences within one language or the use of separate dialects (Ferguson's distinction) to the use of different languages. The latter is the sense used in this chapter.

Diglossia phenomena are truly complex. There are many factors that interfere with its development. As Lienhard (1989) rightly points out, the geopolitical situation and its variations, the system of government, social and cultural policies (e.g. the prohibition or the formalization of native languages) and the interests of different sectors (abandonment or revitalization of indigenous languages by migrants) contribute to modify the forms, content and socio-cultural impact of diglossia. However, in the reductions, the modified Guarani would become the official language: the only one spoken and written (Curbelo 2013). Within the reductions there was never a mass of Spanish speakers, aboriginals always outnumbered Europeans. The status of primary language which Guarani had for the Jesuit missionary system allowed it to spread and consolidate its use in the region, from the dominant Western culture which appropriated it according to their interests (Curbelo & Bracco 2008).

The apparent or real linguistic complicity between church officials and the South American Indians provoked serious concerns in the upper echelons of colonial power. When faced with events like the Andean insurrection led by Tupac Amaru, the Spanish Crown insisted – once more – on the need for an immediate Hispanicization to better control the Indians. Nevertheless, during colonial times, no serious attempts were made in this respect (Lienhard 1989). The only efforts took place in urban centers, by making Spanish the official language for all bureaucratic activities as well as the language in which administration documents were registered.

The aboriginal language was the only system of communication through which links with the marginal sectors were established. Meanwhile, the upper echelons communicated in Spanish. Guarani was typically used by the lower sectors, while Spanish was the language of the state apparatus and the ruling classes. Concerning the emergence of this diglossic relationship, we must keep in mind that it was the result of a violent conquest, so the antagonism between the two systems was very strong.

1.3 Adopted elements

When two cultures with different languages meet, they frequently borrow terms from each other. These borrowed words are loanwords, i.e. words that were transferred from a donor language to a recipient language. One of the first definitions was provided by Haugen, who defined a loanword as "the attempted reproduction in one language of patterns previously found in another" (Haugen 1950: 212). All parts of a language – lexicon, morphology, and syntax – can, in theory, absorb adopted elements, however, only the lexicon provides a sufficient body of data with specific historical content; unfortunately, the potentialities of using borrowed elements as a guide to the historical interactions between societies have for the most part been given limited appreciation, even though they seem to be the most useful kind of linguistic evidence of all (Ehret 1976). The closer and the more intimate the contacts between peoples, the greater the inter-influence of one group upon the other (Kiddle 1952).

Given the close contact that Guarani had with Spanish, it is not surprising to find individual borrowed concepts as well as large semantic categories where loanwords are likely to appear. Missionizing was prominent in the acculturation of the aboriginals, particularly since they made notably successful attempts to use the native languages to win converts to Christianity; in fact, the frequency of loan translation is a result of this technique of persuasion (Kiddle 1952).

Lawrence Kiddle (1952) states that the exchanges of borrowings made between the groups can involve all aspects of the two cultures, whether they be material or non-material, such as customs, religious rites, and superstitions. He believes, just like Ehret, that by studying this phenomenon, we can understand not only the origin of common objects and practices but also the cultural processes by which traits have been diffused. He alleges that the foreign word used in a recipient language enables us to appreciate the development of specific cultures. He considers the case of Spanish particularly interesting, as it offers great possibilities for the study of linguistic and cultural diffusion in the period since the discovery of the New World. Other authors have also pointed out the relevance of the case of Spanish in South America. Stolz & Stolz state that

> the study of Hispanicization phenomena is of utmost importance. This is so not because there is something special about Spanish or any of the indigenous languages influenced by Spanish, but rather because of the almost global extension of the Spanish-speaking areas past and present. The wide areal distribution of Spanish as a contact language offers a next to unique, laboratory-like opportunity to observe perhaps hundreds of near parallel cases of contact between Spanish and an indigenous language. The genetic, typological and areal background of these native languages is far from being homogeneous. The only constant element is the donor language Spanish. A large-scale investigation into Hispani-

cization world-wide could thus become a major testing ground not only for universalist hypotheses but also for more individualized concepts of language contact processes. (Stolz & Stolz 2001 in Elizaincín Eichenberger 2002)

2 The conquest of Guarani

The missionaries' work was the humanist and spiritual counterpart of the military conquest and political domination (Abou 1995). Although the Spanish Crown applied a colonial language policy, there were a series of elements that did not cooperate with such undertaking. According to Meliá (1986), these factors were the weak Spanish emigration to Paraguay, the few tools available to introduce the European language, and the fact that Paraguay remained demographically Indigenous. With respect to the colonial transformation of Guarani, he points to its most salient features:

a. The Guarani language loses semantemes linked to their religion; some words ended up acquiring Christian meanings. Analogous cases can be found in other semantic fields, e.g. politics and other social values.
b. Hispanisms are incorporated, and numerous neologisms are created. At the same time, Spanish became impregnated with Guarani loanwords.
c. While Spanish cannot replace Guarani, it transforms it internally; not only by hispancizing its lexicon but also its grammatical categories. By the end of the 18th century, Creole Guarani was a new linguistic reality regarding the indigenous Guarani at the moment of contact.[3]
d. The Guarani language remained the colloquial language of the Indians and mestizos, whose chances to learn Spanish were minimal.

By reducing Guarani to writing, grammars, dictionaries, catechisms and sermons, the Jesuits implemented a standardization that would also serve as an instrument of manipulation. Guarani would suffer changes in virtually all its fronts, and The Society of Jesus would be responsible for many of them. Nonetheless, the Franciscans were the first to face the challenge of evangelizing the Indigenous peoples of the area that we now call Paraguay.

---

3 Today this creole has evolved to the dialect known as *Jopara*.

2.1 José Luis Bolaños and the first Guarani catechism

The Order of Friars Minor, better known as Franciscans, set foot in the province of Paraguay in 1542. The first to arrive were Fray Bernardo de Armenta and Alonso Lebrón, who founded a chapel in the surrounding area of Asunción, where they tried to indoctrinate the Indians, despite not speaking their language; in 1575 Fray Alonso de San Buenaventura and Fray Luis Bolaños would establish in Paraguay (Durán 1991). By the time these Franciscans arrived in Asunción, the Indians were rebelling all over the province of Paraguay, and they were becoming more and more hostile to the Spaniards. Therefore, the Franciscans decided to not only preach to the Indians but also reduce them into towns, i.e. *reducciones*.

The first stage of this challenging enterprise was hard. According to Félix de Azara (1809), when the Spaniards understood some Guarani they made their best effort to give them an idea of Christianity; they did their best but they could not achieve much. The Indians still associated the *pa'i* or priest with the Spanish oppressor who enslaved them (Durán 1991). Fray Luis Bolaños became interested in Guarani, and together with the help of some natives, colleagues and a soldier (Mitre[4]), he started studying the locals' language. According to Father Diego de Torres Bollo (1610, in Pastells 1949), when it comes to the teaching of the Indians' language, we owe the most to Bolaños, since he was the first to reduce it to art and vocabulary by translating into it the doctrine, the confessionary and the sermons.

It is worth remembering that the fact that Paraguay was an impoverished region made it uninteresting to the Crown. The cartas Annuas of those times state that the clergy did not want to go there. However, by translating the gospel into Guarani, and reducing Indians to towns, Bolaños managed to skip the biggest obstacles of their evangelization, i.e. their language and their dispersion (Durán 1991), making them more functional for the Spanish Crown's interests.

In the Synod of 1603 – one of the most important events of the colonial time – the evangelization of the Indians was lengthily discussed, and it was decided that the teaching of the doctrine would take place in Guarani. In that very Synod, Bolaños' Catechism was approved and named *official, compulsory and unique*. The catechism was composed of the sentences that he would have the Indians recite out. Both Franciscans and Jesuits would have the Indians study this Catechism by heart. Priests were ordered to teach and preach in Guarani, since it was the clearest and most widespread of all languages in the provinces

---

[4] Notes available in Mitre museum's library, Buenos Aires.

(Mateos 1603). What is more, the priests were required i) to know enough Guarani as to administer the sacraments, and ii) to know Father Bolaños' catechism and doctrine by heart in order to pronounce it every Sunday as well as in celebrations, and to teach it to the Indians (Mateos 1603: 341).

Fray Luis Bolaños was probably the first missionary the Indians heard speak in their language. His method allowed for the preaching and teaching of the doctrine in Guarani, which the Jesuits would later tackle with great impetus.

2.2 Guarani becomes a colonization tool

After the Franciscans, in 1610 came the Jesuits, who considered the Guarani language a copious and elegant language that could rightly compete with those of fame (Montoya 1639), i.e. Latin and Greek. Several testimonies highlight Guarani as *a language* and recognize it in all its linguistic dimension clarifying that it has nothing to envy European languages. A French missionary, Father Ignacio Chomé (in Meliá 1976), wrote in a letter that after learning Guarani, he remained astounded by its majesty and power of expression. He explained that each word is an exact definition of the thing in question, providing a definite and clear idea.[5] The Jesuit Felipe Salvador Gilij, in his book *Saggio di Storia Americana* (1782, in Meliá 1992: 24) also assures its magnificence by stating: "non sia dunque maraviglia, che questa lingua parlasi con piacere in tanti regni di America, e che tante Indiche nazioni, abbandonate quasi le loro lingue, preferiscono ad essa el parlare de' Guaranesi".

With regards to education, some Indians were granted the possibility of having access to primary schooling, particularly the children of high ranking officials and caciques. Indian teachers were in charge of those schools, where students learned how to count, read and write (Santos 1992). The latter began with Guarani and would later be done in Spanish, following the Crown's request. Schooling was meant to prepare those who would later occupy important ranks in the community, e.g. secretaries, mayors; but the masses refused to learn Spanish (Meliá 1986). The Jesuits never obliged them to study the European language; as they did not have much interest in the Indians learning it.

---

5 The text reads as follows: "Puedo asegurar, que después de haber alcanzado cierta facilidad en la lengua guaraní, he quedado admirado al comprobar en ella tanta majestad y fuerza de expresión. Cada palabra constituye una definición exacta de la cosa de que se trata, y da de ella una idea precisa y clara" (cited in Meliá 1976: 10).

In the Guarani language, the missionaries saw a privileged place where a more primitive notion of the divine had survived; and precisely because of this relationship with the divine, they respected it (Meliá 1986). Proof of this are the dictionaries, grammars, catechisms, confessionals, sermons and poetry assembled by missionaries throughout their entire stay in the Paraguayan province. Nevertheless, by doing this, they were also contributing to the domination by the Spanish Crown.

Another major issue for the Jesuits was the linguistic unity of Guarani. The Amerindian language was used in an extensive territory; this was the reason why the Spaniards immediately took it as a general language for the colonization and the mission (Meliá 1992). Missionaries, together with the discoverers, immediately perceived the general language character of Guarani, noticing that it proved to be a perfect tool for evangelization, not only because of its geographical expansion but also because its dialects were not far from each other.

3 The reduction and evangelization of Guarani

The many languages spoken in the province of Paraguay received a strong attention by the missionaries, who wrote – and in some cases published – grammars, vocabularies, doctrines, sermons and songs of the Amerindian languages (Santos 1992). These materials were used by new missionaries, who had to learn the natives' language, and by the priests themselves as a tool for their preaching and catechesis.

Any linguistic system has a phonological, syntactic, morphological and lexical sphere. In the case of Guarani, the missionaries reduced each of them. Fray Luis de Bolaños provided Guarani with a graphic system, resulting in a clear representation of the sounds of Guarani. This enterprise was improved a few years later by Jesuit Antonio Ruiz de Montoya. With this endeavor, the missionaries took Guarani from the category of unlettered language to that of language with a written code. By reducing a language to writing, the language and the community that speaks it are endowed with both blessings and punishments. This language now becomes a tool that allows exerting greater control over the society to evangelize; the Christian doctrine needed this. On the other hand, the passage from orality to writing is also a passage to literature. Literature that continues to this day.

It is still unknown how many printings existed in the missions. However, it appears to be the case that there was only one press which was transported among the many reductions, depending on their needs or maybe to familiarize the Indians with this skill (Plá 1975). According to Josefina Plá (1975), the press would have been built in situ, but there is no consensus on the material used. Some authors suggest it was made of hardwood, others copper, and some even propose brass, tin and lead. Despite the existence of the printings, handwritten copies were continued to be made, a task at which – according to a number of sources – the Indians were extremely skilled.

While having an alphabet is the kick-off to provide the Guarani language with a higher status, the existence of a grammar was prevailing. A grammatical reduction was also necessary if there were serious intentions to teach the language. The Jesuits needed instruments to help the missionary rookie in Paraguay acquire the grammatical schemes necessary to understand the Indians and be understood by them. Following the traditions of the time, the first grammars of Guarani were done taking as a model those of Latin and Greek; trying to make it fit the model of the eight parts of speech (i.e. noun, pronoun, verb, adverb, adjective, conjunction, preposition, and interjection). Not surprisingly, by relying on a Latin grammar, the Jesuits could not account for all the peculiarities of the Amerindian language (Meliá 1986). As the missionaries aspired to know the Indigenous language, they modified it, especially towards the Western models (Pulcinelli Orlandi 1993).

Contrary to what one expects when it comes to lexicography, Guarani lexicon was reduced by missionaries who were oblivious to the true being of that language. The reduction at the lexical level was selective as to which terms to incorporate. In fact, the words that could serve the needs of religion were prioritized. But we should not fail to recognize the lexicographical work of Ruiz de Montoya, in his *Tesoro de la lengua guaraní* and Paulo Restivo in the *Vocabulario de la lengua guaraní*. Montoya, in particular, left an invaluable synchronic analysis of the language. Despite their limitations, these works provide us with access to semantic values of Guarani that otherwise would have perished. Missionaries provided Guarani with its very first descriptions. Another example is Isaurralde's work, published in Madrid in 1759. José Insaurralde – another notable Jesuit scholar of the Amerindian language – published two opulent volumes under the title *Ara poru aguíyey haba* (Good use of time), written entirely in Guarani.

The Jesuits modified many Guarani concepts, mainly in the religious realm, e.g. the good and the bad; to this, we should add the modifications on space (e.g. private and public spaces, areas of worship) and political structures (e.g. the figures of the King and the Pope) (Curbelo 2013). Besides, both the soldiers and the missionaries of those colonial times were unaware that the Indians owned a different signifying system, as it was different they did not understand it; this led to a lack of dialogue which would later become the literary and grammatical reduction of Guarani (Myrland 1992).

3.1 The literary reduction

The ethnological literature on the Guarani is deeply marked by the colonial relationship, still not overcome (Meliá 1992). Therefore, the researcher has the task of overcoming the Guarani of history to reach the history of Guarani. It is not an easy job to hear the voice of the Guarani peoples through the Jesuit voices, but with the right methodological approach, it should be possible to approximate the feeling of the reduced Guarani Indian. We must not forget that these sources are virtually all researchers have, to approximate the reality of the Guarani. In other words:

> Com tudo isso, as fontes jesuíticas devidamente desideologizadas e lidas desde a clave hêrmeneutica do «reducionismo» que as caracteriza, seguem sendo, sem dúvida, o mais sério e amplo registro etnográfico sobre os Guarani «históricos». (Meliá et al. 1987)

The main literary work in Guarani, apart from the aforementioned grammars and vocabularies was translation, in particular, religious translation. We must bear in mind that in many Indigenous languages no literature existed, except for the Bible. The Indians did not write down any ritual chant, nor any prayers of their own, nor any myth or legend, even though they had them. The literary reduction could not overcome the colonial domination scheme in which it had been born (Meliá 1986). Over time, written Guarani would gain ground, though very slowly.

In the post-Jesuit period, after the expulsion of the Order in 1768, the Guarani-Jesuitical peoples began to produce their own literature (Chamorro et al. 2011). They wrote letters and above all, for decades, kept their own style, not only in handwriting and spelling but also in social and political thought. One of the most qualified Indigenous reduced representatives was Nicolas Yapuguay, Indian Cacique and musician.

3.2 The borrowing of religious lexicon

The Guarani spoken in the reductions suffered a semantic shift in certain areas of its lexicon, creating neologisms and borrowing Hispanisms – especially in the domain of religious language (Meliá 1986). Religious contexts can be especially revealing for the study of linguistic form and actions since they have the potential of involving people's most extreme and self-conscious manipulations of language (Keane 2007).

The missionaries were trained to be able to communicate and transcribe the foreign languages, paying particular attention to translating the fundamentals of the religious doctrine (Florines Pena 2013). The primary objective was to transmit the strongest ideas of the Christian dogma, i.e. the existence of only one God, the mystery of the Holy Trinity and of the Son of God who came back from death, all this with the ultimate intention of transforming the subjects' ideologies, remarks Florines Pena (2013). To that, he adds that it was never the intention to acquire the Amerindian language fully but to be able to generate simple grammatical structures to fulfill their objective. For instance, the name of Jesus Christ was not translated, but the word *Tupa* is borrowed to convey the idea of God.

Clastres (1993) provides a thorough exposition on the first chronicles about the Guarani religious beliefs and how the missionaries unanimously stated that those of the other side did not have superstitions. According to the Europeans, not only they did not know that there existed a true god – which did not surprise them – but they also did not have false beliefs. This caused amazement in the missionaries, but at the same time, they rejoiced in the fact that their work was simplified as they did not have to fight established beliefs.

There are much more accounts of the Tupi than the Guarani. On the former, Jéan de Léry (in Clastres 1993) points that the Indians do not adore any celestial or terrestrial god, and therefore as they do not have a formula nor an assigned place to meet, they do not pray, neither in public nor privately. Following Léry, religious beliefs were so foreign to them, that when they heard them exposing their theology, the Aboriginals remained in awe. This could be taken as proof that nothing of their own culture could be associated to such discourse. The Franciscan Claude d'Abbeville (in Clastres 1993) was also amazed by the fact that these peoples did not believe in any form of god, they did not perform sacrifices, they did not have priests, altars, temples and ignored what a prayer was.

What we know about the Tupi, should allow us to compensate – to a certain extent – what we do not know about the Guarani. Nevertheless, despite the homogeneity of the Tupi-Guarani culture, we cannot always extend to the latter what we know about the former.

The chronicles insisted on describing the Tupi-Guarani Indian world as non-religious, making them better prepared to receive theirs. Nonetheless, the Tupi-Guarani Indians did have a religion, though there are a plethora of differences with that of the Europeans. In fact, the missionaries borrowed many lemmata from the Aboriginal religion.

The Jesuit Pedro Lozano (in Clastres 1993) pointed out that the Guarani had a certain knowledge of God, and that they had even been able to understand that it was one, as they had given it the name *Tupa*, which means superior excellence. To that, he added that they attributed him the power of thunder and lightning – which scared them a lot – although they never tried to calm it through sacrifices or adoration practices. The missionaries assimilated the Guarani word *Tupa* to that of the Christian god, and *Aña* and *Giropari* to the demon. The Indians find the latter responsible for all misfortunes, be it a war expedition, the failure of a crop or a personal misfortune. Almost identical representations of the Christian devil. On the other hand, the case of *Tupa* needs a more attentive study. The assimilation of *Tupa* with the meaning of the Christian god was a missionary invention. It is evident that they needed a term to express the idea of God, and that their first preoccupation was to find it in the Indian's native language. Notwithstanding, even if some chronicles are right when they award Tupa the meaning of a divine thing, by making it an equivalent of God, they are endowing it with a sense that it did not have. In fact, the Indians believed that the creator of the sky, the earth and the animals on it – though not the sea nor the clouds – is *Monan*. Tupa has no role in the process of creation. Tupa is associated with the great cataclysms. If Monan is the creator, Tupa is the destroyer. But it should be borne in mind that the Tupi-Guarani did not worship any deity. This example proves Kiddle right, in that "when a foreign cultural element is introduced, a native name of a related element may become the name of the borrowed item" (Kiddle 1952: 180). But that is not an isolated example.

The religious practice of the Tupi-Guarani always involved the search of the Land Without Evil, which is intimately related to the idea that the Earth as we know it will be destroyed again, and Tupa as the architect of these destructions, was the true master of their destiny. Therefore, the missionaries were not wrong about the relevance of Tupa; but it is the image of the destroyer that governs the Guarani religion, and not that of the creator. They were mistaken in its significance, as nothing can be more distant in this Indigenous sign from the Christian idea of a creator god. Once again, a reduction was taking place, as the missionaries understood religion concerning the man-god dichotomy. No worship meant no god, and no god meant no religion. By forcing this godly discourse, through the imposition of an alien logic, they were reducing religion to its least significant expression.

When writing about the nature of God, Yves d'Évreux (1864) transcribes the notable arguments of an Indian who appears as an expert in theological debates: Tupa cannot be a man, if he has created everything; if he were a man, he would have been born from another man; Tupa is invisible, etc.

4 Conclusions

Most of what we know about the historical stages of Guarani is owed to the linguistic activities of missionaries. They were the ones to put Guarani into writing, they described its grammar and lexicon, and worked on its standardization to better manipulate them. Colonial missionary work was part of the political colonial rule. In spite of that, many missionaries' work went against the objectives of the official administration. For instance, the desire to translate new concepts into Guarani was not characteristic of the cultural changes enforced by the government representatives (Kiddle 1952).

Beliefs are mediated by the linguistic forms and practices through which they are remembered and transmitted (Keane 2007). The reductions provided a socio-political framework to an ambitious language undertaking; whose relevance could be equated with that of religious conversion or economic development. There is no doubt that speaking the language of the natives enabled the Jesuits to deploy the cultural and religious transformation of their mission. While Spanish penetrated Guarani in several linguistic levels, it fails to do so with complete success. The Spaniards were not able to implement formal instruments and significant social foundations for teaching their language, but they did manage to reserve for it specific semantic fields, which Guarani would never develop (Meliá 1986).

Guarani was not marginalized nor replaced by Spanish; Guarani was absorbed – and therefore altered – by another culture. The missionaries made Guarani their tongue, giving it not only a graphic representation system but keeping it alive. With writing and grammar, the Guarani language was undoubtedly strengthened, but the reduction in its semantics and discourse was made at the expense of irreparable and definitive cultural losses; the Guarani failed to grasp the meaning of important words of their ancient and traditional culture, or saw their significance substantially transformed (Meliá & Nagel 1995). As Bloomfield rightly pointed out: "cultural loans show us what one nation has taught another" (Bloomfield 1933: 458).

The religious conversion was social and cultural. With the evangelization of what we now call Paraguay, the Guarani Indian was deculturized. The fears expressed by Guarani shamans in 1614, at the start of the Jesuit reductions, have become prophetic: "those Indians told us we were spies [...] and that in the books we brought death" (Letters Annuas[6] II, Meliá 1986).

References

Abou, Sélim. 1995. Identité ethnique et identité culturelle. In *L'identité culturelle*, 29–46. Paris: Pluriel.
Azara, Félix de. 1809. *Voyages dans l'Amérique Méridionale*. Paris: Dentu. Retrieved from https://archive.org/details/voyagesdanslam02azar.
Bloomfield, Leonard. 1933. *Language*. New York: Holt.
Chamorro, Graciela, Thiago Cavalcante & Carlos Barros. 2011. *Fromteiras e identidades. Encontros e desencontros entre povos indígenas e missões religiosas*. São Bernardo do Campo: Nhanduti Editora.
Clastres, Hélène. 1993. *La tierra sin mal. El profetismo tupí-guaraní*. Buenos Aires: Ediciones del Sol.
Curbelo, Carmen. 2013. Avañe'ẽ, la "lengua de los hombres". La relación del guaraní con el territorio uruguayo. In Luis Ernesto Behares & Juan Manuel Fustes (eds.), *Aportes sobre la diversidad lingüística del Uruguay*, 95–107. Montevideo: Facultad de Humanidades y Ciencias de la Educación.
Curbelo, Carmen. 2014. Presencia indígena misionera. En Museo de Arte Precolombino e indígena, *Uruguay en guaraní: presencia misionera en Uruguay*. Montevideo: Mapi.
Curbelo, Carmen & Roberto Bracco. 2008. La construcción del espacio misionero y la toponimia en territorio uruguayo. In María Teresa Carrara (ed.), *Cambio cultural en Arqueología Histórica, Actas del Tercer Congreso Nacional de Arqueología Histórica*, 407–413. Rosario: Universidad Nacional de Rosario.
Durán, M. 1991. El catecismo Guaraní de Fray Luis Bolaños y sus disposiciones del sínodo de Asunción de 1603. *Indoafroamérica: cinco siglos de historia franciscana*. Montevideo: CEFRADOHIS.
Ehret, Christopher. 1976. Linguistic evidence and its correlation with archaeology. *World Archaeology* 8(1). 5–18.
Elizaincín Eichenberger, Adolfo Esteban. 2002. Romania Nova: lugar de contacto del español con otras lenguas/culturas. Spanish in Society Conference. Primer Simposio de Lingüística Hispánica del Reino Unido. Guidford, England: Surrey University.
Évreux, Yves de. 1864. *Voyage dans le Nord du Brésil, fait durant les années 1613 et 1614*. Leipzig: Franck.
Ferguson, Charles A. 1959. Diglossia. *Word* 15. 325–340.
Fishman, Joshua. 1967. Bilingualism with and without diglossia; diglossia with and without bilingualism. *Journal of Social Issues* 23. 29–38.

---

[6] The Letters Annuas of the Jesuit Province of Paraguay comprise vital historical sources for the reconstruction of the work carried out by the Company of Jesus in the territories of the River Plate.

Florines Pena, Andrés. 2013. Las lenguas de los pueblos originarios. In Luis Ernesto Behares & Juan Manuel Fustes (eds.), *Aportes sobre la diversidad lingüística del Uruguay*, 95–107. Montevideo: Facultad de Humanidades y Ciencias de la Educación.
Ganson, Barbara. 2003. *The Guaraní under Spanish rule in the Río de la Plata*. Stanford: Stanford University Press.
Haugen, Einar. 1950. The analysis of linguistic borrowing. *Language* 26. 210–231.
Keane, Webb. 2007. Language and religion. In Alessandro Duranti (ed.), *A companion to linguistic anthropology*, 431–448. Oxford: Blackwell Publishers.
Kiddle, Lawrence B. 1952. Spanish loan words in American Indian languages. *Hispania* 35(2). 179–184.
Lienhard, Martin. 1989. *La voz y su huella*. México: Ediciones Casa Juan Pablos.
Mateos, Francisco. 1603. El primer concilio del Río de la Plata en Asunción. *Misionaria Hispánica* 16(78). 257–359.
Meliá, Bartolomeu. 1976. *Guaranies y jesuitas. Ruinas de una civilización distinta*. Asunción: Ediciones Loyola.
Meliá, Bartolomeu. 1986. *El guaraní conquistado y reducido. Ensayos de etnohistoria. Ensayos de etnohistoria*. Asunción: Biblioteca Paraguaya ed Antropología.
Meliá, Bartolomeu. 1992. *La lengua guaraní del Paraguay. Historia, sociedad y literatura*. Madrid: Editorial Mapfre.
Meliá, Bartolomeu & Liane Maria Nagel. 1995. *Guaraníes y jesuitas en tiempo de Misiones*. Asunción: CEPAG.
Meliá, Bartolomeu, Marcos V. de A. Saul & Valmir F. Muraro. 1987. *O Guarani: uma bibliografia etnológica*. Santo Ângelo: Fundação Missioneira de Ensino Superior.
Merello, Enrique. 2015. *El gregoriano perdido de los guaraníes. Ejecución y copiado del canto gregoriano en la "República Jesuítica" del Paraguay*. Asunción: Editorial Arte Nuevo.
Montoya, Antonio Ruiz de. 1639. *Tesoro de la lengua guaraní*. Madrid: Iuan Sanchez.
Montoya, Antonio Ruiz de. 1989. *Conquista Espiritual hecha por los religiosos de la Compañía de Jesús en las provincias del Paraguay, Paraná, Uruguay y Tape*. Rosario: Equipo difusor de Estudios de Historia Iberoamericana.
Myrland, N. 1992. El cristianismo guaraní en los siglos xvi, xvii y xviii. *Boeltín de Historia y Geografía* 9, 97–103.
Plá, Josefina. 1975. *El barroco hispano guaraní*. Asunción: Editorial del Centenario.
Pastells, Pablo. 1949. *Historia de la Compañía de Jesús en la Provincia del Paraguay*. Madrid: CSIC.
Pulcinelli Orlandi, Ení. 1993. La danza de las gramáticas. La relación entre el tupí y el portugués de Brasil. *Iztapalapa* 29. 54–74.
Santos, Ángel. 1992. *Los jesuitas en América*. Madrid: Mapfre.

Wolfram Karg
Construction of (transcontinental) railways as a means of colonization

A corpus-based analysis on the German colonial discourse in postcolonial perspective

Abstract: This paper presents an analysis of comments on the construction of (transcontinental) railways in the context of German colonialism. The comments are taken from minutes of parliamentary debates in the German Reichstag, in articles published by dedicated colonial magazines and also in encyclopedic entries, all of them published in the period between 1900 and 1910. The corpus-based analysis is focused on contrastive-connectives as linguistic expressions of contrasting may serve as a demarcation strategy between various actors in colonial circumstances. In the examples presented in this paper, the demarcation is between Germany and Britain, with railway building serving as sign of power over the respective areas.

Keywords: contrast, connectives, scramble for Africa, Baghdad Railway, effective occupation

1 Historical background

1.1 German traces in Africa's infrastructure

Almost all present-day travel books focusing on African states, such as Tanzania or Namibia, recommend rail transportation to travelers in, at least, some parts of the country. Namibia's *Desert Express* offers convenient package tours, and especially tries to attract customers with promises of an extremely luxury service. In Tanzania, *Pride of Africa*, which is operated by *Rovos Rail*, similarly advertises extraordinary travel experiences tailored almost exclusively to tourists' needs. Most travelers on these trains will not think too much about the historical origins of the tracks on which they travel. The majority of the railway

---

Wolfram Karg, University of Ss. Cyril and Methodius in Trnava, Namestie J. Herdu 2, 91701 Trnava, Slovak Republic. E-Mail: wolframkarg@yahoo.de

lines operated in present-day Africa are remnants of earlier colonial activities in the region. For Tanzania and Namibia, which were colonized by Germany, the railway lines were planned and built by German colonial occupants. Thus a considerable number of station buildings and other facilities clearly show architectural features typical of Europe and, in particular, of Germany, which constitute rather reliable indicators of colonial influence. However, African railways cannot be considered all-out success stories, save in a few exceptional cases (one of these being, at best, the Egyptian National Railway). Due to financial problems, tracks and rolling stock are outdated in many postcolonial countries, and some routes have even had to be closed down completely because refurbishment cannot be carried out due to lack of funds. There is a vast array of possible reasons for this sorry situation, and it is more than likely in many cases that mismanagement by local authorities has played and still plays a vital role.

This essay is, however, not meant to put blame on infrastructural politics and local management within the African railway companies, not least because authentic sources do not provide enough data to solidly support any claims along these lines. Moreover, there is the risk of conveying a misplaced feeling of superiority on the part of Europeans and, at the same time, belittling the mistakes that were made in colonial times. But what is comparatively well documented are the concomitant debates around the planning, the administrative supervision, the funding, and the construction work of railway lines in the German colonies at the time. An examination of those sources is the linguistic basis for this essay, which aims to analyze a theme-based discourse by means of contrast relations.

There are several reasons for the choice of contrast connectives for close inspection. On the one hand, contrast connectives are linguistically well defined so that computational processing of large quantities of data is facilitated (see Rudolph 1996); on the other hand, explicit contrast relations in texts highlight differences of opinion and support the exact delineation of standpoints in relation to each other. The differences of standpoints then can be used to identify constructions of identity since they determine and showcase whether individuals belong to groups with similar or identical positions or not. In order to avoid unsuitable overload of data, it was decided to limit analysis to railway building in a transcontinental context although constructions of identity could be found in quite a number of semantic fields.

Obviously, a short outline of the historical background is essential to provide the basis for investigations of linguistic contrast relations. The following practical part applies theoretical principles of cognitive linguistics to the systematic analysis of contrast relations in colonial texts in order to describe the functioning of contrastive constructions of identities.

1.2 Competition of colonial powers in Africa

The first railway line in Africa was the connection between the two Egyptian ports of Alexandria and Suez (see El-Din 2010: 11). It was the northern starting-point of what later became known as the Cape to Cairo Railway, which linked the northern British territories with their colonies in the south of the continent. Great Britain[1] was far from being the only agent in the area, though. All the imperialist European powers took part in the race for African territorial occupations, since the continent was thought to be rich in natural resources and, at the same time, appeared not to be owned by anyone.[2] Accordingly, Pakenham (1992) chose the title "Scramble for Africa" to describe recklessness and avarice as the driving forces of imperialism. Compared to its competitors the German Empire joined the race at a rather late stage, but tried then to assert its ambitions by means of regiment.

Against this backdrop Chancellor Bismarck convened the so-called "Congo Conference" in November 1884, which dealt not only with the Congo, but also targeted the whole of Africa for an agreement on how to distribute its parts among the European colonial powers. The most important result was that spheres of influence were agreed on and that this agreement was – from the German point of view – binding on all conference participants. A contemporary cartoon illustrated this in a pictorial representation showing Bismarck apportioning a cake with the heads of state from all participating nations watching him (xylograph in *L'illustration* 1885). In actual fact, the Berlin agreement of 1884 was just about legalities and judicial matters and not about determining borders nor about percentages in a general land grab (see Eckert 2013: 141).

---

[1] Throughout this contribution the term *Great Britain* is used to refer to what ultimately became the United Kingdom of Great Britain and Northern Ireland. The historically correct term for the period of the early 19th century would be *United Kingdom of Great Britain and Ireland*, which is rarely used in Germany. In colonial contexts the term *British Empire* could also be used. *Great Britain* reflects the German conception of the predecessing state of today's UK best and is consequently used in all cases in order to avoid confusion through a wide array of terminology.

[2] The concept of owning land was not necessarily known to the colonized inhabitants, creating a rather large cultural misunderstanding about who effectively could use the land for their own purposes.

One of the legal provisions discussed in Berlin was the principle of "effective occupation" (Eckert 2013: 141). It stipulated physical occupation as a prerequisite for the acknowledgement of property rights in the regions concerned. A key element in the process of "effective occupation" was railway building, which not only aimed at providing a means of transportation, but also at effectively asserting the right of occupation in the legal sense defined above. That is why it mattered so much to first set up a network of railway lines. In addition, the railway facilities could later assist the construction of new towns and settlements inclusive of delivering necessary supplies for inhabitants and, in return, move raw materials and agricultural products to the ports. Both purposes were served according to later statistical evidence.[3] In the event of armed conflicts with the local population large quantities of troops and armaments could be deployed, as was the case in the Herero insurrections in the then German South-West Africa, which is now Namibia.

Besides the employment of railways as means of transportation for civil and military goods, they were used to communicate the message of occupation and land appropriation quite similarly to language signs or to indexical signals, which were meant to establish the occupants as the rightful masters of the land.

The Cape to Cairo Railway was not only a demonstration of "effective occupation" by way of linking the northern and the southern British territories, but also served private business activities across the whole continent. It was primarily the businessman and politician Cecil Rhodes who fiercely promoted the railway project even though the idea itself was said to originate from one of his schoolmates. Even the *Daily Telegraph* newspaper, at some stage, claimed to have propagated the idea for the first time citing the adventurer and explorer Stanley as their source of inspiration (Ramutsindela 2007: 13). The benefits from the Cape to Cairo Railway project were manifest when compared to the traditional naval route around the Cape of Hope or a conventional land crossing of the continent. Rail transport would have been by far the fastest option in respect of travel time. Its particular importance for the British Empire derived from their colonial interests in India, which would have been brought into easier reach. A further motive for the railway project was the British claim on a world-wide empire "on which the sun never sets". Although the source of this motto has never been clarified, the policy characterized in this way was evidently adopted by Britain (Morris 1978, Vance 2000, Miller 2003). Germany's attitude towards

---

[3] The German administration's balance sheets for the east-African colony contain a separate entry on the financial profits from railway services; the gains more than tripled in the period between 1904 and 1914 from 171 000 Mark to 653 000 Mark (Volkmann 1920: 616).

this British ambition was ambivalent, as can be seen from the quotations analyzed below. This ambivalence is likely to be the reason why in these passages contrast relations are so frequent, since they resulted from efforts to give shape to a political view which often differed from several others by not more than minor details.

To be sure, there was no general resistance to plans of a transcontinental railway among the social groups concerned in Germany. Rail connections like the Orient Express Service, which was transcontinental in that it connected two continents, give evidence of German attitudes. What distinguished the Orient Express from the African project were two special features: It made use of existing rail tracks and it was operated by a private company, the French CIWL, which depended on each of the public administrations that were responsible for the area crossed by the railway line. CIWL had to sign special contracts with each of them before it could start its service (Reinhardt 2015: 229, Dienel 2009: 115–116).

A second case of transcontinental rail service was the Baghdad Railway, which the Orient Express connected to with Istanbul being the point of junction. The German empire considered this interconnected rail system as a matter of prestige, particularly because railway and steam technologies were regarded as signs of up-to-date progress (Reinhardt 2015: 234). With hindsight, the luxury rail service projects, both the ones that reached only planning stage and those that were actually completed, indicate that the railway system of the future was not just meant to meet basic needs, but were to be developed into a regular and reliable traffic system. The two examples show that the European powers were not only focused on their African interests, but were equally committed to play a respected role as participants in the competition for hegemony among imperialist European powers.

2 The discourse linguistic framework for data analysis

2.1 Debates about railway building as colonial discourse data

Principally, the idea of using railways as a means to the end of "effective occupation" was simple and appeared easy to put into practice. As the building projects, more often than not, were funded by public money in the imperial era, disputes on the costs of colonization arose quite quickly. Such disputes are documented in minutes of parliamentary sessions, in colonial magazines, and in general as well as specific encyclopedias. These texts constitute the source corpus and provide the data for the analysis of contrast connectives and the effects of their use in the identity formation of colonial agents. For this purpose the inquiry is based on just about 1 million tokens from an extended version of the Bremisches Basiskorpus Deutscher Kolonialismus (BBDK), which has been compiled at Bremen University (Warnke & Schmidt-Brücken 2013). The corpus represents the general discourse mode in this inquiry and has to mirror discourse features as precisely as possible (Scherer 2006: 27). For practicability the corpus will be divided up into three sections, which are derived from the way knowledge is constituted: *constitution, argumentation, and distribution* of knowledge (Warnke 2009: 121). Each of the three sections is linked to a particular text genre, the primary communicative function of which relates it with a factor in the constitution of knowledge. According to Warnke & Schmidt-Brücken (2013), the entries in encyclopedias correspond to the constitution phase of knowledge, the parliamentary debates are primarily argumentative, and the magazine articles function mainly as distributors of knowledge because of their comparatively high circulation and the frequency of publication (up to two editions per week). The term "knowledge" in this context does not refer to the stock of information in an individual, but rather to socially shared knowledge. This knowledge is negotiated in discourses in the shape of language-based utterances (see Warnke 2009: 135). In the process of knowledge constitution language is not just the medium that carries chunks of information, but it substantially influences the process of knowledge transfer through choice of words, mode of presentation, and elimination of some parts of information. In this way language is not only *modus operatum*, but also *modus operandi* (Jäger 2007: 21). Therefore the mode of language use is of major significance to discursive practice and, on the other hand, makes discourse a rewarding object of linguistic analysis. In the following section some aspects will be discussed which are concerned with discourse analysis as a legitimate approach in linguistics.

2.2 Colonial discourses as objects of linguistic inquiry

In a study much heeded among linguists, Busse & Teubert (2013 [1994]) posed the question whether discourse is a legitimate object for linguistic research. For specific attention they recommend the following concerns to linguists:

to find out, document, and relate to each other, the linguistic manifestations of alternative views and conceptions, of paradigms of thinking and meaning, and of their epistemic foundations and guiding ideas. (Busse & Teubert 2013 [1994]: 20, transl. by the author)

This agenda determines that discourse analysis, as seen by Busse & Teubert, is to concentrate on the part that language plays in exchanges of opinions, attitudes and views. The emphasis on linguistic priorities seems almost tautological, however, there are undeniably a number of aspects which remain unmentioned but are relevant to the agenda Busse & Teubert have set out. They design their model of linguistic discourse analysis against the backdrop of historical semantics. Consequently, the main focus is on the historical development of concepts and their expression in language; this approach relies on the analysis of individual words in certain contexts. The approach suggested in the following lines is remarkably different, since connectives can hardly be treated as words with a semantic history of their own.

Historical semantics is applicable to expressions only if they carry a clearly determinable meaning and can be described in theoretically defined terms, like in sememe analysis. In this sense, connectives do not have a meaning, at least not one that can change on certain contextual conditions, including historical contexts. It is true that such changes cannot be totally excluded and there are sources which embrace the idea of meaning with connectives (Pasch et al. 2003: 1), however, this cannot be claimed to be generally accepted in linguist circles. With connectives, meaning is less defined through semantic components but through structural function. This is why they were often seen as grammatical phenomena, since they are used as a means to secure coherence in any text without relying on a specific content. What is content-specific in a connected series of propositions are the components of a complex sentence, not the connectives. For this reason, it is the semantic content of the components that will be the linguistic basis in the following explorations, not that of individual words. This approach is based on Foucault's description of the term "Discourse" as "a number of propositions which belong to the same formation system" (Foucault 2013 [1969]: 156). With this definition the foundation stone is laid for a kind of discourse analysis that is based on propositions. By means of an extended concept of sign discourse analysis is no longer dependent on isolated word signs.

Instead, language signs are conceived as propositions, which can consequently be examined as parts of more complex semantic units (Warnke et al. 2014). Propositional discourse analysis opens up the possibility to examine conditions and functions of language in the process of generating and distributing information and knowledge. Thus propositional discourse analysis even reaches out beyond the boundaries of individual content units and makes comprehensive use of theories developed by Foucault (Foucault 2013 [1969], Reisigl 2006, Mills 2007, Warnke 2007) and Bourdieu (1974).

The conceptualization of colonial discourses as objects of linguistic scrutiny mends a gap in research. Faulstich (2009) states in her survey of concept history that chronological studies of language have so far neglected the history of colonialism. In other areas of Germanic Linguistics, hesitant beginnings can be observed in the examination of colonial language use.[4] In German Studies as well as among the general public the reader may, all too often, come across the obviously wrong opinion that German colonialism was too short-lived to be of any significance, or, what is more, people might even not know that Germany had colonies at all. This shows the urgency of a systematic and methodologically well-founded investigation of Europe's and Germany's colonial past to come to terms with this period of language use. The resources are surprisingly extensive for the rather short time they cover, and they are fairly easy to access because many documents have been deposited in archives.

3 Identities of agents indicated by contrast relations

Economically, the German Empire's attempts at colonization did not pay off because the costs were too high and the financial returns did by far not meet expectations (Conrad 2011: 54). Nevertheless, the colonized territories were not given up since they were thought to secure a high status in Europe and the rest of the world. The then Emperor, Wilhelm II, had decided to transform his country into a world power like Great Britain or France. Part and parcel of such a status was the possession of colonies; they could also be used to compare German society favorably with allegedly less developed countries. Particularly in the context of German colonial aspiration, this kind of identity formation gains huge significance because it is seen as consummation and continuation of German nation-building. The proclamation of the German Empire (Deutsches Kaiserreich) in 1871 was an act of national unification absorbing many different independent territories into one nation state (Speitkamp 2014: 16–17) for which a common identity had to gradually develop. How urgent the rise of a German

---

[4] The colonial engagement of Germany lasted just about 50 to 60 years including preparatory activities, actual colonization, and revisionist policies during the interbellum years of the 20s and 30s.

nation state was felt to be, can be seen in the leading role that the German empire adopted at the so-called Congo Conference (Berman 2003, Lindner 2011: 8, Stolz et al. 2011: 8, Schonauer 2012: 13). The sense of impatience expressed itself in what is often referred to as a race, a metaphor also used by Pakenham, to describe this Europe-wide competition for greatness and enhanced international importance. In Germany the search for a national identity consisted of two components: On the one hand, there was the desire to be acknowledged as a world power by other European nations such as Great Britain, France, or Belgium – textual data that belong to this kind of identity include primarily images of equality with other European nations, as can be expected. On the other hand, the conditions met with in the colonized territories were used to contrast them with one's own supposed superiority.

This differentiation corresponds to what Vester (1998) describes as the two tendencies in a human being's development: identification and refutation. Identification denotes the acknowledgment of identical characteristics, whereas refutation is the act of conspicuously contrasting oneself to the other (Vester 1998: 100). A second dichotomy used by Vester (1998) differentiates between the individual and the collective. His usage of the term "Self" refers to personal identity of an individual. In everyday talk, identity is the word that describes this same notion. In colonial theory, however, the concept of identity is applied to nations and is therefore a collective phenomenon. What complicates the matter is the fact that the texts analyzed in this study, though representative of national attitudes, were written by individuals from their own personal perspectives.

Vester (1998) tries to overcome this problem by pursuing a constructivist approach, according to which identity is defined as a process with ever preliminary results (Vester 1998: 96). In the course of such a process individual identity and conformity with a collective are two elements in personal behavior, perception, and reflection. As all this can be practiced individually as well as collectively, the difference between the two forms of identity, individual or collective, boils down to a gradual distinction between the greater effort in the development of individuality as opposed to the more easily available socialization in a community (Vester 1998: 96). But the question remains how to induce collective identities from individual authors.

A close inspection of the texts selected for analysis will reveal that all the contributors to the corpus have written their texts not as private citizens, but as representatives of certain organizations, social groups, or authorities. This is due to the fact that text selection for the corpus was based on the criteria of public relevance or availability. So the authors were very likely to be aware of their public resonance and the fact that they were expected to write on behalf of certain groups of colonial agents (government, opposers of colonization, settlers etc.). This awareness becomes most obvious in parliamentary speeches (notwithstanding the interference of parliamentary script writers) delivered by MPs, who were already seen as representatives of most, if not all, people at that time. Similarly, with texts from periodicals as well as with entries in encyclopedias the target audience of a broad public readership is noticeable. On the other hand, the texts are and remain individual statements, which are representative of collective opinions and views, but were not collectively produced. Arguing from a constructivist point of view, according to Vester (1998), one can conclude that individual and collective identities are in dynamic balance with each other whereby both elements are in constant mutual exchange. What has to be taken into account additionally is the fact that the interaction is language-based and therefore influenced by specific usages of word signs, which may revise or vary meanings of utterances (Jäger 2007).

This additional aspect of identity formation results in a further difficulty by raising the question how such a variable material can be systematically examined. The answer is to concentrate the analysis on a specific linguistic phenomenon. As the notion of contrast has been proposed as one of two factors of identity formation (Vester 1998), it is plausible to conclude personal identities from linguistic contrast relations in texts produced by the respective personalities. It is this that the following analyses are going to do.

According to many linguists *contrast* is not considered to be a linguistic term (Rudolph 1996: 5), and that is why it is not easy to find a straightforward definition in research literature. The most promising approach to this difficulty would be to subsume all relations that express a logical opposition under the term *contrast relations*. Accordingly, *contrast* would be the general term for both *concessivity* and *adversity* (Breindl 2004: 226). A distinction is still necessary between contrast as a grammatical category and contrasting as a speech act, the latter of which is used to relate propositional content. This is what Rezat (2007 and 2009) refers to when she talks about concessivity as a grammatical phenomenon and the corresponding speech act in rhetoric. Contrast connectives or contrast relations are the main tools of contrasting, although this can also be expressed by other linguistic means, like e.g. the coordination of clauses which are in opposition with each other without an explicit connective of contrast. Di Meola (1997) explains this case by claiming that two causative relations underlie its structure implicitly. The following example is to illustrate the distribution of relations. The dotted lines signify the absence of the respective elements.

The clauses which are attributable to A_1 and B_1 express reasons or causes. Clauses of this kind will be called relates or related clauses in the following lines. This terminology results from the structuralist principle, which states that segmented but unclassified units (clauses) are to be distinguished from classified units (relates).

(1) Although Beate[5] is ill, she goes to work, for she has an important appointment.

Beate is ill.   Beate does not go to work.

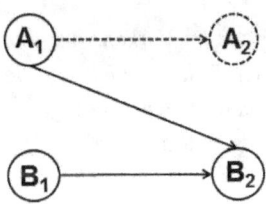

Beate has an important appointment.   Beate goes to work.

Figure 1: Contrast relations as double causative relations (according to Di Meola 1997: 33).

From proposition A_1, which states that Beate is ill, a normal conclusion would be that she does not go to work (König 1991: 634). In the case given here this conclusion does not apply because the speaker claims instead that B., indeed, goes to work (clause B_2). The reason why B_2 applies and not A_2 is added in B_1. In many cases, relations are not expressed explicitly, which directs the focus of attention to the actual incompatibility of cause and effect, or reason and conclusion.

The analysis of causes/reasons which are considered as normal (called *normality standard*) can reveal what the speaker/writer regards as norm. An analysis includes the aspect of what sort of normality standards and deviations from them are related to each other. As, usually, no agents are mentioned, their identity concepts have to be induced from other situationally relevant factors like historical context as well as particular ways in which issues are addressed in a specific context, thus revealing certain attitudes towards these issues. As indicated by the title, in this particular study the focus of analysis will be on transcontinental railway construction.

---

5 Translated from German. *Beate* is a common German first name. Translation by the author.

4 Analysis of selected contrast relations

What follows is an analysis of three items which have been found in the BBDK. First, two items will be given which refer to the Baghdad Railway; another item will be about the Cape to Cairo Railway. The analysis is based on the original German text, for better understanding, all text samples will be accompanied by an English paraphrase.

(2)   *Eine gewisse Konkurrenz im Verkehr mit dem fernen Osten ist dem Suez-Kanal in der Sibirischen Bahn erwachsen, die einen Teil des Personen und Postverkehrsnach Ostasien an sich gezogen hat; noch fühlbarer wird einst der Wettbewerb der Bagdadbahn werden.* <u>Doch</u> *wird dies auf die Rentabilität des Kanals kaum einen wesentlichen Einfluss ausüben. Denn für den Frachtenverkehr nach dem fernen Osten kommen natürlich die viel teureren Eisenbahnen im allgemeinen erst in zweiter Linie in Betracht.* (Kolonie und Heimat 23.05.1909: 5)
[A certain rivalry for the Suez Canal has evolved due to the Siberian Railway, which has attracted some part of the passengers and the mail transport that previously took the Suez route to East Asia. The Baghdad Railway will have an even greater impact on the transport business there. <u>However</u>, this will hardly have a significant influence on the profitability of the Canal. For the naturally costlier railway service is only second choice for freight traffic to the Far East.]

To analyze and classify the clauses in this multiple compound of sentences, it is useful to segment the item into its parts and thus to identify contrast relations and underlying normality standards. The letter labels indicate clauses belonging to the same syntactically complex sentence. Capital letters refer to main clauses, regular letters to subordinate clauses. In the German text passage, word order will be adjusted to grammatical rules when clauses are separated from their syntactic context.

In the above item the following clauses can be identified:

(2)   A.   *Eine gewisse Konkurrenz im Verkehr mit dem fernen Osten ist dem Suez-Kanal in der Sibirischen Bahn erwachsen.*
      Aa. *Die [Sibirische Bahn] hat einen Teil des Personen- und Postverkehrs nach Ostasien an sich gezogen.*
      Ab. *Noch fühlbarer [für den Suezkanal] wird einst der Wettbewerb der Bagdadbahn werden.*

B. Dies wird auf die Rentabilität des Kanals kaum einen wesentlichen Einfluss ausüben.
C. Für den Frachtenverkehr nach dem fernen Osten kommen natürlich die viel teureren Eisenbahnen im allgemeinen erst in zweiter Linie in Betracht.

The connective *doch* (however) marks the contrast relation between the clauses (2A), including the subordinated clauses (2Aa) and (2Ab), and clause (2B). Clause (2A) is to be classified as relate to A_1, whereas clause (2B) is used as relate B_2. This leads to the following normality standard:

(2') Wenn dem Suez-Kanal durch die sibirische Bahn eine gewisse Konkurrenz erwachsen ist und der Wettbewerb der Bagdadbahn [für den Suezkanal] noch fühlbarer werden wird, dann wird dies auf die Rentabilität des Kanals einen wesentlichen Einfluss ausüben.
[If a certain rivalry for the Suez-Canal has arisen due to the Siberian Railway and competition of the Baghdad-Rail [for the Suez-Canal] will enhance, then this will have a considerable effect on the rentability of the Canal.]

Clause (2C) contributes an additional reason how the speaker/writer reaches his conclusion. The entire item emphasizes the anticipated influence of the Baghdad Railway by presenting it as a rival enterprise to the Suez Canal. This form of presentation underlines Germany's target to become a major player in the global power struggle (see Section 1.2). At the same time, the comment reveals that the Baghdad Railway is obviously not expected to be profitable any time soon since rail freight transport is said to be too expensive. Indeed, the only transcontinental railway that was ever operated was exclusively run to provide a passenger service with luxury facilities. Though, at first sight, this text item expresses some pride in a project intended to compete with the famous Suez Canal, the following sentence concedes that railways will not be able to cater for basic needs in the colonies and for goods transport in general. Thus one of the most important arguments for the Baghdad Railway is defeated and the question remains why it should be built at all.[6] In turn, there was the real risk for the Baghdad Railway to lose the competitive struggle with the Suez Canal if the

---

6 The list of possible or actual passengers and their professional backgrounds shows a curious mixture of millionaires, demi-monde ladies, ageing actresses, impoverished gentility (Reinhardt 2015: 229). Whether customers like these were capable of securing the survival of the railway, or whether they were originally the target groups at all is dubitable.

latter had been more successful in both passenger and freight transportation at lower costs. What is more, none of the German colonies were situated along the route of the Baghdad Railway thus denying the local population the ability to make use of it. The analysis of this text item suggests that the writer, perhaps unwillingly, concedes that the railway projects will never be capable of meeting expectations.

Two kinds of expectations were at issue, both of which had to do with freight traffic. On the one hand, further expansion of German industrial production called for new markets; on the other hand, the railway line was supposed to yield profits from transport fares. Unlike the German colonies in Africa, the territory along the Baghdad Railway route was administered by a firmly established ruler, Sultan Abdul Hamid II, who pursued expansionist plans of his own. Imperial Germany had to obtain his permission before construction could begin. As the project would have boosted the Sultan's hopes for renewed invigoration of the Osmanic Realm (Eichholtz 2007: 14–15), the German Empire primarily offered its financial services and was represented by the Deutsche Bank (Fuhrmann 2013: 193).

This is why economic success had higher priority in respect of the Baghdad Railway project than compared to other German railway projects in the colonies, which were designed to support occupation and delivery of goods to colonial territories. If the assessment in text item (3) was correct, all those plans were in vain. But the opening of the first part of that railway line in 1904 (Eichholtz 2007: 13) shows that the author's opinion did not prevail. For our inquiry this case points to the problem that individual statements are often not representative of the general public view.

Like item (2) the following passage also comments on the Baghdad Railway scheme, but it touches on the question of whether or not Great Britain should continue to participate.

(3) *Zunächst ist die englische Regierung so gnädig uns mitzuteilen, daß keinerlei Bedenken gegen den Bau der Bagdadbahn vorhanden sein, „aber" (nun kommt der Haken!) britische Kapitalisten wünschten sich mit Geld daran zu beteiligen!* (Deutsch-Ostafrikanische Zeitung 01.02.1902)
[At first the English[7] Government condescended to tell us that they did not object to the construction of the Baghdad Railway, "but" (and now comes the snag!) British capitalists wished to have a share in its funding!]

---

7 In Germany, *English* is commonly misused as a synonym for *British*.

Construction of (transcontinental) railways as a means of colonization — **183**

The relation between the clauses is built hypotactically and can be segmented in the following way:

(3)   A.   *Die englische Regierung ist so gnädig, uns [etwas mitzuteilen].*
     Aa. *Es sind keinerlei Bedenken gegen den Bau der Bagdadbahn vorhanden.*
     Ab. *Britische Kapitalisten wünschen sich mit Geld daran zu beteiligen.*
     Ac. *Nun kommt der Haken.*

The connective *aber* (but) puts the two clauses (3Aa) and (3Ab) in contrast to each other. According to Figure 1 the following normality standard can be derived:

(3')   *Wenn keinerlei Bedenken der englischen Regierung gegen den Bau der Bagdadbahn vorhanden sind, dann wünschen sich britische Kapitalisten nicht, sich mit Geld daran zu beteiligen.*
[If there are no objections by the British Government against the construction of the Baghdad Railway, British capitalists do not wish to have a share in its funding.]

The proposition that the "englische Regierung" (the British Government) has no objections does not allow for the conclusion that a certain group in British society does not wish to have a share in the project. Instead a reader has to insert a further stepping stone between the two clauses. This semantic addition is hinted at by the unconventional use of quotation marks and by the insertion of clause (4c). The normality standard that can be induced from this missing link may be explicated like this:

(3")   *Wenn keinerlei Bedenken der englischen Regierung gegen den Bau der Bagdadbahn vorhanden sind, dann ist das beruhigend. Wenn britische Kapitalisten wünschen, sich mit Geld daran zu beteiligen, dann ist das ein Grund zur Besorgnis.*
[If there are no objections by the British Government against the construction of the Baghdad-Rail, this is comforting. If British capitalists wish to have a share in its funding, this is a reason to be worried.]

The contrast in this sentence relation does not consist of a cause and its failed effect, but rather by evaluating two different elements in opposite ways as supportive or obstructive to the aim of building the Baghdad Railway. A more extensive explanation why British participation in the project funding is rejected follows immediately after the above quote:

> Hoffentlich sind wir nicht so töricht, an einem guten Geschäft, das wir allein machen können, einen durchaus überflüssigen und nicht grade [sic!] als übermäßig reell bekannten Kompagnon teilnehmen zu lassen. (Deutsch-Ostafrikanische Zeitung 01.02.1902)
> [Hopefully we will not be as stupid as to allow a well-known cheater to step in as a co-operator in a business which we can make all by ourselves.]

The reader of this passage will easily see how much German colonizers and colonial agents felt hindered by Great Britain. This message is not surprising since Great Britain is still today regarded as the greatest colonial power ever and not just in terms of railway construction as a form of territorial invasion (Fuhrmann 2013: 191). However, the drastic words and the sarcasm in both text passages are an unusually open display of dissatisfaction with Great Britain. The author of the text reveals in this way that he is an enemy of British colonial politics even though colonial aspirations are not principally questioned. This identity concept of seeing oneself as an enemy of another colonial power differs from other identity concepts which are more ambivalent and thus less uncompromisingly critical.

Such an identity concept is noticeable in the third text item, which, unlike the previous two, does not refer to the Baghdad Railway but to the Cape to Cairo Railway.

(4) *Eine Bahn soll von Dusile am Nil bis zum Albert-See auf britischem Gebiete führen, und von da westlich vom Albert-Eduard-See und dem Kiwusee nach der Nordwestspitze des Tanganjika gehen. [...] Später wurde <u>allerdings</u> dieser ganze Plan dementirt [sic], da die einstige Verabredung zwischen Wilhelm II und Cecil-Rhodes, derzufolge die Cap-Kairo-Bahn durch Deutsch-Ostafrika zu führen sei, noch zu Recht besteht.* (Deutsche Kolonialzeitung 17.04.1909: 266)
[A railway is to go from Dusile on the Nile to the Albert Lake on British territory, and from there on the west side of the Albert-Eduard Lake and Lake Kiwu to the north-western edge of Lake Tanganjika [...] Later, however, the whole plan was dropped because an earlier agreement between Wilhelm II and Cecil Rhodes saying that the Cape to Cairo Railway had to pass through German East Africa was still legally binding.]

The relation expressed by *allerdings* comes up in a paragraph which assembles an extremely high number of contrast connectives, leading to great confusion with readers. For this reason, in the following lines only one relation was chosen for closer analysis and all inserted relations were excluded. The following clauses are parts of this relation:

(4) A. *Eine Bahn soll von Dusile am Nil bis zum Albert-See auf britischem Gebiet führen.*
B. *Eine Bahn soll von da [dem Albert-See] westlich vom Albert-Eduard-See und dem Kiwusee nach der Nordwestspitze des Tanganjika gehen.*
C. *Später wurde dieser ganze Plan dementiert.*
Ca. *Die einstige Verabredung zwischen Wilhelm II und Cecil-Rhodes besteht noch zu Recht.*
Caa. *Die Kap-Kairo-Bahn ist durch Deutsch-Ostafrika zu führen.*

By way of a preliminary matter, the geographical spots mentioned in this item have to be clarified. The names of lakes referred to here are still in use on maps of this area. What is called Albert-Eduard Lake there is nowadays known as Lac Eduard. Only the place of Dusile remains obscure, the only hint given being its position on the banks of the Nile. This hint, however, helps to reconstruct the route of the railway line as planned; it was to run on a north-south course and was therefore a part of the Cape to Cairo Railway, which is actually mentioned in the second clause.

The semantic relation can be described as contrast between the British plans of building a railway line and a public disclaimer of such plans. From the information given about the route of the railway line a normality standard can be deduced which says that these plans will be put into practice. But clause (4C) contradicts this and is supported by (4Ca), which offers a reason why earlier plans are no longer valid. It is precisely this reason which places this item into opposition to the critical attitude towards Great Britain as expressed in item (3). By way of reference to an alleged agreement between Germany and Great Britain, the German desire for exactly that form of co-operation becomes evident which was rejected with the Baghdad Railway project. Although it would be expecting too much uniformity among German colonial agents to suppose that all of them should have embraced the same opinion about British colonial aspirations, directly opposing positions in very similar questions among German agents raise serious doubts about whether there was a common strategy or at least a generally accepted vision in German society at all. Instead of unanimity the text item shows how ambivalent German attitudes towards Britain were. On the one hand it was trendsetter and colonial scout, on the other hand it was felt to threaten Germany's own colonial ambitions because of its world-wide expansion.

5 Concepts of identity in the colonial discourse on railways

In the text items examined above it becomes evident that there was competition between the German and the British colonial powers for dominance in transcontinental railway construction. On the German side there is a noticeable desire to have a share in the great Cape to Cairo Railway project in order to be counted among the world powers, which was one of the German Emperor's political priorities. On the other hand, the text items referring to the Baghdad Railway reveal the aim to get rid of British dominance and participation, which was rather seen as interference. Tragically, neither railway was ever finished according to the original plans nor were they ever operational. In one text item the reason for the failure was identified as the lack economic benefit, which applies to the Cape to Cairo Railway in much a similar way. Profits could never be expected to cover calculated costs, but, in spite of this, there were nearly no critical voices to be heard about the transcontinental railway projects. On the contrary, the reference to excessive costs for a regular freight transport service does not lead to the obvious conclusion that the hazardous project be cancelled. Whether short-sighted colonial romanticism or a hidden agenda was the reason why plans were pursued over a not insignificant period of time cannot be reliably determined.

The identity concepts noticeable in the text items above are characterized by the principle of competition with Great Britain as the primary opponent. First of all, the Baghdad Railway project would have had to compete with the Suez Canal, which was operated under British supervision; secondly, Great Britain was supposed to be the main profiteer from possible future yields of the project. At the same time Great Britain is referred to as a partner in another railway construction project, the Cape to Cairo Railway, where British dominance would have been unequivocally accepted. Although this seems to aim at a common collective identity of the colonial powers, the great ambivalence in the German attitudes towards their partners rather suggests a lack of coherent strategy. The analysis of the text items indicates general confusion, a lack of planning and a general obsession in terms of accessing and colonizing the target areas. The authors of the selected items do think in national (or nationalistic) categories (e.g. Germany vs. England/Britain), but these categories are not consistently filled, nor is the relationship between the national categories. In the case of the Cape to Cairo Railway, Germany has only the role of carrying out the plans, whereas Great Britain acts as the planning authority. For the Baghdad-Rail,

Germany is in charge of planning, whereas the British Empire is considered an unwanted intruder.

All examined items bear one significant quality; they are merely from the European's perspective. That is to say that those population groups, which lived in the occupied areas and whose lives were subject to the greatest cuts in liberty, did not get any mention in the items of this study. Even a look into further passages taken from the corpus does not reveal any further indication to the local population or their role in the context of colonial railways. This makes this form of railway construction and the discourse about it an exclusively colonialist concept, which only serves economical and ideological purposes. The principle of "effective occupation", which was mentioned at the beginning, adds its share to the conception of colonial railway and their construction as being a means of colonizing rather than of improving living conditions of all parts of the colonial society, including both colonizers and colonized.

References

(a) Primary sources

Deutsche Kolonialzeitung. Organ der Deutschen Kolonialgesellschaft. München. 1909.
Deutsch-Ostafrikanische Zeitung. Publikationsorgan der Wirtschaftlichen Vereinigung von Daressalam und Hinterland. Daressalam. 1899–1916.
Kolonie und Heimat in Wort und Bild. Unabhängige koloniale Wochenschrift. Organ des Frauenbundes der Deutschen Kolonialgesellschaft. Berlin. 1909.

(b) Monographs and articles

Berman, Russel A. 2003. Der Ewige Zweite. Deutschlands sekundärer Kolonialismus. In Birthe Kundrus (ed.), *Phantasiereiche. Zur Kulturgeschichte des deutschen Kolonialismus*, 19–32. Frankfurt a. M.: Campus.
Bourdieu, Pierre. 1974. *Zur Soziologie der symbolischen Formen.* Frankfurt a. M.: Suhrkamp.
Breindl, Eva. 2004. Relationsbedeutung und Konnektorbedeutung. Additivität, Adversativität und Konzessivität. In Hardarik Blühdorn (ed.), *Brücken schlagen,* 226–253. Berlin & New York: De Gruyter.
Busse, Dietrich & Wolfgang Teubert. 2013 [1994]. Ist Diskurs ein sprachwissenschaftliches Objekt? Zur Methodenfrage der historischen Semantik. In Wolfgang Teubert (ed.), *Linguistische Diskursanalyse. Neue Perspektiven*, 2nd edn, 13–30. Wiesbaden: Springer.
Conrad, Sebastian. 2011. *Deutsche Kolonialgeschichte.* München: C. H. Beck.
Dienel, Hans-Liudger. 2009. Die Eisenbahn und der europäische Möglichkeitsraum, 1870–1914. In Ralf Roth & Karl Schlögel (eds.), *Neue Wege in ein neues Europa. Geschichte und Verkehr im 20. Jahrhundert,* 105–123. Frankfurt a. M.: Campus.

Di Meola, Claudio. 1997. *Der Ausdruck der Konzessivität in der deutschen Gegenwartssprache. Theorie und Beschreibung anhand eines Vergleichs mit dem Italienischen.* Tübingen: Niemeyer.

Eckert, Andreas. 2013. Die Berliner Afrika-Konferenz (1884/85). In Jürgen Zimmerer (ed.), *Kein Platz an der Sonne. Erinnerungsorte der deutschen Kolonialgeschichte*, 137–149. Frankfurt a. M.: Campus.

Eichholtz, Dietrich. 2007. *Die Bagdadbahn, Mesopotamien und die deutsche Ölpolitik bis 1918: aufhaltsamer Übergang ins Erdölzeitalter. Mit Dokumenten.* Leipzig: Leipziger Universitätsverlag.

El-Din, Amr Nasr. 2010. Railroads in the land of the Nile. The story of Egyptian railroads. Egyptian railroads and the history of their development. Cairo. http//www.aucegypt.edu (accessed 27 March 2017).

Foucault, Michel. 2013 [1969]. *Archäologie des Wissens.* Transl. Ulrich Köppen. Frankfurt a. M.: Suhrkamp.

Faulstich, Katja. 2009. Deutscher Kolonialismus – (K)ein Thema der Sprachgeschichtsschreibung? In Ingo H. Warnke (ed.), *Deutsche Sprache und Kolonialismus. Aspekte der Nationalen Kommunikation 1884–1919*, 65–96. Berlin & New York: De Gruyter.

Fuhrmann, Malte. 2013. Die Bagdadbahn. In Jürgen Zimmerer (ed.), *Kein Platz an der Sonne. Erinnerungsorte der deutschen Kolonialgeschichte*, 190–207. Frankfurt a. M.: Campus.

Jäger, Ludwig. 2007. Medium Sprache. Anmerkungen zum theoretischen Status der Sprachmedialität. *Mitteilungen des Deutschen Germanistenverbandes* 54(1). 8–24.

König, Ekkehard. 1991. Konzessive Konjunktionen. In Arnim von Stechow & Dieter Wunderlich (eds.), *Semantik. Ein internationales Handbuch der zeitgenössischen Forschung*, 631–639. Berlin & New York: De Gruyter.

L'illustration *Jedem sein Teil.* Wood engraving. 1885. http://www.akg-images.de/C.aspx?VP3=SearchResult&VBID =2UMESQ7RD50YI&SMLS=1&RW =1366&RH=634 (accessed 27 March 2016).

Lindner, Ulrike. 2011. *Koloniale Begegnungen. Deutschland und Großbritannien als Imperialmächte in Afrika 1880–1914.* Frankfurt a. M. & New York: Campus.

Miller, Karl. 2003. Star of the borders. *The Guardian.* http://www.theguardian.com/books/2003/aug/09/featuresreviews.guardianreview3 (accessed 27 March 2016).

Mills, Sara. 2007. *Der Diskurs. Begriff, Theorie, Praxis.* Tübingen: Francke.

Morris, Jan. 1978. Farewell the trumpets: An imperial retreat. *The Norton anthology of English literature.* http://www.wwnorton.com/college/english/nael/20century/topic_1/jamorris.htm (accessed 27 March 2016).

Pakenham, Thomas. 1992. *The scramble for Africa: The white man's conquest of the Dark Continent from 1876 to 1912.* London: Abacus.

Pasch, Renate, Ursula Brausse, Eva Breindl & Ulrich Hermann Waßner. 2003. *Handbuch der deutschen Konnektoren. Linguistische Grundlagen der Beschreibung und syntaktische Merkmale der deutschen Satzverknüpfer (Konjunktionen, Satzadverbien und Partikeln).* Berlin & New York: De Gruyter.

Ramutsindela, Maano. 2007. Transforming landscapes of pain to landscapes of leisure. Reflections on the Cape to Cairo tourism route. In Bob Wishitemi, Anna Spenceley & Harry Wels (eds.), *Culture and community. Tourism studies in Eastern and Southern Africa*, 11–24. Amsterdam: Rozenberg.

Reinhardt, Winfried. 2015. G*eschichte des öffentlichen Personenverkehrs von den Anfängen bis 2014. Mobilität in Deutschland mit Eisenbahn, U-Bahn, Straßenbahn und Bus.* Wiesbaden: Springer.
Reisigl, Martin 2006. Sprachkritische Beobachtungen zu Foucaults Diskursanalyse. In Brigitte Kerchner & Silke Schneider (eds.), *Foucault: Diskursanalyse der Politik. Eine Einführung,* 85–103. Wiesbaden: Springer VS.
Rezat, Sara. 2007. *Die Konzession als strategisches Sprachspiel.* Heidelberg: Winter. (Also 2006 Diss. University of Paderborn).
Rezat, Sara. 2009. Konzessive Konstruktionen. Ein Verfahren zur Rekonstruktion von Konzessionen. *Zeitschrift für Germanistische Linguistik* 37. 470–489.
Rudolph, Elisabeth. 1996. *Contrast: Adversative and concessive relations and their expressions in English, German, Spanish, Portuguese on sentence and text level.* Berlin: De Gruyter.
Scherer, Carmen. 2006. *Korpuslinguistik.* Heidelberg: Winter.
Schonauer, Karlheinz. 2012. *1914 – Protokoll eines gewollten Krieges.* Berlin: Pro Business.
Speitkamp, Winfried. 2014. *Deutsche Kolonialgeschichte.* Stuttgart: Reclam.
Stolz, Thomas, Christina Vossmann & Barbara Dewein. 2011. Kolonialzeitliche Sprachforschung und das Forschungsprogramm Koloniallinguistik. Eine kurze Einführung. In Thomas Stolz, Christina Vossmann & Barbara Dewein (eds.), *Kolonialzeitliche Sprachforschung. Die Beschreibung afrikanischer und ozeanischer Sprachen zur Zeit der deutschen Kolonialherrschaft,* 7–30. Berlin: Akademie Verlag.
Vance, Norman. 2000. Imperial Rome and Britain's language of Empire 1600–1837. *History of European Ideas* 26. 211–224.
Vester, Heinz-Günter. 1998. *Kollektive Identitäten und Mentalitäten. Von der Völkerpsychologie zur kulturvergleichenden Soziologie und interkulturellen Kommunikation.* Frankfurt a. M.: IKO.
Volkmann, Richard. 1920. Deutsch-Ostafrika. In Heinrich Schnee (ed.), *Deutsches Kolonial-Lexikon.* Vol. 3, 616. Leipzig: Quelle und Meier.
Warnke, Ingo H. 2007. Diskurslinguistik nach Foucault. Dimensionen einer Sprachwissenschaft jenseits textueller Grenzen. In Ingo H. Warnke (ed.), *Diskurslinguistik nach Foucault,* 3–24. Berlin & New York: De Gruyter.
Warnke, Ingo H. 2009. Die sprachliche Konstituierung von geteiltem Wissen in Diskursen. In Ekkehard Felder & Marcus Müller (eds.), *Wissen durch Sprache. Theorie, Praxis und Erkenntnisinteresse des Forschungsnetzwerks "Sprache und Wissen",* 113–140. Berlin & New York: De Gruyter.
Warnke, Ingo H. & Daniel Schmidt-Brücken. 2013. Exemplarische Texte und beispielhafter Sprachgebrauch im deutschen Kolonialdiskurs. Zur Konzeption des Bremischen Basiskorpus Deutscher Kolonialismus (BBDK). In Christian Lück, Michael Niehaus, Peter Risthaus & Manfred Schneider (eds.), *Archiv des Beispiels. Vorarbeiten und Überlegungen,* 122–147. Berlin & Zürich: Diaphanes.
Warnke, Ingo H., Janina Wildfeuer, Daniel Schmidt-Brücken & Wolfram Karg. 2014. Diskursgrammatik als wissensanalytische Sprachwissenschaft. In Nora Benitt, Lisa Koch, Katharina Müller, Sven Saage & Lisa Schüler (eds.), *Kommunikation – Korpus– Kultur. Ansätze und Konzepte einer kulturwissenschaftlichen Linguistik,* 67–85. Trier: WVT.

Valentyna Skybina and Natali Bytko
The Raj English in historical lexicography

Abstract: The paper examines the scope and methodology of representation of the English language used in India during the Raj in historical lexicography. In historical dictionaries, a comprehensive documented data on a language/variety history and usage are accumulated. This makes historical lexicography a reliable source for the in-depth analysis of linguistic phenomena in a broad cultural context. As the English language used in India during the Raj, in fact, marks the genesis of Indian English its linguistic analysis might produce valuable data for the better understanding of the historical trajectories of this variety. Several studies of English in India consider the Raj period (e.g. Krishnaswamy & Krishnaswamy 2013; Ram 1983; Sailaja 2009) but mostly focus on socio-political and educational issues. This study draws attention to the Raj English lexis and the dictionaries in which it is defined: *Hobson-Jobson: Being a glossary of Anglo-Indian colloquial words and phrases and of kindred terms etymological, historical, geographical and discursive*, 1886 (further *H-J*) and *Sahibs, Nabobs, and Boxwallahs, A dictionary of the words of Anglo-India*, 1991 (further *SNB*). The methods applied are those of socio-historical linguistics and dictionary criticism. The results obtained suggest that the Raj English dictionaries on historical principles represent the linguistic and socio-linguistic specificity and the sources of the English used in India at that time. They also imply the necessity of compiling a comprehensive dictionary of Indian English on historical principles.

Keywords: the Raj, lexicography, Indian English, socio-cultural context, language evolution, lexical borrowing

1 Introduction

The term Raj pertains to the rule of the British Crown in the Indian subcontinent from 1858 till 1947. However, the British appeared in India much earlier, in the 16th c., when the first Christian missionaries were established. It is since that

---

Valentyna Skybina, Canadian Academy of Independent Scholars, BC Campus, 515 West Hastings Street, Vancouver, Canada. E-Mail: viskybina@gmail.com
Natali Bytko, Zaporizhzhya National University, Tykhvinska str. 15, Kryvyi Rih, 50014, Ukraine. E-Mail: natalibitko@gmail.com

time that the English language has been used in India. Particularly noticeable the presence on English becomes with the advent of the British East-India Co. at the beginning of the 17th c. On this basis, the term 'Raj English' can legitimately be applied to the English language used in India since the middle of the 17th c.

In India, the English appeared in the midst of elaborate civilization with several hundred of deeply established and widely spread languages. Understandably, local people had no need of another language whether for literature or scholarship and certainly not for conversation, trade and religion (Bragg 2003). However, due to political, economic and cultural developments, English was spreading among both the Anglo-Indians[1] and the Hindustani people and a new variety of the language that is nowadays called Indian English started developing (Kachru 1990, Sailaja 2009).

To understand the historical trajectory of Indian English, it is essential to evince characteristics of its earliest forms, primarily the Raj English. One of the most valuable sources for the Raj English research are dictionaries on historical principles that provide not only linguistic but also social, political, and cultural information. Besides, their content reflects the way in which the language was perceived by the dictionaries compilers and, to a certain extent, by a broader English speaking community in India. Moreover, such dictionaries themselves are cultural artifacts and their history adds to the understanding of linguistic phenomena.

This study aims at evincing the historical trajectory and socio-cultural specificity of the Raj English as represented in historical lexicography.

To this end, the very phenomenon of the Raj English is considered in a broad historical and socio-cultural framework. Then two dictionaries on historical principles, *Hobson-Jobson* (Yule et al. 1903 [1886]) and *Sahibs, Nabobs, and Boxwallahs* (Lewis 1991), are portrayed in context with the cultural and linguistic processes of their time and the content of the dictionaries is investigated. Both dictionaries represent the vocabulary of the Raj English, however, *H-J* occupies a special place among the lexicographic publications depicting lexical repertoire of the English speaking India up to the end of the 19th c. Although previous publica-

---

[1] "'Anglo Indian' has two meanings, one essentially historical and one in use today. In the past, the term described Europeans (usually British) who had made India their permanent home and lived there for generations. They were sometimes known as Domiciled Europeans. In its modern usage, however, Anglo Indian refers to people of mixed European and Indian ancestry. This sense of the word received official government recognition in India in 1911. Prior to that, various designations such as "Eurasian" or "Indo-Briton", or more derogatory terms such as "half-caste" or "mixed-breed", were used to describe this population" (Lodrick 2009). For the details see Anand (2011: 525–527).

tions, as will be shown further, accumulated a substantial vocabulary of the Raj English, "*Hobson-Jobson* became the standard-bearer, and no other work has managed to displace it as the premier (though now clearly dated) reference work dealing with Indian influences on English" (Nagle 2011: 6).

H-J has been highly esteemed since after its publication. Thus, in the July 1890 records of the *Royal Geographical Society H-J* was referred to as "[...] a volume that should be in the library of every educated Englishman [...]" (Obituary 1890: 391–393). In 1903 *The Leisure Hour* published a rather comprehensive review of the dictionary characterizing it as

> not only a work of profound erudition, pleasantly free of even a trace of pedantry, [...] not only a very storehouse of information for the student of history and literature, as well as philology, [...] [but] also one of the most amusing, one of the most fascinating books we have seen this long while. (Hobson-Jobson 1886: 599)

No wonder, it has been re-edited many times with the latest edition published in 2016 in New Delhi.

Nowadays, *H-J* is attracting attention of the next generation of researchers. In the 21st c. several studies on the dictionary were published (e.g. Anand 2011; Lambert 2014a; Nagle 2011, 2014; Teltscher 2011; Zimmer 2009). In them, it was revealed "how very important Henry Yule and his *H-J* were to the understanding and documentation of South Asian vocabulary that had been absorbed into the English word-stock" (Nagle 2014: 301). The role of the dictionary in defining this vocabulary in English historical lexicography, primarily in *Oxford English Dictionary*, in which "between 50 % and 75 % of [...] [South Asian words] entries show evidence of Yule's influence" (Nagle 2014: 280) was emphasized (see also Zimmer 2009). The contribution of the dictionary to the education in India, particularly during the Raj, was shown (Teltscher 2011). The cosmopolitan, non-prescriptive character of the dictionary was stressed (Anand 2011). Even the dictionary's rather provocative title was talked over by the reviewers (e.g. Lambert 2014b; Zimmer 2009).

Fundamental changes in socio-cultural and linguistic situation in India, the growing interest in 'new Englishes' in general and in Indian English in particular, entailed the revival of interest to the Raj English. In 1992, a hundred year after the publication of the *H-J*, another dictionary of the Raj English on historical principles, *Sahibs, Nabobs and Boxwallahs. A dictionary of the words of Anglo-India* was compiled by Ivor Lewis and published by Oxford University Press. *SNB* continues the work started by Yule et al., filling in some lacunae and adding the entries drawn from the sources published during the last 60 years of the

Raj, up to 1947. A number of entries have been drawn from later publications, up to 1980s.

The reviews of *SNB* are rather contradictory. Some of the reviews are rather unfavorable. Thus, the reviewer in *Brief reviews of books*, E. G., considers this dictionary to be "largely secondary" and to have "little 'scientific' conception of its subject matter" (E. G. 1997: 225). Lynn Zastoupil also notes that *SNB* "... appears to rely heavily on Hobson-Jobson, and to a lesser extent, to the OED, for most of its words and much of its explanatory material" (Zastoupil 1993: 68). At the same time, the reviewer stresses the value of the historical introduction in which "Lewis raises many intriguing issues" (Zastoupil 1993: 69). Rupert Snell in his laconic review concludes that *SNB* "...is wholly unreliable in its representations of Indian orthographies". He also points out to inaccuracies in derivations and etymologies (Snell 1993: 222). Other reviewers focus more on the strong points. Thus, Alamgir Hashmi gives a very positive review stressing that the dictionary represents "a word-based social history of 'Anglo-India'" (Hashmi 1993: 109), depicts words that vary from "the living use-slang, officealese, other registers, the more creative language – to the solemn burials in textbooks" (Hashmi 1993: 109–110), makes evident the cosmopolitan character and evinces the specificity of the Raj English. At the same time, the problematic character of "dating and updating" (Hashmi 1993: 112) is noted. Olha della Cava indicates that the dictionary's "virtue lies in the fact that in spite of the conciseness it is comprehensive and scholarly; it includes many common words, some of which originated in the twentieth century, and could not have been included in *Hobson-Jobson*" (Della Cava 1994: 413).

2 Historical trajectory of the Raj English

2.1 Historical and socio-cultural context of the Raj English genesis

The history of English in Indian subcontinent can be traced as far back as 1579.

> The first person to think, speak, and write in this language on Indian soil in historical times, most likely, was Father Thomas Stephens, a Roman Catholic who escaped religious persecution in Elizabethan England by joining the Society of Jesus (based in Rome) in 1578, and persuading his superiors to let him sail for the Jesuit mission in India the following year. (Dharwadker 2002: 96)

A few years later, in 1583, several other Englishmen, Ralph Fitch, John Newberry, James Story, William Leeds, were brought to Goa as prisoners by the Portuguese. Since that time on, the British continued coming to the Indian subcontinent as envoys, missioners, trade representatives (Sinha 1978: 2; Lewis 1991: 14). Accordingly, this time, 1579, can be considered the beginning of the English language presence in India (Mehrotra 1998). Those are written sources of this period, mostly epistolary genre samples that allow viewing the end of the 16th c. as the starting point for the genesis of Indian English. Thus, the first lexical borrowings from local languages (in the author's original spelling) can be found in Ralf Fitch's letters.[2] Inclusions of localisms in Thomas Stevens' letters to his father even allow considering them as the first pieces of the English-Indian literature (Ward & Waller 1916: 331–332).

Gradual spread of the English language on the territory of the Indian subcontinent starts in the middle of the 17th c. with the establishment of the British East-India Company that controlled three "Presidency towns": Madras, Bombay, and Calcutta, by the end of the century. It took the Company another century to acquire sovereignty over the large parts of India and neighboring countries having ousted their merchant rivals – Holland and France. Further, following the Indian Rebellion of 1857 and powers transference to the Crown, the new British Raj was generated. As a result, the Crown was controlling approximately 54 % of the area that comprised over 77 % of the population of India thus promoting the spread of English.

With such an expansion, English appeared in the midst of a very complex multilingual and multicultural linguistic situation. Except for more than one thousand local languages and dialects (Baldridge 1996), European languages – Portuguese, Danish, Dutch, as well as French, had already been present on the subcontinent for some time.[3]

Among native languages and dialects those belonging to Indo-Aryan and Dravidian families were the most widely spread while linguistic presence of the Austro-Asiatic and Tibeto-Burman families was much less pronounced. Thus, Indo-Arian languages were spoken in the Western (4 languages), Central (4

---

[2] Ralf Fitch's letters were published in the 16-volume work "The Principal Navigations" by Richard Hakluyt; in it the history of the British seafaring and exploration is presented (Lewis 1991: 14).

[3] The "multitude of languages reflects India's lengthy and diverse history. During the last few thousand years, the Indian sub-continent has been both united under various empires as well as fragmented into many small kingdoms. This has helped spread many common linguistic features among Indian languages without allowing any particular language to become overwhelmingly dominant" (Baldridge 1996).

languages), Eastern (3 languages) and North-Western (5 languages) parts of the area with Hindi, Bengali and Marathi having the majority of speakers. Dravidian languages were the languages of the North (2 languages), Central (2 languages), South-Central (4 languages) and South (5 languages) parts with Telugu and Tamil having the majority of speakers. Tibeto-Burman languages were spoken in the north-east, Austro-Asiatic languages in central and north-eastern parts (Sailaja 2009: 1–10).

In modern history, European languages spread across the Indian subcontinent first as the languages of trade and later as those of colonialism.

Portuguese led by Vasco da Gama were the first Europeans to reach India by sea and to land in Calicut 1498. Only two years later, in 1500, the first European settlement was founded by a Portuguese navigator and explorer Pedro Àlvares Cabral. In 1502 Vasco da Gama started the first trade post. In 1503 Alfonso de Albuquerque set up a Portuguese fort Kochi thus laying the foundation for the eastern Portuguese Empire. Later, immediately after the first Battle of Panipat in 1526 and the establishment of Mughal Empire, Portuguese obtained a trade license from the ruler of Calicut. They then further expanded their presence in the area, particularly along the West (Goa, Diu, Daman, Cannanore, Vasai) and West Bengal. The presence of Portuguese influenced the local linguistic situation in many ways including the formation of the Portuguese based creoles and Indo-Portuguese.

The language accompanying Portuguese in its infiltration into the Hindustan territory was Dutch. Since 1596, the Netherlanders made a series of voyages to India serving the Portuguese in some capacity or the other (Ward & Waller 1916: 29). But it was after the establishment of the Dutch East India Company in 1602 that the Dutch instituted themselves in Coromandel, notably Pulicat, first being given the permission to build a fort and to do trading and then having captured the territory from the Portuguese (Azariah 2007). The years 1616 and 1627 marked the establishment of Dutch Suratte and Dutch Bengal with numerous trading posts within the territories (Parthesius 2010: 45). On these territories, the Dutch appeared in the environment where trade and interaction were conducted in several languages, including Portuguese, Gujarati, Hindi, Sindhi, Marwari, Marathi, Tamil, Telugu, Odia (in Surat), Bengali, Odia, Nepali, Assamese, Chakma, Rohingya, Santali, Urdu (in Bengal), and later in English as well as in a number of mixed and creolized forms. In this complex linguistic situation the Dutch did not see their language as an instrument of empire (Kuipers 1998: 9). With the economic interests to prevail over socio-political, the Dutch administered the colony through a non-European language – one of the languages of local people. As a result, the Dutch language played a minor role in the rapidly developing and changing contact situations.

Danish arrived in India at the beginning of the 17th c., soon after Christian IV, the King of Denmark-Norway, in 1616 issued a charter creating the Danish East India Company (Modern History 1759: 5–6). The Danish held their possessions in West Bengal, Orissa, on the Malabar coast: thus, commercial outposts were established in Oddeay Torre in 1696, Gondalpara in 1698, in Calicut in 1752, in Serampore in 1755. The Nicobar and the Andaman Islands were also declared Danish property in 18th century (Stow 1979: 20). Notwithstanding the Danish dominions in India they presented no linguistic threat nor had any significant influence on the language situation in India.

France was the last European maritime power to participate in trading and military actions in the Indian Ocean in the late 17th century (Cawley 2015: 30) although French trade with East Asia was initiated during the reign of Francis I and the first ship was recorded to arrive in the Indian city of Diu in 1527. Since the second half of the 17th century French enclaves on the Indian subcontinent included possessions of Pondichery district and Karikal on the Coromandel coast; Yanaon and Masulipatam lodge on the coast of Orissa; Mahe and Calicut lodge on the Malabar coast; Chandernagore, lodges of Cassombazar, Dacca, Patna, Balasore in Bengal; Surat in Gujarat (Malleson 1893; Suresh 2010). The influence of the French and the language resulted in the official status of French in the union territories of Puducherry. The status lasted till 1965.

It is evident that the British came to the area with a very complex linguistic and cultural situation so the linguistic consequences for the English language in India lie primarily in the language contacts framework and "the emergence of Indian English as a 'world' variety owes much to this fact" (Nair 2012: 103). The earliest form of this variety was the Raj English. During its history the Raj English, a complex multifunctional dynamic system, not only underwent considerable changes but also developed a high level of sociolinguistic variation.

The complexity of the Raj English was due to its spread into the territories with different linguistic situations and to the extensive use in the bureaucracy.

Multi-functionality of the Raj English is rooted in the diversity of the roles the British played in India. The roles ranged from those of civil servants, law officers, military personnel, marines, medical staff, chaplains, and railway workers to various non-official ones such as merchants and planters, free marines, and missionaries. In all these capacities the British communicated with local people – native speakers of multiple languages and dialects – in the sphere of commerce, administration, legislation, and everyday life.

Sociolinguistic variation was ranging from

broken sort of English spoken by servants or other Indians of little or no "English" education, the English of those who have learnt the language in schools – clerks and the less well educated among the professional Indians who use English daily, such as pleaders and magistrates; ...the almost completely normal English of many Indian writers on the one hand, and the dog English of the schoolboy on the other. (Kindersley 1938: 25)

A separate variety, **Anglo-Indian English**, that emerged among the 'Anglo-Indian' families of rank-and-file British soldiers and others on the one side and lower-caste Indian women on the other (McArthur 2003: 319) was the nativized variety of Indian English (Coelho 1997: 561). In a more technical language, several varieties of English, occupational and regional, that started developing during the Raj, can be singled out.

Boxwalla(h) English is the pidgin variety of broken English used by door-to-door sellers of wares. This variety has considerable code-mixing from one or more languages and a very simplified syntax (Ward & Waller 1916: 512).

Butler English/Bearer English/Kitchen English is a 'minimal' pidgin used by domestic helpers (McArthur 2003: 317). It was used and continues to be used in major metropolitan cities in South Asia where English-speaking foreigners live (Ward & Waller 1916: 511). It was first described with reference to its use in the Madras Presidency (Yule et al. 1903 [1886]: 133–134).

Babu (Baboo) English is the variety of English that first developed as an occupational variety amongst clerks in the Bengali-speaking areas; originally characterized as a form of administrative English, it can now be heard in Nepal, north India, and in some social circles in south India.

The linguistic nature of these varieties is disputable (see McArthur 2003: 317).

Convent English is the variety of English that relates to all Catholic schools and is close to that of the Anglo-Indian schools. Together with Anglo-Indian English this variety contributed to the development of standards for the media and other public activities on an India-wide basis (McArthur 2003: 318–320).

Bengali English, Calcutta English, Dhaka English, Malayali English, Maharashtrian English, Punjabi English, Tamil English are regional varieties of English, often defined with reference to either the state language or mother tongue (or both) of a particular speaker.

Indo-Aryan English is a regional variety used generally in the north.

Dravidian English *is* a regional variety used generally in the south (McArthur 2003: 318).

Development of the above mentioned varieties went in line with the genesis of **Standard/General Indian English** – a 'classical' acrolectal variety of English in India associated with the highly educated people (e.g. Quirk 1958: 13; Sailaja

2009: viii; Lambert 2014a: 113) who acquired English from the native speakers in the British run system of education.

The foundations of the English-language education in India were laid by British missionaries who first taught mostly the kids of the East-India Co.'s employees and some Anglo-Indians (Krishnaswamy & Krishnaswamy 2013: 10; Sinha 1978: 12). Besides, the missionaries also opened orphanages both for European and mixed descent children. Later, in the 18th c., first primary schools for native children were organized. As these schools appeared to be very popular, in Bengal for instance, Free School society of Bengal was established with the aim of providing education to the growing number of students. All around Indian subcontinent educational institutions with the English-language instruction were established. Thus, in 15 years, from 1815 till 1830, the following schools and colleges were opened: Baptist Mission School (1815), Serampore College (1818), London Mission Society's Schools (1818), Calcutta School Society's School (1819), Jaya Narayan Ghoshal's English School in Varanasi (1818), General Assembly's Institution (1830).

The schools became centers of book-printing that also favored the spread of European education including that provided in English. Libraries were opened at these schools, too.

Gradually English started to be perceived by the local people, particularly educated ones, as the language of science and technology, a means to unveil the secrets of the European Enlightenment and an intellectual world lying beyond. The British supported this tendency that led to the English language getting even larger spread among the Hindustani people.

Linguistically, this situation led to further increase in language contacts with all the consequences of this process. The most evident of these consequences was the use of local terms in different spheres of official and non-official communication between the British, Anglo-Indians, and the Hindustani people. The system of education, both religious and secular, also played a significant role in promoting local terms penetration into the English language used in India both in oral and in written speech (see Biswas & Agrawal 1994: 4). "Of all the legacies of the Raj, none is more important than the English language and the modern school system..." (Singh: 2005).

2.2 Lexicographic response

The spread of English in India, its use in different forms and varieties made the problem of miscommunication rather urgent and painful moreover that "the 19th century British encounter with India was marked by a degree of mutual sensitivity to the linguistic and literary dimensions of cultural contact" (Nair 2012: 107).

> When in the East, terms have been used, in the way of business or law, which he (Every Gentleman, whom various circumstances have occasioned to reside in the Honourable East India Company's settlements in Asia) has been unable to comprehend the meaning of; and mistakes have arisen owing to that want of knowledge, which has frequently led persons into disagreeable dilemmas. (Rousseau 1802: iii)

To facilitate the effective communication between multiple groups of users, primarily between the British administration, Anglo-Indians, and Hindustani people, reference works were called forth and "vocabularies of Indian and other foreign words in use among Europeans in the East have not unfrequently been printed" (Yule et al. 1903 [1886]: 120). Colonel Yule mentioned several of them with the earliest one, "Explication de plusieurs mots, don't l'intelligence est necessaire au Lecteur", an appendix to *Voyages et Observations du Sieur de la Boulaye-le Gouvs, Gentlhomme Angeuin*, published in 1653 (Yule et al. 1903 [1886]: 120–121). However,

> The main motivation for the Raj lexicography, was [...] to provide lexical manuals and handbooks for the large network of administrators in a linguistically diverse and culturally pluralistic subcontinent. (Kachru 2005: 50)

Unsurprisingly, the first dictionaries were bilingual; in them, terms in different languages used on the subcontinent were translated into English. The compilers of these dictionaries had a diverse linguistic background and varied level of expertise in dictionary compilation. But with miscommunication being a pressing problem and with the growing need in reference works, every dictionary found its grateful users.

2.2.1 Early dictionaries

One of the earliest dictionaries was *A dictionary of Mohammedan law, and of Bengal revenue terms: with a vocabulary, Persian and English*, published in 1797. It was compiled by Francis Gladwin, a "lexicographer and prolific translator of Persian literature into English" who

> served in the Bengal Army and later [...] became one of the three professors of Persian at Fort William College in Calcutta in 1800, the year of its establishment. He was a founding member of the Asiatic Society of Bengal [...]. (Loloi 2012)

Unlike Francis Gladwin, the compiler of *An Indian glossary: Consisting of some thousand words and terms commonly used in the East Indies; with full explanations of their respective meanings. Forming a useful Vade Mecum, extremely serviceable in assisting strangers to acquire with Ease and Quickness the Language of that Country* (1880), T. T. Robarts was a Lieut. of the Third Regt. of the Native Infantry, E.I. In Colonel Yule's observation, a good deal of the entries for Robarts' glossary was taken directly from the anonymous *"Indian Vocabulary, to which it Prefixed the Forms of Impeachment"* published in 1778 (Yule et al. 1903 [1886]: 120).

Samuel Rousseau, a British Oriental scholar and printer, "a singular instance of patient perseverance in acquirement of ancient languages" (The Gentleman's Magazine 1833: 569), compiled *A dictionary of words used in the East Indies, with full explanations* [...] (Rousseau 1802), "a useful book of reference for the Lawyer, the Writer, the Merchant, and the Military Officer" (Rousseau 1802: viii). This book is useful for contemporary student in philology as well not only in linguistic but also in cultural context. Thus, in the introductory part the author provides "a concise History of the Provinces of Bengal, Bahar, and Orissa"; and he does this "the more readily [...], because Calcutta is the principal seat of the East India trade [...]" (Rousseau 1802: viii). The dictionary articles abound in information in political, historical, economic, religious, and many other spheres (see examples below).

> **Cauffer** This is the term of the greatest abuse. It implies one who has neither the fear of God nor man before his eyes.
> **Cofs** or **Khas**. Land under the immediate superintendence of the government, for want or farmers.
> **Jezia**. A poll-tax, formally levied on all who were not Mahammedans, especially the Hindoos.
> **Tobe Khaneb**. A department of the artillery.
> **Vizeer**. The fifth minister of the empire.

Captain Thomas Roebuck of the Madras Native Infantry, a distinguished Oriental scholar who authored books in 5 languages, compiled *An English and Hindostanee Naval Dictionary of technical terms and sea phrases as also the Various Words of Command Given in Working a Ship & Co. With Many Sentences of Great Use at Sea; To which is prefixed a short grammar of the Hindostanee language* published in 1811. The dictionary appeared to be so popular that 6 additions were published between 1811 and 1882. For one of the editions, revision and corrections were provided by William Carmichael Smyth. The 1882 edition, published under the title *A Laskari dictionary, or, Anglo-Indian vocabulary of nautical terms and phrases in English and Hindustani, chiefly in the corrupt jargon in use among the Laskars or Indian sailors* was revised and enlarged by George Small.

Horace Hayman Wilson, a medical doctor and one of the most distinguished Orientalists of England, spent 24 years in India, mostly in Bengal (Wilson 1902). When the Court of Directors of the East-India Co.

> with their usual praiseworthy desire to facilitate the acquirement of the eastern languages by their servants, decreed, about the end of the year 1842, that a glossary of words in current use in different parts of India should be compiled. (Wilson's Glossary 1857: 354)

Wilson got engaged in the project. In 1855 *A glossary of judicial and revenue terms and of useful words occurring in official documents relating to the administration of the government of British India, from the Arabic, Persian, Hindustani, Sanskrit, Hindi, Bengali, Uriya, Marathi, Guzarathi, Telugu, Karnata, Tamil, Malayalam and other language* was published in London. As the title indicates, the main body of the glossary is comprised by the terms relevant for the British administrative activities. However, being a scholar, Wilson included multiple entries pertaining to local culture, religious practices, as well as to fauna, flora, geography and climate of the Indian subcontinent (Bytko 2015; Wilson's Glossary 1857: 376).

> *Ábádí*, H. The part of the village lands on which the dwellings are erected.
> BHATT, or BHATTA, BHUṬṬ, BHUṬṬA, H. S. A learned Brahman. In some parts of the south of India it especially designates a Brahman who professes a knowledge of the Védas, or belongs to a family in which they have been taught.
> *Bhaṭṭáchárj*, H., Ben., both from the S. *Bhaṭṭáchárya* A learned Brahman; one who teaches any branch of Sanskrit literature. In Bengal it is also applied to any respectable Brahman.
> KAṚBA, otherwise KAḌBA, KAḌBÍBÁR; add, a piece of forest land.

At about the same time, a dictionary of "more modest pretensions and compass than the costly quarto compiled, under the auspices of the East India Company, by the late Prof. H. H. Wilson" (An Anglo-Indian dictionary 1885: 534) was being compiled by George Clifford Whitworth, a Bombay civil service fellow of the University of Bombay. This dictionary, *An Anglo-Indian Dictionary; A Glossary of Indian Terms Used in English, and of Such English or Other Non-Indian Terms as Have Obtained Special Meanings in India* was published in 1885 in London. The compiler admits that "the scope of the work, as regards range of subject, is <...> very wide" (Whitworth 1885: viii). The dictionary is based on written sources and the terms that are not "commonly used in documents which purport to be written in English" (Whitworth 1885: viii) were excluded from the word list. This dictionary, no doubt, was useful for a broad public of its time; for contemporary reader, however, of particular interest is the information on cultural and historical subjects (see some examples below).

Ahmad Sháhi. The name of the branch of the Báhmani dynasty which, on the dismemberment of the letter in 1489 A.D., established itself in Berar. This dynasty lasted till 1574, when Berar was conquered and annexed to the Ahmadnagar state.
Male. The name of a gipsy class in Coorg, said to have come from Malabár.
Pura. [Bengali]. The name of a low cast; they sell fish and vegetables.

A lexicographic product of a different nature, *A Dictionary of Slang, Jargon & Cant Embracing English, American, and Anglo-Indian Slang, Pidgin English, Tinker's Jargon and Other Irregular Phraseology* was compiled and edited in collaboration by two writers – Albert Marie Victor Barrère, Officier de instruction publique, Professor of the Royal Military Academy of Woolwich, author of the "Argo and Slang" and Leland, Charles Godfrey, M. A. Hon., F.R.S.L. Author of "The Breitmann Ballads", "The English Gypsies and their Language". Although the Anglo-Indian component constitutes a rather small part of the dictionary, its emphasis on conversational vocabulary made it very useful in unofficial discourse. The following examples provide an idea of some colloquial lexicon of the Raj.

(Anglo-Indian), from the Bengal and Hindi Bābû, which is properly a term of respects as Master or Mr. <...> In Bengal and elsewhere it is often used among Anglo-Indians with a slight savour or disparagement, as characterizing a superficially cultivated but too often effeminate Bengali. From the extensive employment of the class to which the term was applied as a title, in the capacity of clerks in English offices, the word has come often to signify a native clerk who writes English. <...>
Baboo-English (Anglo-Indian). This term is applied to a peculiar English which is rather written than spoken by the natives in India. It is difficult to describe, not being specially ungrammatical or faulty as regards orthography, and yet it is the drollest dialect of English known.
Teek (Anglo-Indian), exact, close, precise, parsimonious. Hindu thick.
Tiffin (Anglo-Indian and pidgin), luncheon at least in English household. <...>
Vakeel (Anglo-Indian), a barrister.

Thus, the concise overview of the samples of the Raj lexicography given above not only demonstrates the pragmatic character of the lexicography but it also suggests that from the very early time the Raj English was justifiably perceived as a new complex linguistic phenomenon.

2.2.2 The Raj English in dictionaries on historical principles: Then and now

In this chapter, the Raj English is viewed through the magnifying glass of historical lexicography. Two dictionaries on historical principles, *H-J* and *SNB*, are investigated.

In both dictionaries the lexis of the Raj English is displayed in a documented form, thus mirroring the various layers of the vocabulary and the particularities of regional usage. Moreover, complimentary to purely linguistic data these dictionaries provide socio-historical, political, and cultural information. The vast quotation material and etymological data are the source of extensive encyclopedic information. The familiarization with definitions and quotations provides a glimpse on culture, literature and science development; the etymological data reflect the languages contacts and the linguistic transformations triggered by the contacts.

A hundred-year time distance between the dictionaries publication allows observing how the Raj English was perceived by its contemporaries and by the 20th c. lexicographers.

The examination of the dictionaries in context with the linguistic and sociocultural situation of the time of their compilation allows to see the British Raj in two perspectives: the one contemporary to the Raj itself and a modern one.

The method applied in this part of the research consists in dictionary critical analysis with special focus on semantic, sociolinguistic and historical aspects.

Two thousand four hundred and eighty seven dictionary articles from *H-J* dictionary and 3700 articles from *SNB* constitute the data.

2.2.2.1 Dictionaries general characteristics

By the middle of the 19th century the English used in the Indian subcontinent, the Raj English had acquired its individuality.[4] This individuality could be observed in local written and oral discourse as it became a means of communication between the British and Anglo-Indians themselves as well as between those two groups and other groups of local people.[5] By that time, the Raj English had passed the stage of a "technical jargon" (recorded in the dictionaries discussed

---

[4] The unique features of "Anglo-Indian English" were already recognized in colonial days (Lambert 2014b: 65).
[5] The most obvious was the administrative discourse as "the day-to-day management of a nation of 300 million Indians was" conducted by "the 1,300-or-so members of the elite Indian Civil Service" (Buda 1985).

above) and was acquiring variant-forming characteristics. These characteristics can be observed in numerous pieces of epistolary genre, literary works, including those written by Indians[6], documents, dictionaries and other reference books. Internal regional and social variation was also developing.

With the spread of English and its growing variation, comprehension of its distinctive character by both language users and scholars, the dictionary depicting not only terms but all the classes of words which "recur constantly in the daily intercourse of the English in India" (Yule et al. 1886 [1903]: xv) became a necessity.

In 1872, the work on such a dictionary was initiated by two English intellectuals, Sir Henry Yule, a Scottish Orientalist and engineer, and Arthur Coke Burnell, an English scholar in Sanskrit. Fifteen years later, in 1886, *A Glossary of colloquial Anglo-Indian words and phrases, and of kindred terms, etymological, historical, geographical and discursive*, better known sub voce *Hobson-Jobson*, was published.

The objective of the *H-J's* authors was to make a work "of distinctive character, in which something has been aimed at differing in form from any work known to us" as stated in the preface (Yule et al. 1886 [1903]: xv). And they succeeded in compiling a word list of 2487 items that was original, unique and substantiated by 9,782 citations in the 1886 edition.

Ivor Lewis' objective in *SNB* was less pompous, but not less daring:

> to fill in some measure certain lacunae in *Hobson-Jobson* in order to achieve a better balance between the words of the common sort and those in the learned registers of theology, Indology, philosophy and the like. (Lewis 1991: v)

To achieve their goals, Yule et al., according to their "List of Fuller Titles of Books Quoted in the Glossary", used more than 800 sources written in English and other European and non-European languages.

Ivor Lewis, in his turn, based his lexicographic work on *H-J* proper, as well as on *The Oxford English Dictionary*. He also names *Anglo-Indian Dictionary* (1885) by G.C. Whitworth, *Glossary* (1885) by H.H. Wilson, *Indian Words in English* (1945) by G. Subba Rao, *Common Indian Words in English* (1984) by R.E. Hawkins as the sources for the list of words and their definitions when shaping the lexicographic picture on British presence in India from 1600 to 1947. However, Lewis does not specify the entries selection criteria.

---

[6] "The first book written by an Indian in English was *Travels of Dean Mahomet*, a travel narrative by Sake Dean Mahomet published in England in 1793" (Buda 1985).

As stated above, *H-J* comprises 2487 articles that fill 1021 pages; much more humble 266 pages in *SNB* house 3700 entries.

Juxtaposition of the content of these dictionaries reveals the differences and similarities in the compiler's approach both to formal and semantic aspects of the entry words lexicographic representation (see the Table 1).

Table 1: Comparison of the parameters of *H-J* and *SNB*.

Dictionary parameters	H-J	SNB
Part of speech marking	For ~ 93 % of entries	0
Transcription	0	0
Orthographic variants	For 77 % of the entries	For 1/3 of the entries
Usage examples	0	0
Quotations	From 0 to 15	0
Etymology	For 100 % of entries	For 100 % of entries
Types of definitions	Encyclopedic/linguistic (descriptive or explanatory)	Linguistic (descriptive or explanatory)/encyclopedic

2.2.2.2 Generic parameters

In *H-J* ~ 93 % of entries have grammatical marking, namely, part of speech marking. Their analysis shows that the vast majority of entries fall into the category of nouns. Judging by the prevalence of nouns in the dictionary, it is possible to suggest that by the time of the dictionary compilation the process of lexical borrowing into the Raj English was at its early stages.

Phonetic characteristics, transcriptions, are not provided with the exception for a very few entries. This fact, most probable, also indicates that the local additions to English were neologisms at the stage of introduction and thus had either varied or unstable pronunciation. This case is illustrated by the following example:

> **Neelgye, nilghau,** &c., s. Hind. *nīlgāū, nīlgāī, līlgāī,* i.e. 'blue cow'; the popular name of the great antelope <...>.

For 77 % of the lemmas in *H-J* alternative spellings are given that supports the assumptions made above: the Raj English, though rather widely used, was an unstable linguistic entity. Anglicized Victorian spelling of the entry words might also account for this fact. The following examples illustrate the case:

Numda, numna, s. Hind. *namda, namdā,* from Pers. *namad,* [Skt. *namata*]. Felt; sometimes a woollen saddle-cloth, properly made of felt. The word is perhaps the same as Ar. *namaṭ,* 'a coverlet,' spread on the seat of a sovereign, &c.

[1774. – "The apartment was full of people seated on **Naemets** (felts of camel hair) spread round the sides of the room. . . ."-<-> *Hanway, Hist. Account of British Trade,* i. 226.]

1815. – "That chief (Temugin or Chingiz), we are informed, after addressing the Khans in an eloquent harangue, was seated upon a black felt or **nummud,** and reminded of the importance of the duties to which he was called." – *Malcolm, H. of Persia,* i. 410.

[1819. – "A Kattie throws a **nunda** on his mare." – *Trans. Lit. Soc. Bo.* i. 279.]

1828. – "In a two-poled tent of a great size, and lined with yellow woollen stuff of Europe, sat Nader Koolee Khan, upon a coarse **numud**." – *The Kuzzilbash,* i. 254.

[1850. – "The natives use (for their tents) a sort of woolen stuff, about half an inch thick, called '**numbda.**' . . . By the bye, this word '**numbda**' is said to be the origin of the word *nomade,* because the nomade tribes used the same material for their tents" (!) – Letter in *Notes and Queries,* 1st ser.i.342.]

Thus, grammatical, phonetic and orthographic data in *H-J* allows suggesting that by the time the dictionary had been compiled the vocabulary specific for the Raj English was undergoing the early stage of the process of assimilation.

To make inferences on the changes in the quantity of the words belonging to different parts of speech and in the pronunciation of the Raj English lexis in its last 60 years, comparison with the later published dictionaries is necessary. However, this cannot be done, at least now, as *SNB* provides neither grammatical marking nor phonetic characteristics of the entries.

Abkar [18C. H./P. *abkar.*] A maker of strong waters; a distiller (*See* next.)

As for the orthography in *SNB*, the fact that approximately one third of the entries have alternative spelling indicates the spontaneous nature of the processes going on in the Raj English and the prevalence of the oral speech influence on the development of this variety of English.

Prabhu, parbha, parvoe, purvo, parbhu [17C S. *prabhu* 'lord or chief'. The popular name of the 'writer cast' in Western India. <...>

2.2.2.3 Etymology

Etymological references track down the derivational history of the entries and, in their specific form, provide historical and cultural information thus reproducing the history of a language/variety.

The survey of etymologies in *H-J* and *SNB* shedding light on cultural and linguistic contacts of English on the Indian subcontinent exposes the cosmopolitan nature of the Raj English and the intricate pattern of its evolution.

As etymologies of the letter "A" corpus in both dictionaries show, the source languages for the Raj English lexis were multiple and diverse including not only local languages and dialects but also those from the adjacent territories as well as from the languages of previous colonization. At the same time, the main volume of lexical borrowings into the Raj English came from Sanskrit (an Old Indo-Arian language), Hindi (Indo-Arian language), Pashto (a southeastern Iranian language), Malay (a member of the Western, or Indonesian, branch of the Austronesian/Malayo-Polynesian/language family), Malayalam and Tamil (Dravidian languages), Portuguese (a Romance language), Chinese (a branch of Sino-Tibetan language family).

Suryanamaskar [S. *surya*, 'sun' + *namaskar*, 'salutation']. Early morning **Yoga** exercises. [Hawkins, *CIWIE*.] (SNB)

Taka, tucka [19C. H. *takā*; Beng. *tākaā* S. *tantaka*. 'stamped silver money'.] (1) Formerly in Bengal = one rupee. Elsewhere in India valued variously, *See* Tanga, [Broughton (1800), *Letters from a Mahr. Camp.* (ed. 1892), 84; YB.] (2) Now it is a monetary unit in Bangladesh. [*OED*; *Guardian*, 22 Aug 1972, 10/4]. (SNB)

Adigar, adhikar(i) [17C. Tam, *adhikari*;] One possessing authority. A rural headman in S. India; Chief Minister (of Kandyan kings in ancient Ceylon). See **Monegar** and **Patel**. [YB; Knox, An Hist. Rel. of the *Island of Ceylon in the East Indies* (1681),48.] (SNB)

Andor, s. Port. 'a litter' and used in the Old Portuguese writers for a palankin. (H-J)

Andrum, s. Malayāl. *Andrăm*. The form of hydrocele common in S. India. <...> (H-J)

Gruff, adj. Applied to bulky goods. Probably the **Dutch** *grof*, 'coarse.'
[1682-3. – ". . . that for every Tunne of Saltpetre and all other **Groffe** goods I am to receive nineteen pounds." – *Pringle, Diary, Ft. St. Geo.* 1st ser. vol. ii. 3-4.]
1750. – ". . . all which could be called Curtins, and some of the Bastions at *Madrass*, had Warehouses under them for the Reception of Naval Stores, and other **gruff** Goods from Europe, as well as Salt Petre from *Bengal*." – *Letter to a Propr. of the E. I. Co.*, p. 52.

1759. – "Which by causing a great export of rice enhances the price of labour, and consequently of all other **gruff**, piece-goods and raw silk." – In *Long*, 171.

1765. – ". . . also *foole sugar*, lump *jaggre*, ginger, long pepper, and *piply-mol* . . . articles that usually compose the **gruff** cargoes of our outward-bound shipping."-<-> *Holwell, Hist. Events*, &c., i. 194.

1783. – "What in India is called a **gruff** (bulky) cargo." - *Forrest, Voyage to Mergui*, 42. (H-J)

Lamasery, lamaserie , s. This is a word, introduced apparently by the **French** R. C. Missionaries, for a **lama** convent. Without being positive, I would say that it does not represent any Oriental word (*e.g.* compound of *lami* and **serai**), but is a factitious French word analogous to *nonnerie, vacherie, laiterie,* &c.

[c. 1844. – "According to the Tartars, the **Lamasery** of the Five Towers is the best place you can be buried in." – *Huc, Travels in Tartary*, i. 78.] (H-J)

Saphir(e) d'eau [19 C. Fr. *sapphire d'eau*, 'sapphire of water'] A translucent blue variety of cordierite found in Sri Lanka [OED; R. Jameson, *Syst. Mineral* (ed. 1820), 1.174.] (SNB)

It needs to be noted that to establish etymologies the lexicographers used multiple sources and applied different techniques. As a result, in a number of cases etymologies are different for the same words. Thus, in *SNB* etymologies for eleven entries of the letter "A" corpus indicate Arabic as a source language but nine of them give Hindi/Arabic as two possible source languages. In *H-J* etymologies for 17 entries show Arabic as a source language; for seven entries Arabic is indicated as a direct source language and for ten entries not only Arabic is given as a possible source language. The following examples illustrate the case: in *H-J* etymology for AJNĀS, s. shows the word to be a direct borrowing from Arabic, [Ar. plur. of *jins* 'goods, merchandise, crops, etc.' <...>]; in *SNB* two possible source languages are indicated – Hindi and Arabic, [17C. H./Ar. pl. of *jins*, goods, merchandise, crops, etc.].

Therefore, generalizations that would reveal the patterns of the Raj English lexis evolution are not possible to be made at this point. More socio-historical and linguistic studies need to be done. However, some observations can be made. Thus, in *H-J* etymologies of 17 entries out of 95 in the letter "A" corpus give Arabic as a source language (about 18 %) while in *SNB* the numbers are 11 out of 188, respectively (about 6 %). On that account, it is possible to suggest that Arabic loan words had the tendency of falling out of use.

The style of etymologies in *H-J* differs substantially from that in *SNB* and, as a consequence, in many instances the amount of information the user can obtain is incomparable (see the examples below).

H-J:
ABADA, s. A word used by old Spanish and Portuguese writers for a 'rhinoceros,' and adopted by some of the older English narrators. The origin is a little doubtful. If it were certain that the word did not occur earlier than c. 1530-40, it would most probably be an adoption from the Malay *badak*, 'a rhinoceros.' The word is not used by Barros where he would probably have used it if he knew it (see quotation under [GANGA]); and we have found no proof of its earlier existence in the language of the Peninsula; if this should be established we should have to seek an Arabic origin in such a word as *abadat*, *ābid*, fem. *ābida*, of which one meaning is (v. *Lane*) 'a wild animal.' The usual form *abada* is certainly somewhat in favour of such an origin. [Prof. Skeat believes that the *a* in *abada* and similar Malay words represents the Arabic article, which was commonly used in Spanish and Portuguese prefixed to Arabic and other native words.] It will be observed that more than one authority makes it the female rhinoceros, and in the dictionaries the word is feminine. But so Barros makes *Ganda*. [Mr W. W. Skeat suggests that the female was the more dangerous animal, or the one most frequently met with, as is certainly the case with the crocodile.]

SNB:
Abada, badak [16C = Pg. *abada*, Mal. Badak.]

2.2.2.4 Semantic parameter

In a dictionary's semantic block, the meaning of lemmas is defined. In historical dictionaries typical definitions are descriptive and explanatory; cross references and references to the quotations are widely used. A key point to consider is that definitions, etymology and quotations, taken together, uncovering the history of every entry, indirectly reveal the history of the underlying notions and phenomena. Nevertheless, some compilers of historical dictionaries turn to encyclopedic definitions if they believe that both types of information are crucial for the dictionary potential users.

As *H-J's* target users were first of all British, the compilers most likely believed that to function effectively in India they needed not only a working knowledge of the language they shared with the Anglo-Indians but also some understanding of the cultural environment. Most probable, that is why the majority of definitions in this dictionary include a very heavy encyclopedic component. Such definitions and the quotations provide a variety of information: geographical, historical, social, political, often with proper names and dates. The history of the notions underlying lexical items and their usage pertain not only to the culture of the people speaking the language the lexeme was borrowed from (directly or indirectly) but also to the culture and social milieu of the British in India and the adjacent areas:

> **Kuzzilbash,** n.p. From Turki *kizi-büsh,* 'red head'. This title has been since the days of Safavi dynasty (See **Sophy**) in Persia applied to the Persianized Turks who form the ruling class in the country, from the red caps which they wore. The class is also settled extensively over Afghanistan. Many of them used to take service with the Delhi emperors; and not a few do so now in our frontier cavalry regiments. (*H-J*).

Although the dictionary articles in *H-J* do not contain any usage examples, the majority of them include a number of quotations (see the above example), up to 15 in some dictionary articles, that show the lemmas use in real context. These quotations, given in chronological order, are drawn from written sources in numerous languages: those in Arabic and other Asian languages are given in translation. As a result, the dictionary acquires not only lexicographic but also historical and cultural significance.

The definitions in *SNB* are of several types: (1) explanatory; (2) cross references; (3) the combination of explanatory definition and cross reference; the meanings of polysemantic words are enumerated:

> **Rumna** [18 C. H. *ramnā*, S. *ramana*, 'causing pleasure'.] A 'chase' or reserved hunting ground. [YB; Vansittart, *Narrative Bengal* (1760-64), I. 63]
> **Surrow** *See* **Serow.**
> **Rusa** [19 C. Malay, *rūsa*.] The East-Indian red-deer, a sub-genus of *Cevus*. See **Babi Roussa**. [Beveridge, *Hist. India* (1862), I. Introd. II]

Judging by the definitions, this dictionary is mainly linguistic in nature; although articles may provide some non-linguistic information, it can hardly be called purely encyclopedic. This is particularly evident when compared with the definitions of the analogous entries in *H-J*:

> **Gallevat, gallivant, galley-watt** (17C. Pg. galeota. Obs. 'A large boat used in Eastern seas having a triangular sail as well as oars [OED]. Like a **Grab** but smaller. Sea **Jalebote** (Jolly-boat). [OED & YB; Downton in Purchas (1618; 1625-26), 1, 501]. (*SNB*)

Gallevat, s. The name applied to a kind of galley, or war-boat with oars, of small draught of water, which continued to be employed on the west coast of India down to the latter half of the 18th century. The work quoted below under 1717 explains the *galleywatts* to be "large boats like Gravesend Tilt-boats; they carry about 6 Carvel-Guns and 60 men at small arms, and Oars; They sail with a Peak Sail like the Mizen of a Man-of-War, and row with 30 or 40 Oars... They are principally used for landing Troops for a Descent..." (p. 22). The word is highly interesting from its genealogical tree; it is a descendant of the great historical and numerous family of the *Galley* (galley, galiot, galleon, galeass, galleida, galeoncino, &c.), and it is almost certainly the immediate parent of the hardly less historical *Jolly-boat*, which plays so important a part in British naval annals. [Prof. Skeat takes *jolly-boat* to be an English adaptation of **Danish** *jolle*, 'a yawl'; Mr. Foster remarks that *jollyvatt* as an English word, is at least as old as 1495–97 (*Oppenheim, Naval Accounts and Inventories, Navy Rec. Soc.* viii. 193) (*Letters*, iii. 296).] If this be true, which we can hardly doubt, we shall have three of the boats of the British man-of-war owing their names (*quod minime reris!*) to Indian originals, viz. the *Cutter*, the *Dingy*, and the *Jolly-boat* to **catur, dingy** and **gallevat.** This last derivation we take from Sir J. Campbell's *Bombay Gazetteer* (xiii. 417), a work that one can hardly mention without admiration. This writer, who states that a form of the same word, *galbat*, is now generally used by the natives in Bombay waters for large foreign vessels, such as English ships and steamers, is inclined to refer it to *jalba*, a word for a small boat used on the shores of the Red Sea (see *Dozy and Eng.*, p. 276), which appears below in a quotation from Ibn Batuta, and which vessels were called by the early Portuguese *geluas*. Whether this word is the parent of *galley* and its derivatives, as Sir J. Campbell thinks, must be very doubtful, for *galley* is much older in European use than he seems to think, as the quotation from Asser shows. The word also occurs in Byzantine writers of the 9th century, such as the Continuator of Theophanes quoted below, and the Emperor Leo. We shall find below the occurrence of *galley* as an Oriental word in the form *jalia*, which looks like an Arabized adoption from a Mediterranean tongue. The Turkish, too, still has ḳālyūn for a ship of the line, which is certainly an adoption from *galeone*. The origin of *galley* is a very obscure question. Amongst other suggestions mentioned by Diez (*Etym. Worterb.*, 2nd ed. i. 198 <–> 199) is one from GALEO/S, a shark, or from GALEW/THS, a sword-fish – the latter very suggestive of a galley with its aggressive beak; another is from GA/LH, a word in Hesychius, which is the apparent origin of '*gallery*'. It is possible that *galeota, galiote*, may have been taken directly from the shark or sword-fish, though in imitation of the *galea* already in use. For we shall see below that *galiot* was used for a pirate. [The *N.E.D.* gives the European synonymous words, and regards the ultimate etymology of *galley* as unknown.] (H-J)

Very demonstrative of the specificities of the Raj English are the results of the semantic analysis of the definitions in both dictionaries.

This analysis showed that entries in both dictionaries fall into a relatively similar lexical thematic groups: "Material culture" (with further subdivision), "Toponymy", "Flora", "Fauna", "Religion".

Table 2: Thematic categories of entries in *H-J* and *SNB*.

Lexical thematic category	*H-J* (% to the total quantity of entries)	*SNB* (% to the total quantity of entries)
Material Culture	53.5	73.4
Toponymy	22.1	1.7
Flora	14.8	12.3
Fauna	5.4	5
Religion	2.6	6.3
Miscellaneous	1.6	1.3

As numbers in Table 2 show, the most numerous group of entries (54 % of the total amount of the entries under investigation in *H-J* and 73.4 % in *SNB*) belongs to the category of "Material Culture". In both dictionaries, this category falls under several subcategories: "objects of everyday life", "people and their occupation", "associations/organizations", "activities and titles", "means of watercraft", "products and drinks". In *SNB*, additional subcategories can be distinguished: "traditions" and "processes", "terms" and "knowledge", "measurement" and "money, revenue", as well as abstract notions. The widespread presence of material culture terms in the Raj English was noted by the dictionary compilers.

Interestingly, the number of toponyms in *SNB* is 13 times smaller than that in *H-J*. This fact might account for a high level of assimilation of loanwords-geographical terms in Indian English. However, it can also result from different word-list selection criteria applied by the compilers of *H-J* and *SNB*.

Despite extensive biodiversity of the Indian subcontinent, surprisingly small is the quantity of flora and, particularly, fauna terms in both dictionaries. This fact might reflect the specificity of the Raj English as a colonial language.

The increase in the terminology of religion can be connected to the changes in the ratio British/Anglo-Indian speaker of the Raj English in favor of the latter.

3 Conclusions

The Raj English, the forerunner of the Indian variety of English, originated in the bowels of the British colonial bureaucracy in India. Through its history, the Raj English absorbed multiple elements from its linguistic and cultural environment. Gradually, it evolved from a technical dialect of administration, legislation, and commerce into a language of education, technology, and literature. The Raj English evolution has been delineated in numerous dictionaries with *Hobson-Jobson*, a dictionary on historical principles, being the pinnacle of this process. Publication of another Raj English dictionary on historical principles, *Sahibs, Nabobs and Boxwallahs*, a hundred years after Hobson-Jobson suggests that this period of the Indian English evolution is recognized as crucial and at the same time underestimated.

The research showed that parameters of both dictionaries were determined by the demands of the target audience – British administration in colonial times and a broad Indian English-speaking and learning community nowadays. Although both dictionaries define lexis of the Raj period they differ in the methods of entries selection and in definitions. *Hobson-Jobson* abounds in encyclopedic information while *Sahibs, Nabobs and Boxwallahs* provides mainly linguistic facts.

Due to the significance of the Raj English for the formation of the Indian variety of English and an important role of lexicography in this process Indian English lexicography demands further research. It is also evident that compilation of a comprehensive dictionary of Indian English on historical principles will give a powerful impulse to further research and theoretical substantiation of the essential parameters of Indian English.

References

(a) Monographs and articles

Anand, Ari S. 2011. Cosmopolitanism in Hobson-Jobson: Remaking imperial subjects. *Comparative Studies of South Asia, Africa and the Middle East* 31(2). 521–537.

Azariah, Jayapaul. 2007. *My biography – Palliacatta, the Pulicat 1400 – 2007*. Chennai: CRNIEO.

Baldridge, Jason. 1996. *Reconciling linguistic diversity: The history and the future of language policy in India*. http://www.ling.upenn.edu/~jason2/papers/natlang.htm (accessed 25 March 2017).

Biswas, Arabinda & S. P. Agrawal. 1994. *Development of education in India: A historical survey of educational documents before and after independence*. New Delhi: Concept Publishing Company.

Bragg, Melvyn. 2003. *The adventure of English: The biography of a language*. London: Hodder & Stoughton.

Buda, J. K. 1985. The literature of British India. *Otsuma Women's University Faculty of Literature Annual Report* XVII. http://www.f.waseda.jp/buda/texts/litindia.html (accessed 25 March 2017).

Bytko, Natali. 2015. Anglojazichnaja uridicheskaja terminologia Indii v leksikograficheskoi presentazii [English juridical terminology in Indian dictionaries]. *Volgograd National University Bulletin*. Philology 2. 108–117.

Cawley, Charles. 2015. *Colonies in conflict: The history of the British overseas territories*. Newcastle upon Tune: Cambridge Scholars Publishing.

Coelho, Gail M. 1997. Anglo-Indian English: A nativized variety of Indian English. *Language in Society* 26(4). 561–589.

Dharwadker, Vinay. 2002. English in India and Indian literature in English: The early history, 1579–1834. *Comparative Literature Studies* 39(2). 93–119.

Della Cava, Olha. 1994. Lewis, Ivor. *Sahibs, Nabobs, and Boxwallahs: A dictionary of the words of Anglo-India*. Bombay & New York: Oxford University Press. 1991. In Eileen McIlvaine. *Selected Reference Books of 1993–1994. College & Research Libraries*. 55(5). 413.

Dodwell, Henry H. 1929. *The Cambridge history of the British Empire*. Vol. 4, *British India 1497–1858*. Cambridge: Cambridge University Press.

E. G. 1997. Review of: *Sahibs, Nabobs, and Boxwallahs: A dictionary of the words of Anglo-India. Journal of the American Oriental Society* 117(1). 224–225.

Hashmi, Alamgir. 1993. South Asia in English lexicography: Currying up (Blood-Pudding) English Teek-Hai! *Chicago Review*. 39(2). 108–113.

Hobson-Jobson. 1886. *The Leisure Hour*. Jan.1877–Oct.1903. 599–601. http://proxy.lib.sfu.ca/login?url=https://search-proquest-com.proxy.lib.sfu.ca/docview/3707782?accountid=13800 (accessed 25 March 2017).

Kachru, Braj B. 1990. *The alchemy of English: The spread, functions and models of non-native Englishes*. Champaign: University of Illinois Press.

Kachru, Braj B. 2005. *Asian Englishes: Beyond the canon*. Hong Kong: Hong Kong University Press. http://books.google.com/books?id=ksHUa14iV34C&pg=PA14&source=gbs_selected_pages. (accessed 25 March 2017).

Kindersley, A. F. 1938. Notes on the Indian idiom of English: Style, syntax, and vocabulary. *Transactions of the Philological Society* 37(1). 25–34.

Krishnaswamy, N. & Lalitha Krishnaswamy. 2013. *The story of English in India*. New Delhi: Cambridge University Press.

Kuipers, Joel C. 1998. *Language, identity, and marginality in Indonesia: The changing nature of ritual speech on the island of Sumba*. Cambridge: Cambridge University Press. http://assets.cambridge.org/97805216/24084/excerpt/9780521624084_excerpt.pdf (accessed 25 March 2017).

Lambert, James. 2014a. Diachronic stability in Indian English lexis. *World Englishes* 33(1). 112–127.

Lambert, James. 2014b. A much tortured expression: A new look at 'Hobson-Jobson'. *International Journal of Lexicography* 27(1). 54–88.

Loloi, Parvin. 2012. Gladwin, Francis. *Encyclopædia Iranica*. http://www.iranicaonline.org/articles/gladwin-francis (accessed 25 March 2017).

Lodrick, D. O. 2009. Anglo-Indians. *Worldmark encyclopedia of cultures and daily life.* http://www.encyclopedia.com (accessed 25 March 2017).

Malleson, George B. 1893. *History of the French in Indian from the founding of Pondicherry in 1674 to the capture of that place in 1761*. London: W. H. Allen. https://archive.org/details/historyoffrenchi00mallrich (accessed 25 March 2017).

McArthur, Tom. 2003. *The Oxford guide to World English*. Oxford: Oxford University Press.

Mehrotra, Raja R. 1998. *Indian English: Texts and interpretation*. Amsterdam & Philadelphia: John Benjamins.

Modern History: Being a continuation of the universal history. Book XIV. Chap. VIII. The commerce, colonies, and companies, which the Danes have heretofore maintained, or still support, in the East Indies. 1759. London: Printed for S. Richardson, T. Osborne, C. Hitch, A. Millar, John Rivington, S. Crowder, P. Davey and B. Law, T. Lingman, and C. Ware. https://books.google.co.kr/books?id=9wr3sSLfOlsC&pg=PA1&hl=ko#v=onepage&q&f=false (accessed 25 March 2017).

Nagle, Traci C. 2011. *Correspondence: The epistolary and textual influence between James A. H. Murray's "Oxford English Dictionary" and Henry A. Yule's "Hobson-Jobson"*. Indiana University: ProQuest Dissertations Publishing.

Nagle, Traci C. 2014. The visible and invisible influence of Yule's Hobson-Jobson on Murray's Oxford English Dictionary. *International Journal of Lexicography*. 27(3). 280–308.

Nair, Rukmini Bh. 2012. Bringing English into the 21st century: A view from India. *International Journal of Language, Translation and Intercultural Communication* 1(1). 103–122.

Obituary of the Year. 1890. *Proceedings of the Royal Geographical Society and Monthly Record of Geography* 12(7). 391–393. http://www.jstor.org/stable/1801230 (accessed 25 March 2017).

Parthesius, Robert. 2010. *Dutch ships in tropical waters: The development of the Dutch East India Company (VOC) shipping network in Asia 1595–1660*. Amsterdam: Amsterdam University Press.

Quirk, Randolph. 1958. Linguistics. In Beatrice White & T. S. Dorsch (eds.), *The year's work in English studies,* 33–53. London: Oxford University Press. https://archive.org/stream/yearsworksinengl009214mbp/yearsworksinengl009214mbp_djvu.txt (accessed 25 March 2017).

Ram, Tusli.1983. *Trading in language: The story of English in India*. Delhi: GDK Publications.

Sailaja, Pingali. 2009. *Indian English*. Edinburgh: Edinburgh University Press.

Sinha, Surenda P. 1978. *English in India: A historical study with particular reference to English education in India*. Patna: Janaki Prakashan.

Singh, Manmohan. 2005. Of Oxford, economics, empire, and freedom. *The Hindu*. July 10. http://www.thehindu.com/2005/07/10/stories/2005071002301000.htm

Snell, Rupert. 1993. Sahibs, nabobs, and boxwallahs: A dictionary of the words of Anglo-India by Ivor Lewis. *Bulletin of the School of Oriental and African Studies, University of London*, 56(1). 202. http://www.jstor.org.proxy.lib.sfu.ca/stable/620370 (accessed 25 March 2017).

Stow, Randolph. 1979. Denmark in the Indian Ocean, 1616–1845. An introduction. *Kunapipi* 1(1). http://ro.uow.edu.au/kunapipi/vol1/iss1/3 (accessed 25 March 2017).

Suresh, A. 2010. *Politics and social conflicts in French India: 1870–1939*. Puducherry: Department of History Pondicherry University thesis http://dspace.pondiuni.edu.in/jspui/bitstream/1/1782/1/T05396.pdf (accessed 25 March 2017).

Teltscher, Kate. 2011. The floating lexicon: Hobson-Jobson and the OED. In Indra Sengupta & D. Ali (eds.), *Knowledge production, pedagogy, and institutions in Colonial India*, 41–57. New York: Palgrave Macmillan US.

The Gentleman's Magazine and Historical Chronicle. 1820. XC. (2). London: John Nichols and Son, 569. https://books.google.com.ua/books?id=2nJKpRjYVugC&printsec=frontcover&source=gbs_ge_summary_r&cad=0#v=onepage&q&f=false (accessed 25 March 2017).

Ward, Adolphus W. & Alfred Rayney Waller. 1916. *The Cambridge history of English literature*. Vol. 14. Cambridge: Cambridge University Press.

Wellington, Donald C. 2006. *French East India companies: A historical account and record of trade*. Oxford: Hamilton Books.

Wilson, Horace Hayman. English Orientalist. 1902. *Encyclopedia Britannica*. http://www.1902encyclopedia.com/W/WIL/horace-hayman-wilson.html (accessed 25 March 2017).

Wilson's Glossary. Art. IV. 1857. *The Calcutta Review* 29. 354–376. https://books.google.com.pe/books?id=DZ0IAAAAQAAJ&printsec=frontcover&source=gbs_ge_summary_r&cad=0#v=onepage&q=a%20glossary%20of%20words%20&f=false (accessed 25 March 2017).

Zastoupil, Lynn 1993. Review of: *Sahibs, Nabobs and Boxwallahs: A dictionary of the words of Anglo-India*. *Journal of Asian History* 27(1). 68–69.

Zimmer, Ben. 2009. The story behind "Hobson-Jobson". https://www.visualthesaurus.com/cm/wordroutes/the-story-behind-hobson-jobson/

(b) Dictionaries and glossaries

An Anglo-Indian dictionary. 1885. A glossary of Indian terms used in English, and of such English or other non-Indian terms as have obtained special meanings in India. *The Athenaeum*. 3026. 534–535. http://proxy.lib.sfu.ca/login?url=https://search-proquest-com.proxy.lib.sfu.ca/docview/9130377?accountid=13800 (accessed 25 March 2017).

Barrère, Albert M. V. & Charles Godfrey Leland. 1897. *A dictionary of slang, jargon & cant embracing English, American, and Anglo-Indian slang, pidgin English, gypsies' jargon and other irregular phraseology*. London: George Bell & Sons.

Gladwin, Francis. 1797. *A dictionary of Mohammedan law, and of Bengal revenue terms: With a vocabulary; Persian and English*. Calcutta: From the press of Thomson and Ferris. http://www.iranicaonline.org/articles/gladwin-francis (accessed 25 March 2017).

Lewis, Ivor. 1991. *Sahibs, Nabobs, and Boxwallahs: A dictionary of the words of Anglo-India*. Bombay & New York: Oxford University Press.

Robarts, T. T. 1800. *An Indian glossary: Consisting of some thousand words and terms commonly used in the East Indies; with full explanations of their respective meanings. Forming an useful Vade Mecum, extremely serviceable in assisting strangers to acquire with Ease and Quickness the Language of that Country*. London: Printed for Murray and Highley, Fleet Street; Stewart, Piccadilly; and Collins, Change Alley.

Roebuck, Thomas, William Carmichael Smyth & George Small. 1882. *A Laskari dictionary, or, Anglo-Indian vocabulary of nautical terms and phrases in English and Hindustani, chiefly* in the corrupt jargon in use among the Laskars or Indian sailors. London: W. H. Allen & Company.

Roebuck, Thomas. 1811. *An English and Hindostanee naval dictionary of technical terms and sea phrases as also the various words of command given in working a ship & Co. With many sentences of great use at sea; to which is prefixed a short grammar of the Hindostanee language*. London: W. H. Allen & Company.

Rousseau, Samuel. 1802. *A dictionary of Mohammedan law, Bengal revenue terms, Shanscrit, Hindoo, and other words, used in the East Indies: With full explanations; the leading word of each article being printed in a New Nustaleek type*. London: Printed for J. Sewell, Cornhill; Murray and Highley, Fleet Street; and the Editor, Wood Street, Spa Fields.

The Indian vocabulary. To which is prefixed the forms of impeachment. 1788. London: John Stockdale.

Whitworth, George Clifford. 1885. *An Anglo-Indian dictionary: A glossary of Indian terms used in English, and of such English or other non-Indian terms as have obtained special meanings in India*. London: K. Paul, Trench.

Wilson, Horace Hayman. 1855. *A glossary of judicial and revenue terms and of useful words occurring in official documents relating to the administration of the government of British India, from the Arabic, Persian, Hindustani, Sanskrit, Hindi, Bengali, Uriya, Marathi, Guzarathi, Telugu, Karnata, Tamil, Malayalam and other languages*. London: W^M.H. Allen and Co.

Yule, Henry, Arthur Coke Burnell & William Crooke (eds.). 1903. *Hobson-Jobson: A glossary of colloquial Anglo-Indian words and phrases, and of kindred terms, etymological, historical, geographical and discursive*. London: J. Murray.

Brigitte Weber
Anglo-Norman: Language contact and obsolescence

Abstract: Anglo-Norman, listed as 'French of the Channel Islands' in the *Ethnologue* appears to be threatened. The UNESCO *Atlas of the world's languages in danger* categorizes its dialectal names *Jerriais* and *Dgernesiais* as "severely endangered". Due to contact with the more dominant language English, seen as the route to economic advantage, the continuing existence of Anglo-Norman seems to be under pressure. During the Middle Ages, from the 11th to the 14th centuries, however, it was the language of the élite in England and was still used for legal purposes until the 16th century. This paper offers a diachronic approach to language development and contact from Roman Britain and Gaul to this day. Changing attitudes towards different language situations are considered. It is the aim of this paper to identify a possible revitalization of Anglo-Norman on the Channel Island

Keywords: spoken Latin, varieties of Old French, medieval multilingualism, codification, Channel Islands Norman French.

1 Introduction

A central issue in the study of language contact is the relationship to other areas of linguistics such as typology, language history, dialectology, sociolinguistics, and pidgin and creole studies. The present research of the Anglo-Norman language involves aspects of all these fields of study based in part on an abundance of adequate literature (Hickey 2010, as a representative example). First the topic and context will be developed, and items of previous research will be reviewed. Anglo-Norman as one of the Medieval French dialects was spoken in the North of France and in Britain before and after the Norman Conquest in 1066. It was used for communication, for documentary sources and as a language for literary texts until the end of the 15th century. In the case of Law French, however, it has survived until this day: "la reine le veult" can still be

---

Brigitte Weber, Alpen-Adria University Klagenfurt, Department of English, Universitätsstr. 65–67, 9020 Klagenfurt, Austria. E-Mail: weber_loets@yahoo.co.uk

heard in the Houses of Parliament. Loanwords of this medieval French variety are still to be found in the English language such as "bailiff" on the Channel Islands for example. Anglo-Norman or alternatively called Anglo-French[1] between the Wars (Short 2013: 470) lives on today as a mainly spoken language on the Channel Islands and is also referred to as 'Insular Norman' (Jones 2014), 'Guernesiais'/'Guernsey French' (Sallabank 2011), 'Norman French' – 'Jèrriais' and 'Serquiais' (Liddicoat 1994) to cite some examples.

This language, introduced to medieval Britain as a result of the Norman colonialization, comprises two main functions: that of a spoken vernacular and that of a written language with a flourishing literature. At the beginning of the 12th century during the reign of Henry I, literature was mainly written in Latin, yet the beginning of an island French literature initiated with the poetic works of Philipe de Thaon (1113), further with an anonymous play *Le jeu d'Adam* (around 1150), *the life of St. Brendan* (1106), the heroic poem *Chanson de Roland*, *La Vie de Saint Alexis* (a translation of a Roman legend), *Les Lais de Marie de France* (Littérature Courtoise). They are based on Anglo-Norman manuscripts of the eleventh and twelfth centuries. There is great diversity among the manuscripts, depending on the scribe's origin.

Typologically Anglo-Norman seems to have been a language with a wide range of variation. Short (2013: 31) argues that Anglo-Norman, being an imported language, could theoretically fulfill the role of a lingua franca and points out that it must have been the same wherever it was used. This idea is supported by Higden yet rejected by Susan Crane (Short 2013: 31) who claims that French in England was the reverse of a lingua franca in that "it limited rather than facilitated access to the domains in which it was used". Folena (2015: 261), in his study of Old Venetian, also considers conservativeness a possible characteristic of colonial languages.

In the multilingual situation of language contact in the Middle Ages, Anglo-Norman went through a process of simplification. There is general agreement in the literature that language contact is associated with the linguistic process of simplification and the best examples are the pidgin and creole languages (Trudgill 2011: 15). Schlieben-Lange (1977: 81–101) suggests that all Roman languages emerged as creoles. Yet Thomason & Kaufman (1988: 306) conclude in their chapter *French influence on Middle English and the question of creolization*

---

[1] Menger (1904: 4) states that "Anglo-Norman" seems to designate more aptly the early period of the dialect, while "Anglo-French" as used by some scholars would better apply to the latter part of it. Neither defines the entire period.

that – after thorough research – creolization was unlikely on social grounds and that the degree of French influence was meaningful, but moderate and fairly commonplace. They accept morphological simplification, though (Thomason & Kaufman 1988: 310).

Language contact between English and French has existed from the Middle Ages in Europe and overseas. At a certain stage a variety of Anglo-Norman in Britain used to be called "faus franceis de l'Engleterre".[2] Today we have new coinages which rather non-native speakers are creating. Among many others there are *"franglais"* and "camfranglais".[3] As David Crystal states in his encyclopedia of the English language (Crystal 1995: 115), code-mixing takes place to some degree everywhere that English is spoken alongside another language and is a normal feature of bilingualism. The mixed varieties are given blended names to show their origins, such as *Franglais* (French and English), *Camfranglais (*as mentioned above*:* Cameroon Pidgin + English + French), or others like *Spanglish* (Spanish and English), or *Anglikaans* (Afrikaans and English) just to mention a few among many others. These varieties are widely spoken but unusual in writing. I agree with Ian Short (2013: 17) in that he states that Anglo-Norman is not the assimilation of the French and English language, to form the mixed dialect termed the Anglo-Norman – in spite of a definition in the *Oxford companion to the English language* (McArthur 1992: 69) "a contact language mixing French and English". French clerics translating non-literary English texts introduced French structure and vocabulary into the English language, though. The Anglo-Norman language lives on as 'insular' as well as 'mainland Norman', in the latter to a lesser extent, though. It is the indigenous language of the Channel Islands where different varieties are spoken in each island. The variety spoken in mainland Normandy is in contact with the related, structurally similar *oïl* variety of French, serving as an example of dialect contact (Jones 2014: 6).

Julia Sallabank, Reader in Language Policy and Revitalization at the School of Oriental and African Studies, University of London, finds that "the Norman vernacular of the Channel Islands has scarcely been developed or modernized in the last fifty years" (Sallabank 2002: 217). In an article in *Shima* (Sallabank 2011) she examines the island varieties of Norman and concludes that they are now highly endangered. She then discusses efforts to preserve the linguistic heritage of the islands' culture and considers revitalization measures.

---

2 Trotter (2005: 3).
3 French: *boycotter, tester* including **Cam**franglais from the former colony Cameroon: *Quand on waitait le professeur* < *on attendait*.

Suzanne Romaine (2010: 320) shows two possible choices for groups in contact to communicate: The first is the use of a lingua franca both groups share. The second option is to learn the other group's language(s). In case of equilibrium between the groups, stable multilingualism may result, as was often the case in the Middle Ages. Romaine further points out that bilingualism, where it is asymmetrical, and where the more powerful group imposes its language on a subordinate group, contact often leads to language shift or loss. This seems to be the case with insular Norman in contact with English. Considerable research has been devoted to the development of Anglo-Norman from the Middle Ages to this day mainly indicating that this viable language was slowly progressing towards a total takeover by English.

Language contact, however, may also result in different forms of innovation. In Heine & Kuteva (2005) contact-induced change is described via abundant contemporary evidence of the influence of a linguistically dominant source variety on the grammar and vocabulary of a contact variety and thus adding to it. Examples are considered from Italian, Pennsylvanian German, Finnish, Singaporean English, to name but a few. In Maltese an example is presented with an extension of meaning for the preposition *fuq*, originally meaning *on* in a spatial sense only, replicating the use of the English preposition 'on television', 'on holiday', 'on the advice of' (Ingham 2010: 12). Ingham applies this perspective to an analysis of the structural convergence of Anglo-Norman (Ingham 2010: 13) and French.

The aim of this paper is to focus on innovations relating to contemporary Anglo-Norman in order to identify a revival of this language or a possible emergence of a new language. The following processes regarding language contact, language development and change will be studied: Contact and borrowing, contact and code-switching, contact and dialectology, all in a diachronic perspective. The remainder of this paper is divided into three sections: First of all, (Section 2) From the Latinization of Gaul to the codification of French, then (Section 3) The linguistic situation in Britain and finally (Section 4) Norman on the Channel Islands.

As can be seen on the map below, both Gallia and Britannia were parts of the Roman Empire. Their respective language situation and change will be examined in the following sections.

2 From the Latinization of Gaul to the codification of French

The name for the language Latin is derived from the area of Latium, today 'Lazio', a region around Rome. Latin spread from the Romans' language to the whole of Europe and is still the basis of modern languages, of academic disciplines like law, of sciences for physicists, chemists and medical doctors. It was used in alchemy and witchcraft during the renaissance period and represents an important element in today's children's literature like *Harry Potter*.

Before going into detail with the spread and development of Latin in Gallia, some details about the name of the language "Anglo-Norman" will be given.

Map 1: The Roman Empire (https://commons.wikimedia.org/wiki/File:Roman_Empire_125_general_map. SVG).

The name **Norman** originates from "northmen", the Vikings of Scandinavia. They settled in northern England and seem to have terrified Gaul for several decades. In Roman Gaul they established a dense settlement in the lower stretches of the Seine, around its mouth. This area was ceded to them in 911. There they created a remarkable dukedom based in Rouen where they developed their own variety of the Gallo-Romance language (Lodge 2001: 65). In the 11th century the Dukes of Normandy set up colonial kingdoms in Sicily and England. The latter will be discussed in section III. The Norman Territory in Roman Gaul is the present-day region of Normandy in north-west France, divided into five 'départements'. Some 75 square miles of the Norman territory form a small archipelago lying in the English Channel (Jones 2014: 2), off the west of the Cotentin peninsula.

Menger (1904: 3) states that we need not think that the term "Anglo-Norman" refers exclusively to the dialect of the province of Normandy as used in England. He further points out that according to history men from many parts of France took part in the expedition of William the Conqueror and that the essential basis of the original French in England was Norman and Norman influence had been at work in England 24 years before the advent of the Conqueror; that is during the reign of Edward the Confessor.

> The dominant political influence in England was that of Norman leaders, and the literary men of France most likely to be attracted to England were Norman men of letters [...] Anglo-Norman seems to designate more aptly the early period of the dialect, while Anglo-French as used by some scholars would better apply to the latter part of it. Neither defines the entire period. (Menger 1904: 4)

Menger analyses in detail 35 Anglo-Norman texts, among them *Laws of William the Conqueror, Roland, Brandan, Adgar, Bible translations,* just to name some examples. Anglo-Norman literature written in the French of medieval England is rather limited.

2.1 From Gallo-Romance to the varieties of French

The distribution of Gaulish place-names seems to be the only indication with regard to the areas inhabited by the Gauls, and with regard to the old Gaulish language, some traces can still be found in modern French designating plants, trees and agricultural implements as for example *charrue* ('plough'), *charpente* ('timber framework'), *benne* ('bucket') (Lodge 2001: 40). The military conquest of Gaul by the Romans began towards the end of the 2nd century BC. Communities like Gaul remained diglossic for a long time, with Latin acting as the official language and with numerous local vernaculars continuing to serve the needs of local populations. According to Ferguson (1959: 325–340) one language variety

(Latin) is labeled High (H), used in formal contexts, the other variety (a local vernacular) is labeled Low (L) and used in informal contexts. He distinguishes H and L by categorizing their use into: *functions, prestige, literary heritage, acquisition, standardization* and *stability* (Lodge 2001: 14). In Britain, however, the use of Latin as a spoken language replacing Celtic was probably very limited. The Roman Empire may be seen as a multilingual and multicultural community rather than as a sociolinguistic monolith built around a Latin free of variation (Lodge 2001: 33ff.). It seems that the Latin language was diffused in the western empire more in its informal, colloquial form than in that of the high prestige standard.

In Gaul, during the period of the Roman Empire, the language of the state expanded. Large parts of the population took up Latin as their first language, also due to the strong central power. In the Roman Empire the number of languages diminished (just as has been the trend in world history for several millennia).

The usual way for a language to disappear is what probably happened in Roman times:
- a gradual shift from one language to another,
- families become bilingual,
- in a later generation, the children start with the new language;
- later people stop learning the original language first;
- in the end, people stop learning the original language at all.

The social reasons for shifting to a new powerful language even today are often similar to the ones in the Roman Empire: Education and culture, religion, contacts with important people, good jobs, money and power, these are important matters for most people. All those things are easier to come by if you speak a rich and powerful language. Language shifts and extinction of languages are quite frequent in modern times. The later history of Latin, however, is an interesting example of the opposite process, the birth of **new languages**.

Latin and Roman culture survived after the crash of the Roman Empire in spite of Germanic intruders during the 6th and 7th centuries. Latin remained the only written language. In the seventh and eighth centuries very few texts were produced and their language is often quite strange. The writers wanted to write in the classical manner, but their lack of education made that impossible, and what they wrote down is sometimes not even comprehensible.

The following figure (Figure 1 below) shows the relationship between written and spoken Latin in Gaul (realized as "code graphique" and "code phonique"). The two varieties diverged in the 3rd century B.C. (see Berschin et al. 2008: 62).

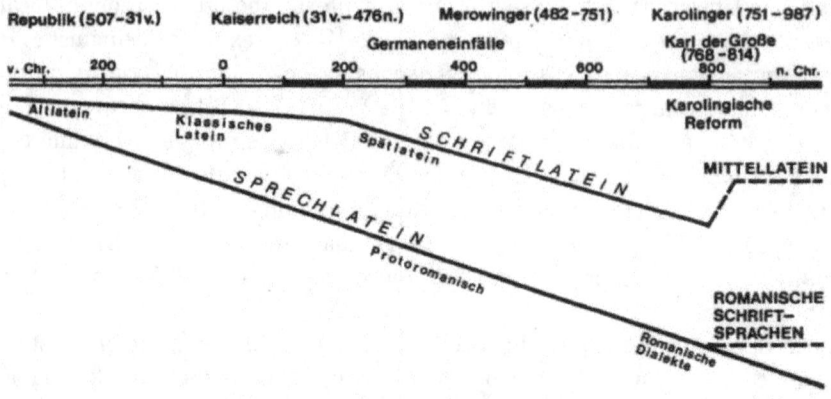

Figure 1: "Zweisprachigkeitsthese" (Berschin et al. 2008: 62).

As we can see on the figure, from the middle of the 8th century on there is a tendency to a cultural renewal characterized by a turning towards antiquity: *The Carolingian Renaissance*, an orientation towards Rome and the Pope. It reintroduced the classical Latin as written by Cicero without possible oral communication any longer.

Each corner was left to itself, and external contacts were reduced to a minimum. The consequences for language can be anticipated: Each region developed its own speech habits. Within a few centuries after the collapse of the Roman Empire Latin was transformed into a multitude of regional and local dialects. In the Latin essay *De vulgari eloquentia*, the Italian poet **Dante Alighieri** classified the Romance languages identifying them by their word for 'yes' in **oïl** language (in the north of Gaul), **oc** language (in the south) and **si** language on the Apennines Peninsula (de).

2.2 Local languages and their documentation

The Roman language, also called *Rustica Romana Lingua*, was officially recognized in a document for the first time in 813 and set against Latin together with German vernaculars. It was in the resolution of the *Council of Tours*. Some hundred years later, in 1539, in the region of Picardy, in the *Decree of Villers-Cotterêts*, Latin was suppressed even for legal texts and documents. Another important step with linguistic significance were *The Oaths of Strassbourg* in 842, pledges of allegiance and cooperation between Louis the German and Charles the Bald, both grandsons of Charlemagne, written in medieval Latin, OHG, OF. These oaths were composed to settle the sons' disputes regarding the succession of the Emperor Louis the Pious and they swore their oaths in *Teudisca* and *Romana lingua*. The orality of their vows reveals the linguistic variety of the particular geographical region they originate from. It is a legal text. The Oath in *Romana Lingua* contains characteristics independent from Latin, as for example articles, but there are still a number of Latin elements. Latin was not understood any longer and so the oaths were written in vernacular. Latin was only the language of the elite.

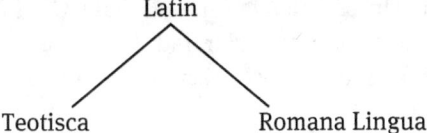

Innovations, seen as errors are included in the initially spoken language. Peter Koch (1993: 39–81) develop a schema for the typology of the first written texts which were also meant to be read (written texts with a final oral aim/performance). The different types of texts can be classified according to closeness or distance. They study orality and writing of speech: Oral or written code, both from 'immediate communicative' to 'distant communicative'. Oral texts may belong to the distant communicative, if they are meant to be read. Written texts may belong to the immediate communicative, if they are personal, like letters for example.[4] An example may be the reading of lyric poetry at court or the reading of/listening to account books, lists, description of the interior of a ship or a last will, anything without a textual structure.

In the Middle Ages the text type of **Skriptae** has been preserved from different areas. More elaborated texts/manuscripts appeared later: the scribe (copyist) contributed to (diatopic) variation. Sometimes several words were written as one. The elaborated text type of Christian Hagiography with the *Séquence de Sainte Eulalie* (Bibl. de Valenciennes) is destined for oral recitation with ~880 verses. It seems to originate from the regions of Picardy-Wallonia. The spelling/orthography mixes Latinisms, archaisms and regional features. The value of sounds can be guessed due to rhyming. Writing does not reflect phonetic reality. Another early Romance text is a bilingual sermon called *Fragment of Jonas*. It is a collection of personal notes preparing a sermon containing an appeal for fasting. A further manuscript is the Anglo-Norman *Vie de Saint Alexis*, a Roman

---

4 More information in 'lecture notes': Vorlesung Prof. Wilhelmer, Romanistik WS 2016 AAU Klagenfurt.

legend, written in England in decasyllables. It has been scholarly well analyzed. Gaston Paris dates it around 1040. Eventually there emerge three prestige varieties in the *lingua d'oïl*:

- **The King's French** or *francian* around Paris. Particularly through the crusades the King's French played a vehicular role across Europe's aristocracy. It became the administrative language of a vastly extended kingdom.
- **The Picard** variety in the north. Picard was seen as a "langue véhiculaire d'origine urbaine" as it emerged in one of the most urbanized regions of Europe and was first used for administrative purposes mainly. For the acquisition of this business language special dialogues for trading were made up (lecture notes). It was a vehicular trade language and influenced the
- **The Anglo-Norman** variety spoken in England and Normandy due to trading. See Section 3.

The *langue d'oïl* in Latin was referred to as **lingua gallica/gallicana** and in French as **françois.** Roger Bacon distinguished four main dialects writing in the 1260s: Picard, Norman, Burgundian, Parisian and French. They were mutually intelligible, although distinct. He emphasized that they were all the same language, namely French.

2.3 The way to standardization

In his study *French. From dialect to standard,* Anthony Lodge (1993) adopts a sociolinguistic approach for the diachronic study of one of several dialects on its way to standardization. The method is suggested by the Scandinavian linguist Einar Haugen in his publication: *Dialect, standard, nation* (Haugen 1972 [1966]). According to Haugen there are two types of process at work in standardization: social processes and linguistic processes. The first involve modifications to the status of a particular variety in a certain speech community which is adopted as the standard. He calls this *selection*. One dialect is chosen for privileged use in the political and economic sphere. Usually it is the dialect of the dominant group in the society in question. This variety has to gain acceptance throughout the relevant population. With regard to linguistic processes Haugen distinguishes two processes here: *elaboration of function* and *codification*. The linguistic tools to perform its extended range of functions are the development of a written form, of the syntax required in written documents and a lexicon in order to function in a wider range of fields. The four steps on the way to standardization thus are:

1. *selection of norms* (which characteristics can be declared the norm of spoken vernaculars and of the writing system);
2. *elaboration of function* (H/L variety) involves an extensive 'Ausbau' and intensive use in many domains;
3. *codification* involves the writing of grammars, dictionaries;
4. *acceptance* implies the hope that the respective language will be used in many areas;
5. *maintenance* of the standard (added by Lodge).

The final chapter consists of a discussion about the problems of the "Maintenance of the standard" in contemporary France (Lodge 2001: 27). In this study the "way to standardization" traces the success story of the **Francian** dialect.

3 The linguistic situation in Britain

Before 1066, a monastic revival had started in France. Many English monks came to study their generating close contacts between the two cultures and thus French loanwords can be found in Old English by this time like *prisun* 'prison', *castel* 'castle', *cancelere* 'chancellor', *prude* 'proud', *prutness* 'pride' (Crystal 1995: 27). Latin ecclesiastical as well as general loans exist from that time:

clericus > *cleric* 'clerk'	*persicum* > *persic* 'peach'
credo > *creda* 'creed'	*hymnus* > *ymen* 'hymn'
crucem > *cruc* 'cross'	*declinare* > *declinian* 'decline'

The largest corpus from the Old English dialects is the one written in the West Saxon dialect. It reflects the political and cultural importance of this area, the kingdom of Wessex. Some other important vernacular varieties are Northumbrian, Mercian and Kentish. Latin left its footprints not only in the language, also in British culture. It is rather in the written form it lived on. Even French, taught in England after the conquest, was taught in the same way as Latin was. This means that French grammar was taught like Latin grammar.

3.1 The French language in medieval, multilingual England

"La *Romania submersa* dans les îles britanniques: Après 1066/Die verlorene Romanität auf den Britischen Inseln: Nach 1066".[5] This is an exhaustive yet concise contribution about the linguistic history of the Romania by the American linguist Douglas A. Kibbee, affiliated to the University of Illinois. The introduction as to the concept of Roman: the Roman conquest in the 1st century AD, Christianization in the 5th century and the Norman Conquest from the eleventh to the 15th century, is followed by a detailed chapter on the "external" linguistic history in five sections, and a shorter chapter on the "internal" linguistic history focusing mainly on the phonology of Anglo-French ("français insulaire"). In the subsequent chapter named "scientific problems", Kibbee reveals the difficulty for a characterization of this variety (Kibbee 2003: 723) due to the dialectal diversity of the first texts. Some features originate from the West, others from Picardy. They are just identified as "Norman". Kibbee believes that the explanation for this diversity can be found in the diversity of William's army. Even the courtesans accompanying the wives contributed to this diversity originating from different areas. This can be traced in later texts and documents. Kibbee then raises the question if unknown syntactic structures in texts of the thirteenth and fourteenth centuries suggest a special insular development of French or an error relating to a person without sufficient knowledge of the French language. Looking at 13th century literature, different types of variation can be found as for example in the *Chanson de la Première Croisade d'après Baudri de Bourgueil* (Gabel de Aguirre 2015) due to graphic/phonetic, morphologic, syntactic and lexical varieties based on manuscripts as for example the *Oxford Bodl. Hatton 77 (H)*, an Anglo-Norman scripta from the middle of the 13th century. Variation occurs even in the same diatopic domain.

Legge (1976: 87) underlines the dialectal aspect of everyday vocabulary but considers a certain unity within the literary language. She finds that many Anglo-Norman writers' names of the twelfth and thirteenth centuries are derived from Norman place names where they used to settle on the lands of their Norman Lords as the bishop of Bayeux, the viscount of Avranches for example. The fiefdoms remain the same and thus guarantee the unity of the language. Legge also underlines the peaceful character of the Norman Conquest which she does not call *conquête* ('conquest') but *acquêt* ('acquisition'). She also reports on

---

5 This is a section from *Romanische Sprachgeschichte. Histoire linguistique de la Romania. 3. Teilband.* Edited by Gerhard Ernst, Martin-Dietrich Gleßgen, Christian Schmitt & Wolfgang Schweickard.

Edward the Confessor's good relationship with the Normans. Soldiers and clerics have come to England before 1066 but have not left many linguistic traces. On the contrary, they had to learn English in order to correct the toponymic orthography of the Doomsday Book investigators. After the conquest the remaining Normans exert a certain influence on the English language. Legge reports on the bailiffs introducing *cart* for *char*, *carry for charier*, *cattle* for *cheptel and* many more.

In the 11th century, as stated in Section 2, the Norman/Anglo-Norman variety of Old French dialects was spoken in the North of France as well as in England. This language contact resulted in a change of sounds and lexical items in England. In the 12th century, during the reign of the House of Plantagenets, the Francian dialect was favored as the King's French and a number of older Anglo-Norman forms were replaced as for example *charité* for *carité*. Others exist side by side with a difference of meaning:

Anglo-Norman *cacher* 'catch' – Francian *chacier* 'chase';
Anglo-Norman *wage* 'wages' – Francian *gage* 'gage', 'gauge'

Loanwords in the English language of the 12th and 13th centuries are not very numerous and originate from the military sector, from administration, the holding of court and ecclesiastical life: *bataille, prisoun, citee, complainte, manciple, pork, beef, mutoun, ureisoun, cloister* (Pinsker 1974: 8). More loanwords are taken over from France with monks, priests, merchants and traders until 1204. With John Lackland's loss of Normandy, however, the gentry in England loses their estates and cultural background, the Anglo-Norman language seems to have drifted apart more and more from the King's French and starts to be ridiculed. As we can see in some of Chaucer's verses in the description of the *Prioresse* in the prologue to the *Canterbury Tales*:

And French she spak ful faire and fetisly
After the scole of Stratford-atte-Bowe
For Frensh of Paris was to hir unknowe.

3.2 The teaching of French

The American linguist Douglas A. Kibbee, author of several linguistic textbooks like the *History of linguistics* (Kibbee 2007), *Language and the law* (Kibbee 2016) and many more, dedicated himself intensively to the situation of the French language in England from 1000–1600. On this topic he published *For to Speke*

Frenche Trewely (Kibbee 1991). In England the French language is taught to Anglophones and the first textbooks are only word lists. Kibbee divides the centuries after the Norman Conquest into four main periods as far as the role of French is concerned, maintaining that "instruction in French seems to arise with the development, during Period III but especially in Period IV, of schools of *dictamen*[6] associated with the University at Oxford" (Kibbee 1991: 41). His 'Period III' is 1258–1362 and 'Period IV' 1362–1470, so, if this statement were correct, it would mean that there was no demand at all for the teaching of French in England for at least two centuries after the Conquest. He goes on to say that: "The first significant teaching tools for French were the bilingual and trilingual *nominalia* to which the orthographic treatises were added slightly later in Period III" (Kibbee 1991: 41). This primacy attributed to the *nominalia* as the earliest branch of the French language to be taught would imply that, even after two hundred years of French rule, the only perceived barrier to the understanding of French by the English was a shortage of vocabulary that could be remedied by the few surviving *nominalia* from the later 13th century, and, therefore, that a knowledge of basic French grammar could be taken for granted amongst the literate classes in England for generations after the Conquest. This is because any *nominale* is no more than a static body of potential knowledge until the addition of grammar, in particular verbal morphology and prepositions or flexions, turns it into actual knowledge by giving it temporal and spatial context, thus making possible its use in linguistic exchanges. In the absence of that context the *nominale* is useful only for inventories, lists of goods or people and the like. Rothwell (2001: 6) observes that

> thanks to *Teaching and Learning Latin* it is clear that the grammatical terminology of both French and English is in place and in active use long before the thirteenth century, and the considerable volume of imaginative writing in French all through the twelfth century in England testifies to the presence of a not inconsiderable public that understands French at that time.

The appearance of a little treatise on the French verb at the beginning of the 13th century, followed by Bibbesworth's *Tretiz* later in the century, a very early example of an Anglo-Norman pedagogical poem, confirms that the need for instruction in both French grammar and vocabulary continues to be felt in different sections of the population in response to changes in English society: The number of French-speaking families in England diminished over the years, familiari-

---

6 Early 16th century; from Post-Classical Latin *dictamin-*, *dictamen* dictate, bidding, utterance from Classical Latin *dictāre* + *-men*.

ty with the language declined, but its continuing use amongst the landed gentry in managing their estates and its enduring position as a language of record in the steadily growing area of administration meant that it had to be taught. A further instruction book called *La manière de langage* (1873) is composed in the later 14th century to help the English traveler abroad find his way around France. Yet, providing much vocabulary useful in many different situations, these imaginary conversations with French people make no mention of how the words in their lists are to be pronounced. A French grammar was composed by Johan Barton: "Donatus and the Teaching of French in Medieval England", as a final product called *Donait François* (Colombat 2014).

Rothwell (2001: 18) concludes that

> in the long run the enduring mark left on English by all the medieval teaching of French was limited to the domain of vocabulary, but in the later Middle Ages, without impinging on the entrenched position of English as the only national language, the remaining presence of an acquired form of French, together with the residual prestige of Latin, helped produce a mixed language that survives in a host of business documents, accounts, inventories and the like. This language uses English, French and Latin.

3.3 New vocabulary analyses

A new perspective for vocabulary analysis is suggested by the lexicologist Rothwell (1975: 41–49). In his view background knowledge is essential for the deep understanding of certain lexical items. Specific cultural, historic or environmental information is required for a genuine interpretation. In the next section some examples will be picked out to show the importance of general knowledge, the way of medieval life, to set an example.

Rothwell reports on changing conditions of study and signs of change. He points out that since the end of the Second World War two important new factors have been exerting growing influence on the study of Anglo-Norman. In the first place, a transformation is coming about on the textual scene. On the one hand the Anglo- Norman Text Society has produced an increasing number of literary texts conforming to the high standards of modern editorial practice, while other institutions have continued to publish numerous volumes of legal and administrative texts in Anglo-Norman. This means that textual material is becoming available in sufficient quantity and quality upon which modern research can be based. Secondly, there have been changes in many aspects of linguistic research, including work in Anglo-Norman. Rothwell suggests that new tools now exist for the study of Anglo-Norman and new materials on which to use them. In his article *Anglo-Norman perspectives*, Rothwell (1975: 43ff.)

dedicates himself to the areas of Anglo-Norman vocabulary and syntax and points out that both of these are far from completely explored and claims that in certain aspects of both there can be seen either an influence of English on French or evidence of an independent development of French on English soil. Since, however, questions of vocabulary lend themselves more readily to treatment within a small compass he will confine himself there. As a simple illustration of the kind of question that may be asked by anyone investigating the development of Anglo-Norman vocabulary Rothwell takes the history of the English word *noon*. He further shows that this does not figure in the lists drawn up by Pope (1944) in her paper on the Anglo-Norman element in today's English vocabulary, perhaps because its development seems, on the surface at least, too clear. Rothwell's findings are the following: In form, *noon* is simply a variant spelling of the standard Old French *nonne*, the ninth canonical hour, situated traditionally in mid-afternoon. Etymologically, it goes back to the Roman reckoning of time. The two authoritative dictionaries of Old French are both quite clear as to the meaning of the word: for both Godefroy (1880–1902) and Tobler (see Långfors 1930) it means 3 p.m., the hour at which the office of Nones was supposed to be recited in religious houses. Neither is aware of the fact that *noon* in English means midday and not mid-afternoon. At first sight it might appear that English alone is responsible for this shift of meaning and that we are dealing with a case of insular development marking off Anglo-Norman from continental French. A closer look at the dictionaries mentioned, however, shows that both are obviously wrong in maintaining that *nonne* meant only 3 p.m. in medieval France. Rothwell criticizes them stating that their own quotations prove them wrong, even without taking into account a whole mass of documentary evidence both have ignored (Rothwell 1959 and 1966). One of Godefroy's (1880–1902) quotations in support of his translation 'trois heures de l'après-midi' is this: *trois heures puis noesne*. *Puis* here means 'after', thus giving, presumably, the meaning 'three hours after three o'clock'. 'Three hours after noon' would make better sense, noon being the axis of the day. In Tobler we read that *nonne* was used figuratively in medieval French for the peak or zenith of a man's life ("figurlich von der Hohezeit des Lebens"). The obvious connection between the **high point of life** and **the high point of the sun** (emphasis mine) at noon is not made. The more one examines the evidence in the case of *nonne*, the more difficult it becomes to accept the one single meaning given for it in the dictionaries. This is, in fact, just one of the many cases where an understanding of medieval life is not merely a necessary part of the lexicologist's equipment, but the key to the solution of the problem. The fact is that *nonne* was linked to the *hora solvendi jejunii* – the ending of the fast – in medieval monasteries, and until well into the 14th century time was reckoned not by nationally regulated clocks as nowadays but by purely local estimation and the ringing of bells to mark different parts of the ecclesiastical day in individual religious houses. Once this is realized, the movement of *nonne* from mid-afternoon to midday becomes perfectly understandable: it seems evident that it is the medieval monk's empty stomach on the very numerous fast days that leads him to ring Nones earlier than he strictly ought to in order to get his meal.[7] It would be strange indeed if only English stomachs had rumbled out the message in the monasteries that it was high time to ring Nones. Rothwell finds that the *Französische Etymologische Wörterbuch* (VII, 189) clearly shows by reference to sources up and down France that the same movement forward in time took place on the continent just as in England, and the rough equivalence of *nonne* and *midi* must have been widespread. He holds that our modern English *noon* is therefore not just an Anglo-Norman word borrowed after the Conquest, but a linguistic survival – a fossil – from a state of affairs common to the life of medieval England and medieval France. Rothwell also suggests that the problem with regard to *noon* has arisen only because *nonne* has disappeared from use in normal every-day French, replaced by *midi*, and he argues that modern English *noon* (like all the other hours of the day) is now firmly fixed to a series of radio 'pips'[8] that measure out our day with scientific accuracy, far removed from the vague approximate canonical hour that meant so much to medieval religious on both sides of the Channel.

Rothwell (1975: 44) looks at another example of the way in which the simple notion of 'borrowing' from one language to another "needs to be clothed in the flesh of social reality" before it becomes meaningful. This is provided by our words for the points of the compass. Just as medieval man experienced great difficulty in determining time with any precision until the arrival of striking clocks on public buildings, so his handling of the concept of direction was very confused until well after the end of the medieval period. The simple statement that our present system of cardinal points, now in general use in Western Europe, is of Germanic origin and has been borrowed into the Romance languages largely through Anglo-Norman, tells us little. It is not merely that the direction of borrowing is here reversed, running from England to the continent, rather than from France across the Channel to Britain: it is rather that an abstract system of orientation used by a sea-faring people, the British, for crossing wide

---

7 Bilfinger, G. 1892. *Die Mittelalterlichen Horen* (cited in Rothwell 1975: 44). "Horen" are Goddesses in Greek Mythology supervising time management.
8 A radio station.

stretches of water out of sight of land and landmarks has gradually displaced a whole series of local systems of direction, many of them linked to purely local landmarks in France and so ill-suited to use outside a particular area. Related to this, Rothwell shows another example: The boatmen on the Rhone have for centuries indicated 'east' and 'west' by *empire* and *royaume*, but these terms make sense only in the historical and geographical context of the river which formed the boundary between the Holy Roman Empire to the east and the Kingdom of France to the west. The modern *est* and *ouest*, free from such local ties, can be used in any area. What is borrowed here is not just a set of terms; it is nothing less than a different outlook on the physical environment.

4 Anglo-Norman of the Channel Islands

According to the researcher Sallabank, expert in endangered languages (Sallabank 2013), the Anglo-Norman varieties of the Channel Islands have scarcely been developed or modernized in the last fifty years. Even if there is a large body of literature, (some of which is quoted in the introductory chapter), many people are of the opinion that the (Anglo-Norman) local vernacular is not a written language. They call it "patois" which used to be the majority language until the late 19th century with French as the High diglossic partner. The spread of English, with its economic power and monopoly of the mass media, has displaced French and led to Jèrriais, Guernesiais, Serquiais being threatened with extinction. In an article Sallabank (2011) discusses speakers' literacy practices, attitudes towards the writing of the local varieties of Anglo-Norman and suggests various attempts at orthographic systems, leading to a wider discussion of the place of writing and literacy in the survival of endangered languages.

4.1 Geographical and historical background

The Channel Islands are famous for their cows, dairy products, sweaters, tomatoes and potatoes, and are popular in Europe as a tourist destination. Many visitors remain unaware that they also have their own language, which is now highly endangered (Sallabank 2002).

The Channel Islands belong to the British Crown but not to the United Kingdom and have never been full members of the European Union. They are self-governing with regard to internal affairs, with their own parliaments. Guernsey has a population of just under 60,000 (2001 census) and a land area of 62 km². It is about 80 miles/130 km from Weymouth, the nearest British port, but only 30 km from Dielette, the nearest French port (see the map below). This geographical proximity to France, but political allegiance to Britain, lies at the heart of the sociolinguistic situation.

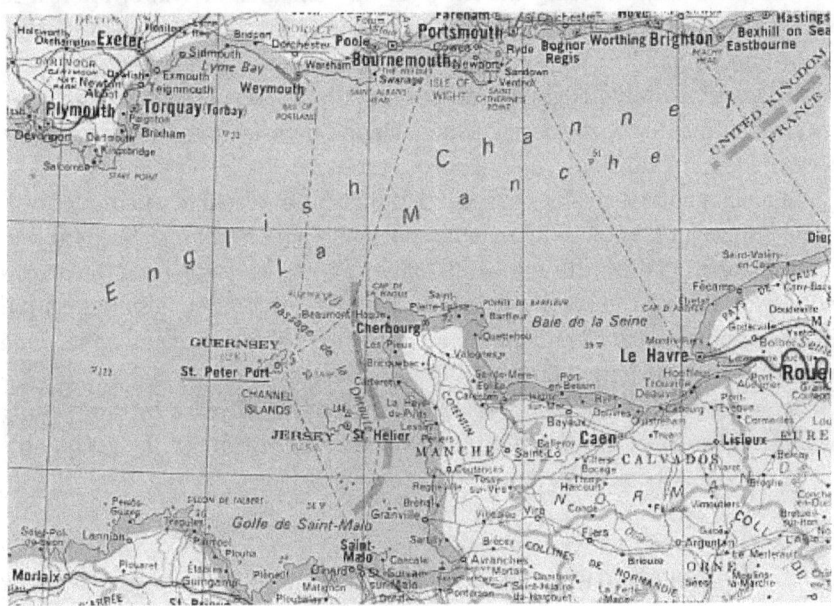

Map 2: The Channel Islands (in Sallabank 2002: 218).

The Channel Islands were formally annexed by Normandy in 933, and their relationship with England started in 1066, when Duke William of Normandy conquered England. King John lost mainland Normandy to Philip Augustus of France in 1204, but the Channel Islands remained loyal to the English Crown, for which they were rewarded with autonomy and tax privileges which became very important to their economies, as they eventually developed into offshore banking centers and tax havens. The islands were strategically important and fought off numerous attacks from France until the 19th century.

As discussed above, in the Middle Ages Norman was an important international language in France, England, Italy, and even in the Middle East during the Crusades. It had a large body of literature, the most well-known of which are *Le Chanson de Roland,* and *Le Roman de Rou* and *Le Roman de Brut* by Wace, who proudly proclaimed that he came from the neighboring island of Jersey. Sallabank (2002: 221) cites Bédier (1968: 250), editor of the *Chanson de Roland,* that we do not possess a single document from the 12th century which was written in the Parisian region. Up to the late 19th century (including during the high period of Norman culture), the majority of the inhabitants of the Channel Islands were illiterate, like the majority of people everywhere. Guernesiais was not thought worthy of being written until the Romantic revival of interest in local vernaculars and folklore in the 19th century. At that time numerous other vernaculars, which had been equally low in status, were standardized, and are now accepted as fully-fledged languages for all purposes. French, as the more powerful partner in the diglossic relationship in Guernsey, was the *Dachsprache* in Kloss's terms (1967).

Some language revivalists suspect that the lack of teaching Guernsey history and culture in schools is intended to prevent a nationalist movement and to increase identification with the UK (Sallabank 2002: 224). However, the President of the largest Guernsey cultural society, *La Société Guernesiaise,* stated: "It's very important to keep the tradition – we are losing our identity and some people think we are part of England."

Remains the question: Standardization: yes or no? If yes, which standard? Even if it takes time, the Anglo-Norman vernaculars are on the right way. This will be shown in the next section.

4.2 Some new features of Insular Norman

"Mette a haout dauve la grippe des Angllaïs" (Convergence on the island of Guernsey)

4.2.1 Guernésiais influence on the English of Guernsey (Jones & Esch 2002: 146)

– The **definite article** appears in contexts in which it is not normally used in standard English:
    – with names of languages
       *My father knew **the** good French and **the** English and **the** patois*
       *They never did **the** Guernsey French at school*
    – adverbials of direction and position in combination with street-names
       *He's got a chain of h'm shops in the, in **the** Fountain street*

- adverbials of time expressing a regular repetition
  *He gives the news out on the wireless in h'm in patois on **the** Friday*
  *And we go to **the** Saturday evening like – old time dancing*
- before the noun 'school' and the idiomatic expression 'to go by bus':
  *But I mean that [Guernsey French] wasn't helpful in **the** school, you see.*
  *It was always by **the** bus we went.*

- **Preposition 'to'** used in the English of Guernsey (EG) to describe motion towards a location, but also to specify static location:
  *There's some of them candles **to** the Forest museum. He is **to** town. He bought it **to** Creasey.*

  Position: [ʒə dmœr a sai pjɛr pɔr]   I live in Saint Peter's Port
  Destination: [ʒə ve a sai pjɛr pɔr]   I go to saint Peter's Port

- The **present tense** is used instead of the present perfect:
  There's nearly a thousand years we are British (I y a v'chin quâsi mille aens qué nou-s-est Britanniques)
  I'm in charge of it for 24 years
  That's h'm what over 30 years she is dead

4.2.2 English influence on Guernesiais

- **No-one** *(autchun)* historically requires a plural verb in Guernesiais. In one third of all cases a singular verb was used.
- **Dates: Cardinal** numbers are maintained, but there is **English word order:** *lé tchinze d'estembre/estembre lé tchinze.'*
  English: 'September the fifteenth'; 'the fifteenth of September'
- **When:** English: *I will tell you when I **come** back*
  Guernesiais : *Jé vous dirai quànd j'r'**viandrai*** (only in 46 percent of contexts)
- **The verbal system: lexical semantics.**
  L'église est couraïe par la paraesse – 'The church is **run** by the parish'
  Chena fait l'affaire pus difficile – 'That makes the thing more difficult'
  L's jonnes n'ètaient pas trop emportaïs dauve l'idée – 'The young people weren't too carried away with the idea'
  La langue va – 'The language is going' (i.e. disappearing)
  Nou saït l's fermiers – 'We know the farmers' (saver/counnitre)
  Not' desnaït fut attendu par 230 personnes – 'Our dinner was attended by 230 people' (G attendre > to wait for)
  J'té manqué – 'I miss you' (tu mé mànques > you to me miss?)

- **Calques**
  I met Mr. Pope yesterday – Is it? (Est-che?)
  I am always starving, me –' j'ai terjous fôim, mé
  Lé pénni quaï (cassé) – 'the penny dropped'
  Nou c'mmenche les gens jonnes – 'we start people young' (E and G historically differ in terms of word order)
  La piaeche ouéque l'hotael est – 'The place where the hotel is'
  Jé ne pouvais pas ouir autchun – 'I couldn't hear anyone' (G lexical items inserted in underlying English syntax)
- **Calquing of prepositions**
  Prepositions used in contexts with which they were not historically associated.
    - **Pour:** *Payer pour* – 'to pay for'
      J'fus civil servant pour 25 onnaïes – 'I was a civil servant for 25 years'
      Nou n'a pas etaï en Serk pour longtemps – 'We haven't been to Sark for a long time'
    - **Hors:** *Chena mit l's éfànts hors* – 'That put the children out'
      Copaïr hors – 'to cut out'; *J'fus hors* – 'I went out'; *hors de six O levels, il avait passaï riocque daeux* – 'out of six O levels he had only passed two.
      With the meaning of English 'off':
      Le switch est hors – 'the switch is off'; *I gardit lé jour hors* – 'He took the day off'; *Nou 'tait mux hors* – 'we were better off'
    - **Bas:** *J'mettrai lé naom bas* – 'I'll put the name down'
      M'n père a copaï bao l'arbre – 'My father has cut down the tree'
    - **Haout:** *Mette a haout dauve mé* – 'to put up with me'
      l'a baailli a haout l'école – 'he has given up school'

5 Conclusions

This paper is concerned with the emergence and development of one variety of the Old French dialects: Norman. It is a Romance language containing some Norse elements, such as terms relating to the sea, as for example *hou* 'island', *dicq* 'embankment', 'dyke', *vraic* 'seaweed', *halaï* 'to haul', *banque* 'low cliff', 'beach' (Sallabank 2011: 20). As shown in Section 2, the then called Vikings secured a permanent foothold on Frankish soil and became part of the area where the "Romana lingua" was spoken. They came to be known as 'Normans' and extended their rule westward to the districts of Lower Normandy where the Norman language variety emerged. After 1066, when England became part of the French kingdom, language contact between Norman and English resulted in an influence of Norman on the English language, still to be seen today (see Section 3.1)

Legge (1976: 86) identifies the language contact between (Anglo)-Norman and Picardian as vital for the development of Anglo-Norman. The trade with wool with the north-east of France has reinforced the Picard element already present. Thus the English words *chivalry, orison, waver (gaufre)* belong to the second wave of influence (Legge 1976: 87). It is noteworthy that in Anglo-Norman *e* preceded by *s* plus consonant was still instable and appears in 'school', 'spirit', 'sponge'. The characteristic stress of Picardian results in agglutination of an initial vowel with the vowel of the article which has had an influence on place names until today: Spital Fields, Spital of Glenshee.

The Anglo-Norman language has survived in spite of political suppression and negative attitudes, especially on the Channel Islands. There have been activities for the revival of the lowstatus vernacular like lessons, evening classes and festivals as the *Fête d'la Vieille Langue Normande*. Dictionaries are being compiled.

Processes of linguistic change are making the English and Norman French more similar to each other and more distant from the mainland varieties – although Norman French was in close and prolonged contact with Middle English (Baugh & Cable 2013: 127–149). It seems that the contemporary linguistic situation has arisen through convergence rather than common inheritance. A hypothesis about the emergence of a new language variety seems legitimate.

References

Baugh, Albert C. & Thomas Cable. 2013. *A history of the English language*. London & New York: Routledge.
Bédier, Joseph (ed.). 1968. *La chanson de Roland*. Paris. Piazza.
Berschin, Helmut, Josef Felixberger & Hans Goebl. 2008. *Französische Sprachgeschichte*. Hildesheim [u.a.]: Olms.
Colombat, Bernard. 2014. *Barton, Johan, Donait François*. Paris: Classiques Garnier.
Crystal, David. 1995. *The Cambridge Encyclopedia of the English language*. Cambridge: Cambridge University Press.
Ernst, Gerhard, Martin-Dietrich Gleßgen, Christian Schmitt & Wolfgang Schweickard (eds.). 2003. *Romanische Sprachgeschichte. Histoirè linguistique de la Romania. Ein internationales Handbuch zur Geschichte der romanischen Sprachen. Manuel international d'histoire linguistique de la Romania*. Berlin & New York: De Gruyter.
Ethnologue: Languages of the world. 2005. 15th edn. Dallas: SIL.
Ferguson, Charles.1959. Diglossia. *Word* 15. 325–340
Folena, Gianfranco. 2015. *Culture e lingue nel Veneto medievale*. Padova: Libreria universitaria.

Gabel de Aguirre, Jennifer. 2015. *La « Chanson de la Première Croisade » en ancien français d'après Baudri de Bourgueil*. Heidelberg: Winter.
Godefroy, Frédéric. 1880–1902. *Dictionnaire de l'ancienne langue française*. 10 volumes. Paris.
Haugen, Einar. 1972 [1966]. Dialect, language, nation. Reprint in J. B. Pride & Janet Holmes (eds.), *Sociolinguistics. Selected Readings*, 97–111. Harmondsworth: Penguin.
Heine, Bernd & Tania Kuteva. 2005. *Language contact and grammatical change*. Cambridge: Cambridge University Press.
Hickey, Raymond. 2010. *The handbook of language contact*. Oxford: Blackwell.
Ingham, Richard, 2010. *The Anglo-Norman language and its contexts*. Woodbridge: Boydel.
Janson, Tore. 2004. *A natural history of Latin*. Oxford: Oxford University Press.
Jones, Mari C. 2014. *Variation and change in Mainland and Insular Norman*. Leiden & Boston: Brill.
Jones, Mari C. & Edith Esch. 2002. *Language change: The interplay of internal, external and extra-linguistics factors*. Berlin & New York: De Gruyter.
Kibbee, Douglas A. 1991. *For to speke Frenche trewely. The French language in England, 1000–1600. Its status, description and instruction*. Amsterdam & Philadelphia: John Benjamins.
Kibbee, Douglas A. 2003. La Romania submersa dans les iles britanniques: après 1066/Die verlorene Romanität auf den Britischen Inseln: nach 1066. In Gerhard Ernst, Martin-Dietrich Gleßgen, Christian Schmitt & Wolfgang Schweickard (eds.), *Romanische Sprachgeschichte. Histoire linguistique de la Romania. Ein internationales Handbuch zur Geschichte der romanischen Sprachen. Manuel international d'histoire linguistique de la Romania*, 717–726. Berlin & New York: De Gruyter.
Kibbee, Douglas A. 2007. *History of linguistics 2005. Selected papers from the Tenth International Conference on the History of the Language Sciences (ICHOLS X), 1–5 September 2005, Urbana-Champaign, Illinois*. Amsterdam & Philadelphia: John Benjamins.
Kibbee, Douglas A. 2016. *Language and the law: Linguistic inequality in America*. Cambridge: Cambridge University Press
Kloss, Heinz. 1967. 'Abstand languages' and 'Ausbau languages'. *Anthropological Linguistics* 9. 29–71.
Koch, Peter. 1993. Pour une typologie conceptionnelle et médiale des plus anciens documents/monuments des langues romanes. In Maria Selig, Barbara Frank & Jörg Hartmann (eds.), *Le passage à l'écrit des langues romanes*, 39–81. Tübingen : Gunther Narr.
La manière de langage. Qui enseigne à parler et à écrire le français. Modèles de conversation composés en Angleterre a la fin du XIVe siècle e publiés d'après le MS du musée Britannique Harl. 3988. 1873. Paris: Franck.
Långfors Arthur. 1930 Tobler-Lommatzsch, Altfranzösisches Wörterbuch, 1928. (Compte rendu). *Romania* 56(222). 290–291.
Legge, Mary Dominica. 1976. L'anglo-normand: langue coloniale? In Marcel Boudreault & Frankwalt Möhren (eds.), *Actes du XIIIe Congrès International de Linguistique et de Philologie Romanes tenu à l'université Laval (Québec, Canada) du 29 août au 5 septembre 1971*, 85–91. Québec: Les Presses de l'Université Laval.
Liddicoat, Anthony J. 1994. *A grammar of the Norman French of the Channel Islands*. Berlin & New York: De Gruyter.
Lodge, R. Anthony. 1993. *French. From dialect to standard*. London. Routledge.
Lodge, R. Anthony. 2001. *French from dialect to standard*. London: Routledge.
McArthur, Tom. 1992. *Oxford companion to the English language*. Oxford: Oxford University Press.

Menger, Louis Emil. 1904. *The Anglo-Norman dialect: A manual of its phonology and morphology with illustrative specimens of the literature*. New York: The Columbia University Press.
Pinsker, Hans Ernst. 1974. *Historische Englische Grammatik*. München: Max Hueber.
Pope, Mildred K. 1944. *The Anglo-Norman element in our vocabulary. Its significance for our civilization*. Manchester: Manchester University Press.
Romaine, Suzanne. 2010. Contact and language death. In Raymond Hickey (ed.), *The handbook of language contact*, 320–339. Oxford: Wiley-Blackwell.
Rothwell, William. 1959. The hours of the day in Medieval French. *French Studies*, 13(3). 240–251.
Rothwell, William. 1966. A further note on *Nonne*. *French Studies* 20(3). 223–225.
Rothwell, William. 1975. Anglo-Norman perspectives. *The Modern Language Review* 70(1). 41–49.
Rothwell, William. 2001. The teaching and learning of French in later Medieval England. *Zeitschrift für französische Sprache und Literatur* 111(1). 1–18.
Sallabank, Julia. 2002. Writing in an unwritten language: The case of Guernsey French. *Reading Working Papers in Linguistics* 6. 217–244.
Sallabank, Julia. 2011. Norman languages of the Channel Islands. Current situation, language maintenance and revitalization. *Shima: The International Journal of Research into Island Cultures* 5(2). 19–44.
Sallabank, Julia. 2013. *Attitudes to endangered languages: Identities and policies*. Cambridge: Cambridge University Press.
Schlieben-Lange, Brigitte. 1977. L'origine des langues romanes: un cas de créolisation? In Jürgen Meisel (ed.), *Langues en contact – pidgins – créoles – Languages in contact*, 81–101. Tübingen: Gunter Narr.
Short, Ian. 2013. *Manual of Anglo-Norman*. Oxford: Anglo-Norman Text Society.
Thomason, Sarah G. & Terrence Kaufmann. 1988. *Language contact, Creolization, and genetic linguistics*. Oxford: University of California Press.
Trotter, David. 2005. L'anglo-normand: variété insulaire, ou variété isolée? Anglo-Norman: Insular or isolated? *Médiévale* 45. 3–12.
Trudgill, Peter. 2011. *Sociolinguistic typology*. Oxford: Oxford University Press.
UNESCO Atlas of the world's languages in danger: www.unesco.org/languages.atlas/.

Index of Authors

Aberdeen, Lucinda 118
Abou, Sélim 157
Adam, Lucien 143
Adick, Christel 117
Agha, Asif 18
Agrawal, S. P. 199
Ammon, Ulrich 5
Anand, Ari S. 192f.
Andersen, Erik Langer 52f.
Anderson, Benedict 115
Anderson, John M. 17, 47
Azara, Félix de 158
Azariah, Jayapaul 196

Bade, Klaus J. 116f.
Baissac, Charles 141, 145, 147
Baldridge, Jason 195
Barrère, Albert M. V. 203
Batoma, Atoma 14
Baugh, Albert C. 241
Bédier, Joseph 238
Berg, Lawrence D. 44f., 51, 59
Berman, Russel A. 176
Berschin, Helmut 226
Beyer, Jürgen 29
Bischof, Heinz 66
Biswas, Arabinda 199
Bloomfield, Leonard 165
Bobé, Louis 59, 61f., 64f.
Bollig, P. Laurentius 93f., 96ff., 113, 109ff.
Bouman, P. J. 36
Bourdieu, Pierre 175
Bourquin, Alexandre 145
Boyer, Henri 145
Bracco, Roberto 155
Bragg, Melvyn 192
Breindl, Eva 178
Bro-Jørgensen, J. J. 28f.
Buda, J. K. 205
Busse, Beatrix 43f.
Busse, Dietrich 174f.
Bytko, Natali 202

Cable, Thomas 241
Calvet, Louis-Jean 149
Carter, Paul 45
Castro Varela, María do Mar 14
Cavell, Janice 48
Cawley, Charles 197
Chamorro, Graciela 162
Clastres, Hélène 163f.
Coelho, Gail M. 198
Colombat, Bernard 233
Conklin, Alice L. 116
Conrad, Sebastian 176
Costantini, Dino 116
Crampton, Jeremy W. 44
Crowley, Roger 3
Crystal, David 2, 5f., 221, 229
Curbelo, Carmen 154f., 162

Del Boca, Angelo 77, 81f.
Della Cava, Olha 194
Deppermann, Arnulf 118
Dewein, Barbara 15, 45
Dharwadker, Vinay 194
Dhawan, Nikita 14
Di Meola, Claudio 178f.
Dienel, Hans-Liudger 173
Dietrich, Adolphe 139, 141ff.
Durán, M. 158

Ebert, Verena 77
Eckert, Andreas 171
Ehret, Christopher 156
Eichholtz, Dietrich 182
Elbert, Samuel H. 98, 106, 113, 109ff.
El-Din, Amr Nasr 171
Elizaincín Eichenberger, Adolfo Esteban 157
Engelberg, Stefan 121, 128
Ernst, Gerhard 230
Errington, Joseph 149
Esch, Edith 238
Évreux, Yves de 165

Faulstich, Katja 176
Ferguson, Charles A. 155, 224

Index of Authors

Ferguson, Ronnie 3
Finlayson, Douglas 51
Fishman, Joshua 155
Florines Pena, Andrés 163
Folena, Gianfranco 4, 220
Foucault, Michel 175
Fuhrmann, Malte 182, 184

Gabel de Aguirre, Jennifer 230
Ganson, Barbara 154
Garde, Thomas Vilhelm 43f.
Genft, Christof Ernst 65
Gladwin, Francis 200f.
Godefroy, Frédéric 234
Goodenough, Ward H. 98, 106, 113, 109ff.
Grant, Shelagh 59, 62, 64f.
Guillorel, Hervé 36

Hannemann, Emil Friedrich 122f., 125
Harder, Kelsey B. 118, 121
Harpham, Geoffrey Galt 149
Harré, Rom 118f.
Hashmi, Alamgir 194
Haugen, Einar 156, 228
Havard, Gilles 28, 32
Heine, Bernd 222
Helander, Kaisa Rautio 49
Helmich, Heinrich 119, 127ff.
Heyden, Ulrich van der 31
Hickey, Raymond 219
Hiery, Hermann Joseph 23
Higgins, Anthony K. 46ff., 55
Holm, John 140
Hulzen, Johan van 28

Ingham, Richard 222
Iturrioz Leza, Jose-Luis 121

Jäger, Ludwig 174, 178
Jansen, Jan C. 149
Jones, Mari C. 220f., 224, 238
Jónsson, Finnur 53

Kachru, Braj B. 192, 200
Käser, Lothar 96, 98
Kaufman, Terrence 220
Kausch, Oskar 16, 18ff., 28, 35

Keane, Webb 163, 165
Kellemeier-Rehbein, Birte 94
Kibbee, Douglas A. 230ff.
Kiddle, Lawrence B. 156, 164f.
Kindersley, A. F. 198
Kleivan, Inge 45ff., 50, 52f., 56, 59ff.
Kloss, Heinz 238
Koch, Peter 227
König, Ekkehard 179
Krämer, Augustin 99ff.
Krämer, Philipp 141ff., 145ff.
Krishnaswamy, Lalitha 191, 199
Krishnaswamy, N. 191, 199
Kuipers, Joel C. 196
Kuteva, Tania 222

Labanca, Nicola 16, 77
Lambert, James 193, 199, 204
Langenhove, Luk van 118
Långfors, Arthur 234
Laude, Norbert 16, 28, 31
Laursen, Dan 46, 48f., 51
Legge, Mary Dominica 230f., 241
Leith, Dick 5
Leland, Charles G. 203
Lewis, Ivor 192ff., 205f.
Liddicoat, Anthony J. 220
Lidegaard, Mads 35
Lienhard, Martin 153, 155
Lindner, Ulrike 176
Littke, Peter 28, 32, 35f.
Lodge, R. Anthony 224f., 228f.
Lodrick, D. O. 192
Loeffen, Volker 117
Loloi, Parvin 200
Loomba, Ania 46
Lucius-Hoene, Gabriele 118
Lupi, Luca 82
Lynnerup, Niels 53

Malleson, George B. 197
Marcato, Carla 77
Marcus, Geoffrey Jules 54f.
Markham, Albert H. 56f.
Masoin, Fritz 35
Mateos, Francisco 159
Mattiesen, Otto Heinz 28

McArthur, Tom 198, 221
McCaskill Popini, Eloise 56
Mehnert, Wolfgang 117
Mehrotra, Raja R. 195
Meliá, Bartolomeu 155, 157, 159ff., 165f.
Menger, Louis Emil 220, 224
Merello, Enrique 154
Messling, Markus 148f.
Metzeltin, Miguel 32
Meyer, Gustav 142
Meyers, Debra 22
Miccoli, Paolo 32, 76, 85, 87f.
Michiels, Albert 16, 28, 31
Mignolo, Walter D. 149
Miller, Karl 172
Mills, Sara 175
Moghaddam, Fathali M. 118
Møller Kruse, Lisathe 46, 61
Möller, Lucie A. 16, 19ff.
Montagnon, Pierre 36
Montoya, Antonio Ruiz de 154, 159ff.
Morris, Jan 172
Mota, A. Teixeira da 32f.
Mückler, Hermann 96
Mufwene, Salikoko 145
Myrland, N. 162

Nagel, Liane Maria 165
Nagle, Traci C. 193
Nair, Rukmini Bh. 197, 200
Nicolaisen, Wilhelm 51, 63f.
Nübling, Damaris 15, 17, 47, 50, 52, 64f., 77
Nuttall, Mark 45, 47f., 50, 52, 56, 59, 62

Olsen, Carl Christian 46, 48f.
Onedera, Peter 25
Orosz, Kenneth J. 125
Osterhammel, Jürgen 149
Ostermann, H. 48

Pakenham, Thomas 171, 177
Parthesius, Robert 196
Pasch, Renate 175
Pastells, Pablo 158
Payack, Paul J. J. 6
Pélissier, René 32, 36
Petersen, Robert 44, 62

Pinsker, Hans Ernst 231
Plá, Josefina 161
Poyen-Bellisle, René de 140f., 146f.
Pulcinelli Orlandi, Ení 161
Pümpel-Mader, Maria 118, 120f., 128

Quirk, Randolph 198

Ram, Tusli 191
Ramutsindela, Maano 172
Randa, Alexander 27, 31
Reinhardt, Winfried 173, 181
Reisigl, Martin 175
Rella, Christoph 30f.
Rezat, Sara 178
Robarts, T. T. 201
Roebuck, Thomas 201
Rogers, Robert F. 23, 25
Romaine, Suzanne 222
Room, Adrian 16, 28f., 32ff., 36
Rothwell, William 232ff.
Rousseau, Samuel 200f.
Rudolph, Elisabeth 170, 178

Said, Edward W. 115, 149
Sailaja, Pingali 191f., 196, 198
Sallabank, Julia 220f., 236ff., 241
Santos, Ángel 154, 159f.
Scherer, Carmen 174
Schlieben-Lange, Brigitte 220
Schmidt-Brücken, Daniel 118, 120, 131, 135, 174
Schonauer, Karlheinz 177
Schöner, Mathias 121
Schuchardt, Hugo 139, 141ff., 146, 148
Schulz, Matthias 77
Schulze, Mathias 118
Schuster, Susanne 94
Short, Ian 220f.
Simone, Raffaele 5
Singh, Manmohan 199
Sinha, Surenda P. 195, 199
Sjögren, Bengt 28, 32
Snell, Rupert 194
Sokop, Brigitte 21, 32
Sousa, Silvio Moreira de 141
Speitkamp, Winfried 25, 176

Spivak, Gayatri Chakravorty 115, 132
Stein, Peter 143
Stewart, George R. 51
Stolberg, Doris 127
Stolz, Christel 157
Stolz, Thomas 15, 44ff., 50f., 54, 60, 66, 68, 76, 78, 121, 140, 149, 157, 177
Stow, Randolph 197
Struwe, Kamma 31
Stuart, George R. 51
Sturmfels, Wilhelm 66
Sugita, Hiroshi 98, 106, 113, 109ff.
Suresh, A. 197

Tappenbeck, Hans 18f.
Teltscher, Kate 193
Teubert, Wolfgang 174f.
Thomason, Sarah G. 220f.
Topping, Donald 24
Trabant, Jürgen 148
Traversi, Carlo 77
Trotter, David 221
Trudgill, Peter 220
Turiault, Jean 141

Val Julián, Carmen 29
Van Langendonck, Willy 17
Vance, Norman 172
Vedovelli, Massimo 4
Vester, Heinz-Günter 177f.
Vidal, Cécile 28, 32
Vinson, Julien 141
Volkmann, Richard 172
Vuolteenaho, Jani 44f., 51, 59

Waller, Alfred Rayney 195f., 198
Ward, Adolphus W. 195f., 198
Warnke, Ingo H. 15, 43ff., 50, 60, 66, 68, 76, 121, 140, 174f.
Weber, Brigitte 18f.
Whitworth, George Clifford 202, 205
Wienberg, Marina 93f.
Wilson, Horace Hayman 202, 205

Yule, Henry 192f., 198, 200f., 205

Zastoupil, Lynn 194
Zimmer, Ben 193
Zimmermann, Klaus 94

Index of Languages

Afrikaans 221
Amharic 28
Anglo-Norman/Anglo-French 219ff., 228, 230ff., 238, 241
Arabic 94, 202, 209ff.
Assamese 196

Bengali 196, 198, 202f.

Cameroon Pidgin 221
Chakma 196
Chamorro 23ff., 94
Chinese 6f., 208
Chuukese 94, 96ff., 102, 104, 106, 109ff.
Creole
– Antillean ~ 140
– Mauritian ~ 141, 145
Danish 46, 49, 62ff., 195, 197, 212
Dutch 28, 60ff., 68, 143, 195, 197, 208

English 5ff., 47, 50, 55ff., 61, 64, 67f., 98, 103f., 105, 111f., 122f., 141, 143, 145, 180, 182, 192f., 194ff., 210, 212, 214, 219ff., 229, 231ff.
– Anglo-Indian ~ 198, 203
– Babu/Baboo ~ 198, 203
– Boxwalla(h) ~ 198
– Butler/Bearer/Kitchen ~ 198
– Dravidian ~ 198
– General Indian ~ 198
– Indian ~ 192f., 195, 197f., 214
– Indo-Aryan ~ 198

Finnish 222
Florentine 3
Francian 228f., 231
French 6, 9ff., 35f., 140f., 143ff., 147f., 195, 197, 209, 219ff., 228ff.
– Norman ~ 220, 241

German 20ff., 49, 65ff., 76f., 94, 99ff., 102, 104, 106, 111f., 117, 122f., 127, 176, 179f., 222, 226

Greek 2, 127, 159, 161
Greenlandic 44, 46, 49, 51
Guarani 154ff.
Guernesiais/Guernsey French 220, 236, 238f.
Gujarati/Guzarathi 196, 202

Hebrew 127
Hindi 196, 202f., 208ff.

Insular Norman 220, 222, 238
Irish 7, 9
Italian 3ff., 9, 76, 78f., 83ff., 222

Japanese 9
Jèrriais 220, 236
Jopara 157

Kalaallisut 46
Karnata 202
Korean 8

Latin 2f., 8, 16, 23, 100, 159, 161, 220, 223ff., 232f.
Latvian 31

Malay 208, 210f.
Malayalam 202, 208
Maltese 222
Marathi 196, 202
Marwari 196

Nepali 196
Norse 50, 52ff., 68, 240

Odia 196

Pashto 208
Persian 198, 202
Picardian 241
Pohnpeian 97
Polish 7, 35
Portuguese 7, 9, 29, 32, 141, 143, 195f., 208, 212

Rohingya 196
Romanian 9

Sanskrit 202, 205, 208
Santali 196
Serquiais 220, 236
Sindhi 196
Spanish 8f., 23ff., 28ff., 37, 141, 153ff., 165, 210, 221

Tamil 196, 198, 202, 208
Telugu 196, 203
Trukese 98, 106
Tuscan 3

Urdu 196
Uriya 202

Venetian 220

Index of Subjects

Anglicization 17
archives 99, 122, 134, 142f., 176
anthroponyms 10, 20, 22, 25, 54f., 58, 61, 63, 68, 88ff.

Baghdad Railway 173, 180ff.
bilingualism 3, 8, 153f., 221f.
borrowing 156, 162, 195, 206, 208, 209, 222, 235

choronyms 19
classifier 16, 17, 50f., 54, 59ff., 63, 65f., 68, 76, 79ff.
code-mixing 198, 221
code-switching 222
colonial discourse 11, 76, 84, 146, 148, 173f., 176, 185
colonial linguistics 1, 11, 94, 139, 147, 149f.
colonial rule 14, 45, 62, 116, 149, 165
colonialism 2, 10, 13ff., 17, 21, 26, 29, 37, 44f., 56, 75f., 82ff., 89, 115f., 126, 135, 149f., 176, 196
colonies 2, 4, 15f., 17, 21, 34, 37f., 45, 47f., 52, 77, 80, 97, 116, 140, 144, 148, 170f., 176, 181f.
colonization 2, 4f., 11, 14, 36, 45f., 49, 52, 59, 62, 64f., 79f., 84f., 159f., 173, 176f., 208
compound 15, 50, 53f., 57ff., 63, 66, 68, 180, 209
Congo Conference 171, 176
connectives 170, 173, 175, 178, 184
contrast relations 170, 172f., 176ff.
corpus 14, 173f., 177, 186, 208ff., 229
creole language 10f., 139ff., 157, 196, 219f.
Creolistics 11, 139ff., 143f., 146f., 149f.

decolonization 44, 77, 150
derivation 16, 120, 194, 208, 212
determiner 50f., 54f., 57, 60f., 63, 65f., 68
dialects 155, 160, 195, 197, 208, 219, 226, 228f., 231, 240
dictionaries 93f., 98, 101, 104, 106, 109ff., 157, 160, 192, 200, 204ff., 210f., 213f., 229, 234, 241

diglossia 154f.
discourse 37, 45, 118, 122, 140f., 146, 149, 163ff., 170, 174f., 187, 203, 204

endonyms 23, 50, 56, 76
ethnonyms 14
etymology 46, 59f., 206, 208ff., 212
Europeanization 15f., 153
evangelization 153, 158, 160, 165
exonyms 16, 50, 56, 60, 65, 76ff., 86f., 89, 118f., 121
expedition 3, 18, 35, 46f., 81ff., 99, 164, 224

fascist period/phase 10, 76ff., 80, 82ff.

genericity 118ff., 124, 131, 135
grammar(s) 93, 98, 102, 109f., 141, 148, 157, 160ff., 165, 201, 222, 229, 232f.

hagionyms 22ff.
Herero insurrections 172
Hispanicization 155f.
hybrids/hybrid forms 50, 56, 76, 78
hydronyms 19

identity 118f., 134f., 170, 173, 176ff., 184ff., 238
imperialism 2, 46f., 171

koiné/koneization 2ff.

language contact 11, 157, 197, 199, 219ff., 231, 240
lexicography 11, 161, 191ff., 200, 203f., 214
lingua franca 4f., 7ff., 220, 222
loanwords 94, 135, 156f., 213, 219, 229, 231

macrotoponym 15, 49f., 76ff., 84ff., 90
mapping 44, 56, 59
microtoponym 76f., 85ff.
missionaries 10, 35, 44, 64, 66f., 78, 93ff., 100, 111, 116f., 119ff., 128ff., 135, 140, 153f., 157, 160f., 163ff., 191, 197, 199, 209

Index of Subjects

missionary linguistics 94
missionary activity/work 2, 10, 48, 95ff., 165
missions/missionary societies 18, 22, 48, 65ff., 81, 94f., 116f., 122f., 129, 133ff., 140, 160, 165
– Bethel Mission 95, 122
– Capuchin Mission/Order of Capuchin 93, 96f.
– Franciscans 154, 157ff.
– Herrnhut Mission 35
– Jesuits Mission 25, 194
– Liebenzell Mission 96, 98
– Neuendettelsauer Mission 95, 117
– Rhenish Mission Society 10, 95, 115f., 124ff.
– Societas Verbi Divini 117
– Steyler Mission 96
– Vereinte Evangelische Mission 122

naming 10, 13f., 17, 22, 30, 38, 44ff., 49, 55, 59, 61, 64, 67f., 78, 80ff., 87, 89f., 118f., 121, 126
native language 11, 31, 100, 117, 148, 153, 155f., 160, 164, 195, 197, 199, 221
natives 127, 129f., 132, 134, 158, 165, 201, 203, 207, 212

(effective) occupation 171ff., 182, 187, 213
oronyms 19

pidgins 10, 198, 203, 219
place names 13ff., 17f., 25, 44ff., 49ff., 76, 84, 121, 224, 230, 241
place-making 13f., 30, 43, 45, 76
place-naming 10, 14, 19, 26, 29f., 33ff., 37, 44, 78
positioning 118f., 130f., 133f.
prestige 3, 7f., 59, 68, 154, 173, 225, 228, 233
proper names 14, 17, 19, 53, 211

qualitative/quantitative approach 17, 38, 50

racialist discourse/paradigm 139ff., 146

semantics 15, 88, 165, 175, 239
spaces 14, 53f., 59, 84, 115, 161
standardization 157, 165, 225, 228f., 238
stereotyping 118ff., 124, 135
suffix/suffixation 16, 62f., 102

toponomasticon 16ff., 22f., 25ff., 32, 35, 38, 44f., 47, 49
toponomastics 14ff., 23, 30, 76
toponym(y) 3, 10, 14, 18, 20, 24ff., 30, 32ff., 36f., 43, 45f., 49ff., 76ff., 121, 213f., 231

Index of Toponyms

Alaska 32, 36, 47
– Kenai Peninsula 32
– Kodiak Island 28
Albania 4
Amára 79
Andaman Islands 197
Angola 32, 36
Argentina 4
Austria 16, 26, 35, 141f., 148

Belgium 4, 16, 31, 177
Bismarck Archipelago 20, 95, 116, 124
Bolivia 4
Brandenburg-Preußen 16, 26f., 31
Brazil 4, 36, 154

Cameroon, *see also* Kamerun 8, 18, 125, 221
Canada 4, 32, 47, 55
Caroline Islands 95f.
– Pohnpei 96f.
Carthage 2
Cephalonia 3
Chad 36f.,
Channel Islands 10, 220ff., 236ff.
Chile 4
China 6ff., 96
Chuuk Islands 94ff.
– Tol 96ff.
Colombia 4
Constantinople 3
Corfu 3
Crete 3
Croatia 4
Cyclades, the 3
Cyprus 3
Congo Belge 16, 28, 35
Courland 16, 26f., 31

Dalmatia 3
Danish Virgin Islands 28
Denmark 16, 28, 45, 48f., 62, 64, 197
Deutsch-Neuguinea 20
Deutsch-Ostafrika 18, 184f.
Deutsch-Südwestafrika 15

Egypt 3, 171
– Alexandria 171
– Suez 171
Eritrea (Africa Orientale Italiana) 4, 28, 75, 78f., 84
Ethiopia 4, 77ff., 83, 85ff.
– Addis Abeba 76, 79, 86ff.
– Adua 81, 89
– Galla 79f.
– Harar 79
– Sidama 79f.
Euboea 3

Finland 5
Florence 3
France 4, 16, 28, 32, 36, 38, 140, 143, 176f., 195, 197, 219ff., 224, 229, 231, 233ff., 241

Germany 4, 16, 20f., 23, 26, 29, 95f., 116, 125, 170ff., 176f., 181f., 185f.
Greenland 10, 35, 43ff.
– Nanortalik 66
– Narsaq 52, 56
– Nuuk 66, 48f., 52
Guadeloupe 148
Guinea Portuguesa 33
Guinea Española 28

Iceland 45, 47, 52
India 8, 11, 19, 172, 191ff.
– Bangalore 8
– Bombay 195, 202, 212
– Calcutta 195, 200f.
– Calicut 196f.
– Cannanore 196
– Coromandel 196
– Diu 196f.
– Daman 196
– Goa 195f.
– Gondalpara 197
– Madras 195, 198, 201
– Orissa 197, 201
– Serampore 197, 199
– Vasai 196

Ireland 5f., 19, 171
Istanbul 173
Istria 3
Italy 16, 36, 77, 79ff., 89f., 237

Japan 4, 17, 116

Kaiser-Wilhelmsland 20, 32, 35, 95
Kamerun, *see also* Cameroon 17
Kiautschou 19

Libia/Libya 4, 16, 78, 86, 89
– Tripoli 76, 86ff.

Madagascar 35, 144
Malta 4
Manus Island 94
Mariana Islands/Marianas 17, 23ff., 37, 95f., 116
– Guam 23, 25, 38, 94, 116
– Saipan 24f., 94
– Rota 24f.
Marshall Islands 95, 116
Martinique 141
Mascarene Islands 11, 143
– La Réunion 11, 143ff.
– Mauritius 11, 32, 143f.
– Rodrigues 143
Methoni 3
Monaco 4
Mozambique 28, 36, 144, 147

Namibia 169f., 172
Nauru 116
Nepal 198
Netherlands, the/Holland 16, 21, 96, 195
New Guinea 116f., 121ff., 126f.
New Zealand 4, 9, 33f., 36, 116
Newfoundland 28
Nicobar Islands 31, 197
Norway 47f., 197

Palau 96, 116
Papua New Guinea 33
– Friedrich-Wilhelmshafen 20, 117
Paraguay 4, 153ff., 157f., 160f., 165
Peru 4
Philippines 23
Portugal 16, 28, 32f., 36

Queensland 33

Rome 2, 76, 88, 125, 194, 223, 226
Russia 16, 29

Salomon Islands 95
Samoa 95, 116
Sicily 2, 224
Slovenia 4
Somalia 4, 32, 36, 78f., 84
Spain 2, 17, 23, 26, 36, 38
Spitsbergen 48, 59, 61
St. Barthélemy 28, 32
Sweden 16, 26, 28, 32
Switzerland 4

Tanzania 169f.,
Tobago 31
Togo 18

UK/United Kingdom 4, 17, 34, 171, 237
Uruguay 4
USA/United States 6ff., 16f., 23, 140

Venezuela 4
Venice 2f.

Zakinthos 3

www.ingramcontent.com/pod-product-compliance
Lightning Source LLC
Chambersburg PA
CBHW070308230426
43664CB00015B/2677